The Twelve Teas™ of Christmas

EMILIE BARNES

PAINTINGS BY SANDY LYNAM CLOUGH

HARVEST HOUSE™ PUBLISHERS

EUGENE, OREGON

The Twelve Teas™ of Christmas

Copyright © 1999 by Harvest House Publishers
Eugene, Oregon 97402

www.harvesthousepublishers.com

Library of Congress Cataloging-in-Publication Data

Barnes, Emilie.
    The 12 teas of Christmas / Emilie Barnes ; paintings by Sandy Lynam Clough.
        p.   cm.
    ISBN 0-7369-0052-7
    1. Afternoon teas.   2. Christmas cookery.   I. Title.
TX736.B36964   1999
641.5'68—dc21

99-14124
CIP

For information regarding Emilie Barnes's speaking schedule or how you may purchase the cookie cutters featured in "Bake Me a Story" (page 82), please send a self-addressed, stamped business envelope to:

More Hours in My Day
2150 Whitestone Drive
Riverside, CA 92506

All works of art reproduced in this book are copyrighted by Sandy Lynam Clough and may not be reproduced without the artist's permission. For information regarding art prints featured in this book, please contact:

Sandy Clough Studios
P.O. Box 85
Powder Springs, GA 30127
(800) 447-8409

Design and production by Garborg Design Works, Minneapolis, Minnesota

Scripture quotations are from: the Holy Bible, New International Version®. Copyright ©1973, 1978, 1984 by the International Bible Society. Used by permission of Zondervan Publishing House; and The Living Bible, Copyright © 1971 owned by assignment by Illinois Regional Bank N.A. (as trustee). Used by permission of Tyndale House Publishers, Inc., Wheaton, Illinois 60189. All rights reserved.

Harvest House Publishers, Inc., is the exclusive licensee of the trademark THE TWELVE TEAS.

Printed in Hong Kong.

03 04 05 06 07 08 / NG / 10 9 8

Contents

If teacups could talk
And teapots could sing,
Especially at Christmas,
They would tell us some things...
Of family and friends,
Carolers and trees,
Sharing the warmth of the season
With twelve special teas.

SANDY LYNAM CLOUGH

A Celebration of Friendship

Starting off the holiday season with a heart full of welcome

*You are invited to begin the Christmas season
with a very special tea party
given in celebration of our friendship.*

Every year I love to see the signs that point to winter's approach—spirited late-afternoon windstorms that send fiery orange-and-yellow leaves scurrying off the trees, the transition from breezy cotton to cozy flannel sheets, wool sweaters, and warm coats brought forth from trunks and drawers. There's an excitement that permeates the chill in the air, a growing feeling of anticipation, a heightened expectation of things yet to come. Christmas is on the way!

During the Christmas season, we celebrate all that is good. We send others our most sincere wishes of peace, joy, and love. From giving gifts to decorating our homes to offering extra smiles and words of encouragement, we're

DID YOU KNOW?

The name "Christmas" comes from the Latin "Christes Masse" of Christ's Mass. It grew out of the Roman Catholic feast day by that name in approximately A.D. 100.

helping add to the feeling of goodwill that embraces the holiday season. In our interaction with those around us—family both immediate and extended, friends new and old, coworkers and members of the small groups to which we belong—we are given one opportunity after another to make someone else's Christmas a little more meaningful, a little more memorable, a little more beautiful.

One of the best ways to start the season off in festive fashion is by inviting a group of special people to begin the celebration with you—a few close friends, a study group, your sisters, the people in your department at work. And a tea party is a celebration just perfect for the occasion. In a salute to both companionship and Christmas, a Celebration of Friendship tea party helps you kick off the holidays on a proper note, preparing your heart and your home for the days of joy to come.

A Word about Tea

Raise a cup of tea as a toast to good health! Tea drinking is a delightful habit to cultivate. Not only does the ceremony of teatime lift spirits, the health benefits are yours to enjoy as well! Tea helps relieve fatigue, lift the spirits, and stimulate the mind. A cup of tea contains zero calories (add approximately 40 for a cup taken with milk and sugar), yet provides you with several of the complex vitamins. Six cups a day gives you ten percent of your daily requirements.

Menu for a Celebration of Friendship tea party—

Nut Bread with Three-Apple Butter
Tuna Pinwheels
Cranberry Streusel Cake
Best Tasting Brownies

RECIPES

Three-Apple Butter

1 pound unsalted sweet butter
1 Granny Smith apple, quartered
  with core and skin
1 Winesap apple, quartered with
  core and skin
1 Macon apple, quartered with
  core and skin

(You may use any combination of cooked
apples, as long as some are tart and some
are sweet.)

Place all ingredients in a heavy 4-quart saucepan. Cook 30 minutes over medium-low heat, lowering heat as apples cook, and stirring occasionally. Force mixture through a sieve or stainless steel strainer. Cool, cover saucepan, and refrigerate. Makes 3 cups.

CHRISTMAS TIMELINE
Early 4th Century: The earliest recorded observance of Christmas.

Tuna Pinwheels

1-pound loaf of unsliced, day-old
  white bread (fresh-baked will
  be difficult to cut)
1/2 cup unsalted butter, room
  temperature
your favorite tuna salad

Neatly cut off all crust from loaf of bread. Lightly spread butter to edges of one side. Cut lengthwise into very thin slices. Spread buttered slice with tuna salad. Roll up lengthwise, jelly roll-style. Wrap in foil. Repeat until loaf is finished. (You should have about 6 rolls.) Refrigerate for at least an hour; butter will harden and hold rolls together. Before serving, cut each roll crosswise into about 5 slices. Makes about 30 pinwheels.

Cranberry Streusel Cake

STREUSEL MIXTURE:
  3/4 cup packed light brown sugar
  1 teaspoon cinnamon
  1/4 cup flour
  1/4 cup butter or margarine

In a small bowl, cut and mix together above ingredients, then set aside.

CAKE MIXTURE:
  1/2 cup butter or margarine
  2 eggs
  1 cup sour cream

1 cup sugar
1 teaspoon vanilla

Beat cake ingredients together in large bowl. Gradually add to the above mixture the following dry ingredients:

2 cups flour
1 teaspoon baking soda
1 teaspoon baking powder
1/2 teaspoon salt

Wash 1 bag of fresh or frozen cranberries and set aside. Preheat oven to 350 degrees. Grease an angel food cake pan. Spread half of cake mixture into pan, followed by half of streusel mixture and half of cranberries. Repeat with other half batter, then cranberries, then streusel. Bake 1- 1 1/4 hours.

Best Tasting Brownies

1 family-size package Duncan Hines fudge brownie mix with chocolate syrup
2 large eggs
2 teaspoons water
1/4 cup oil
1 cup chocolate chips
1 cup chopped walnuts
1 cup white mini marshmallows

Combine all ingredients. Bake at 350 degrees for 30 minutes.

READYING THE ROOMS

To help get yourself—as well as your guests—in the Christmas spirit, pull out your boxes full of holiday decorations and jot down a list of the main areas of your house, inside and out, you'd like to dress up for the holidays. If possible, it's fun to have a friendship tea on the very first day of December to put everyone in good spirits for the twenty-four

A PILE OF PRESENTS

Not all Christmas packages need to be wrapped up in paper! Gather up your decorative pillows and gift-wrap them for the holidays. Choose some satin or organdy ribbon (three inches is a good width) in colors that match your pillows. Tie the ribbon onto the pillows, complete with cheery bows, and return them to their respective places, properly dressed in Christmas finery!

days to follow. Your guests will come away from your party inspired to decorate their own homes with cheery lights and welcoming wreaths of red and green to refresh the soul after a hard day of work or a particularly taxing afternoon.

Start your transforming with the outdoor lights. Perhaps you'd like to try the elegant look of all-white lights this

What is the Christmas spirit? It is the spirit which brings a smile to the lips and tenderness to the heart; it is the spirit which warms one into friendship with all the world, which impels one to hold out the hand of fellowship to every man and woman.

ANONYMOUS

year, or you might opt to go with strings of brightly colored bulbs. Red and white strings of lights bring the whimsy of candy cane villages to mind. Wind lights artfully around trees and bushes (and hope that it snows soon so they glow softly through the powdered branches!); line rooftops and windows with lights to transform your home into a gingerbread chalet. Wrap a lamppost with lights, or string them along a fence. You'll be heartened as the days grow shorter, for your Christmas lights will glow even brighter!

Now it's time to head inside to open up the boxes and pull out your favorite

MAKE A CHRISTMAS CARD BULLETIN BOARD

Instead of piling Christmas cards received into a basket or drawer, turn them into a part of your Christmas decorating. Stretch plain-colored or holiday-print fabric over a standard tack board, attaching it to the back of the board with thumbtacks. Next, lay matching ribbons (grosgrain ribbon always looks nice) in a crisscross pattern across the board, also securing them in the back with thumbtacks. For the frame, paint stock molding in colors to match or find a charming vintage frame at an antique or secondhand shop. As your cards come in, slide them under the ribbons to form a friendship-filled holiday display.

ornaments and decorations. Americans didn't always get the season underway by rescuing holiday boxes from attics and garages! Not until the middle of the nineteenth century did many of the familiar Christmas decorations become common in our country. We have the Victorians to thank for the fanciful ornaments of Christmas—nutcrackers and gingerbread men, candy canes, glittering glass balls, even romantic sprigs of mistletoe.

Even if you're still waiting a week or so to get your tree, you can fill your home with the sights and smells of Christmas. Head to a nearby garden store or into the great outdoors to pick up branches of evergreen, balsam, or juniper. Outline mirrors with the fragrant branches, arrange them on mantels and in windowsills, on tabletops and bookshelves. It's pretty to add small, simple ornaments—gold or silver balls, for instance—for a touch of merriment. Or showcase your holiday collectibles in among the branches—snow villages, collections of angels, and of course your Christmas teacups!

You can also make your own teatime

centerpiece that easily bridges the transition from autumn to winter. Find a medium-sized woven basket, wooden box, or even a terra-cotta planter, and fill it with green moss or evergreen branches. Then arrange half a dozen fat yellow pears or shiny red apples on top. And tie a red-and-green ribbon on the basket handle or around the planter for added color.

For a tea party held in the dining room, weave Christmas-colored ribbons throughout the chairs or hang small stockings on chairbacks. Wrap small boxes in Christmas paper and use them as placecards, writing each guest's name on a tag. (You can even put a small gift inside—a chocolate truffle, a little box of tea, a handmade ornament.) Natural-colored paper, one with an interesting texture, also works well for placecards. Use a silver or gold calligraphy pen to add some sparkle.

To make your friendship tea party *really* seem English, hold it in your living room. (You can call it the "drawing room" just for fun.) Top a high, round table with a long skirt to make an official tea table, and pull chairs and sofas into a cozy circle facing the fireplace and each other. Turn off the overhead lights, relying only on lamplight and the fire to provide a soft, intimate glow. And dress the furniture in the room for Christmas using merry red or green slipcovers and pillow covers.

Add a few more touches—indoor wreaths and garlands, bows tied on candlesticks and plenty of candles in seasonal colors and scents set about, cozy throws and cheery table runners, a Nativity scene or a special Advent calendar, a gathering of family photos decorated with bows and greens—and your home is brimming with welcome and good cheer!

CUSTOMS OF CHRISTMAS

One of our first holiday tasks is the writing and sending of Christmas cards. The custom began in Great Britain around 1840 with the advent of the "Penny Post"—the first public postal delivery system. Legend tells that a procrastinating Englishman named Henry Cole actually started the tradition. In 1843, he found himself behind in his correspondence with friends and wanted to set things right with a cheery Christmas note to end the year. His resourceful idea led to a mass marketing of holiday cards, particularly after 1860 as printing methods improved. In Britain, sending season's greetings jumped in popularity when a card could be posted in an unsealed envelope for just one half-penny—half the price of a regular letter. In 1865, Bostonian Louis Prang printed and sold the first Christmas card in the United States. The images and the message have remained fairly constant throughout the years—pictures showing the Christmas story or other seasonal scenes along with wishes of a merry Christmas and a happy new year.

Include your friendship tea invitations along with your Christmas cards if you send them out early enough, or you can even devote a portion of your tea party to Christmas-card-writing if you're gathering together with a group of like-minded and time-pressed friends! Provide colorful pens, festive rubber stamps, and holiday music for a relaxing time of catching up family and friends on the year's happenings.

THE SECOND TEA OF CHRISTMAS

A Celebration of Family

Building tradition while spending holiday time together

*You're invited to a togetherness tea party
full of fun, games, treats, and hugs—
a party just for our family!*

When I think of Christmas, I think of family. During the Christmas season, families need to make a place in their lives for the ritual of sharing. This is the time when memories are made, old traditions are carried out, and new traditions are created. Perhaps Dad always reads *A Child's Christmas in Wales* on Christmas Eve, or everyone gathers in the family room to watch "It's a Wonderful Life" the day after Thanksgiving. Maybe you and your children bundle up in your warmest attire and head into the mountains to get your Christmas tree on the first weekend in December. Or perhaps you're like a lot of families, who would love to start forming and sharing traditions but, in the

DID YOU KNOW...?

It was Queen Victoria's influence that allowed children to play more and work less. The queen held parties at Christmastime especially for children, encouraging them to take part in the festivity of the season.

12

midst of the gift shopping and the card writing and the goodie baking, haven't quite arrived at that point.

And speaking of rituals, did you know that tea parties aren't just for adults? Children get excited about tea parties, too! After all, what child doesn't love playing dress-up, receiving a colorful party invitation, playing games, and eating yummy treats? A Celebration of Family tea provides a time for parents and children to come together in an afternoon or evening of fun. Together you'll share in the anticipation of the season, talk about the meaning of Christmas, and build tradition.

Send tea party invitations to your children and your spouse! You can slip them under their door, hide them with the day's letters, or even send them in the "real" mail. If you're single, you can "adopt" some children of your own—your nieces and nephews, the kids down the street, a few of the grade schoolers at your church. Try to keep it cozy, though. And enjoy your hearty cup of togetherness tea!

A Word about Tea

Tea drinking is an activity that the whole family can enjoy! While children should not drink caffeinated beverages, herbal teas are both yummy and good for little ones. Lavender tea can calm cranky youngsters. Chamomile, one of the best-loved herbal teas, is an ideal bedtime tea.

Its gentle flavor and aroma contain a completely natural sedative that helps soothe you to sleep. If you're using loose tea leaves instead of tea bags, simply measure two teaspoons of tea leaves per four-cup pot. Steep twenty minutes, then strain well. And enjoy a family tradition of togetherness!

Menu for a Celebration of Family tea party—

Ham-Filled Sandwiches
Assorted Cheeses
Christmas Tree Bread
Fruit Salsa

RECIPES

Ham-Filled Sandwich Spread
1/2-pound cooked ham
1 large dill pickle
4 hard-cooked eggs
2 teaspoons mustard
3 tablespoons mayonnaise
salt and pepper to taste

Combine ham, pickle, eggs, and mustard in food processor. Moisten with mayonnaise. Season with salt and pepper.

Christmas Tree Bread
2 packages active dry yeast
1/2 cup warm water
1 1/4 cups buttermilk
1/2 cup sugar
2 eggs
2 teaspoons baking powder
2 teaspoons salt
5 1/2 cups flour
1/2 cup margarine, softened

Dissolve yeast in warm water in large mixing bowl. Add buttermilk, sugar, margarine,

eggs, baking powder, salt, and 2 1/2 cups flour. Beat on low speed, scraping bowl constantly, for 30 seconds. Beat on medium speed, scraping bowl occasionally, for 2 minutes. Stir in remaining flour. Dough will be soft and slightly sticky. Turn dough onto well-floured surface; knead until smooth and elastic, about 5 minutes. Divide dough in half (to form two trees); shape one half at a time into eighteen 2-inch balls. Form tree shape with balls in rows of 5, 4, 3, 3, 1 on lightly greased cookie sheet. Roll remaining 2 balls together for trunk of tree. Cover; let rise in warm place for 1 hour. Bake at 350 degrees until golden brown, 20-25 minutes. Remove from cookie sheet and cool. Beat 2 cups powdered sugar, 2-3 tablespoons water or milk, and 1 teaspoon vanilla until smooth. Decorate trees with frosting. Trim with candied fruit.

Fruit Salsa
2 medium Granny Smith apples
1 1/2 cups fresh strawberries
1 kiwi, peeled
1 small orange
2 tablespoons brown sugar
2 tablespoons apple jelly

Peel, core, and chop apples. Hull strawberries and slice. Peel, core, and chop kiwi. Grate 2 tablespoons orange zest, squeeze rest of orange to equal 1/4 cup of juice. Stir all of the above with brown sugar and apple jelly in a bowl. Terrific on bread and muffins!

FAMILY ORNAMENTS TO MAKE TOGETHER

If you live in the woods or in the country, it might be fun to make old-fashioned ornaments to reflect your family's current roots. Use buttons to make cute, rustic ornaments. All you'll need for this project is glue, cardboard, and a bunch of buttons. Cut shapes like gingerbread men, candy canes, and snowmen out of the cardboard. Now glue the buttons onto the cardboard—black buttons for gingerbread eyes, small red and white buttons for candy cane stripes, orange buttons for a snowman's nose. You can further embellish your creation with colored pens. Make sure you decorate both sides, then hang your new ornaments with a small piece of twine.

If you live near the water, you can display a shell tree! Gather seashells, gold and silver or pastel spray paint, metallic-tone beads, fake pearls, dried flowers, and ribbon. Spray paint the shells and let them dry. Then glue on ribbons, beads, pearls, and dried flowers. Great for a tropical Christmas!

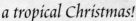

READYING THE ROOMS

A wonderful way to build tradition *and* decorate your house for the holidays is to devote a portion of your Celebration of Family tea to trimming the Christmas tree. If you haven't yet purchased your tree, go into the mountains or to a nearby Christmas tree farm (many give candy canes and hot cocoa to youngsters or offer free horsedrawn wagon rides; check your local newspaper for farms that offer fun activities). The trip will become a ritual in itself! If you are unable to cut your own tree, make sure the whole family goes together to pick out a tree at a lot. Many schools and charities sell precut Christmas trees,

CHRISTMAS TIMELINE
1510: A decorated Christmas tree displayed in Riga, Latvia.
1610: Tinsel invented in Germany.

A SEASON OF ANTICIPATION

It's fun to create your own family Advent calendar. Here are three ideas for a season of anticipation—

- **Open the Door:** *Draw a Christmas scene on a sheet of construction paper, and sketch 25 little doors on it. Mark the doors 1-25, then cut three sides so they open and close just like a real door would. Now place this sheet of paper over another sheet of paper. Draw a picture or write a Christmas saying behind every door. Glue the first sheet (the one with the doors) over the second sheet (the one with the pictures or sayings). If the doors don't stay closed, you can use small pieces of tape.*

- **A Season of Sweets:** *Choose 25 pieces of individually wrapped hard candy. Tie each candy to a piece of twine, a strand of red or green yarn, or a thin piece of torn Christmas fabric. Then hang all the strings of candy on a coat hanger, a drapery rod, or even on the Christmas tree. Take turns enjoying a piece of candy every day. As the candy supply diminishes, Christmas is getting closer!*

- **Christmas Chain:** *Make a paper chain out of red and green construction paper. Before you connect and glue the pieces in the chain, number them 1-25. You can also write a little message, a part of the Christmas story, or the promise for a small treat on each one. Break off a piece of the chain every day of Advent.*

and it's always nice to support a good cause during the holidays.

Be sure to gather some branches for additional decorating. Another option is to purchase a tree with a balled root. It won't drop nearly as many needles as a freshly cut tree, and you can plant it in your yard when Christmas is over.

As you're headed out to get your tree, you can tell the children about the origins of this now-familiar symbol of Christmas. Its story comes to us from Germany, where the theologian Martin Luther cut and decorated the first Christmas tree for his children back in

A Teddy Bear for the Tree

Materials:

For each bear, you'll need:

- one Christmas ball ornament
- four 1/2" pom poms
- three 1/4" pom poms
- one 2" pom pom
- one pair googly eyes
- scrap of red felt
- hot glue gun and
  glue sticks

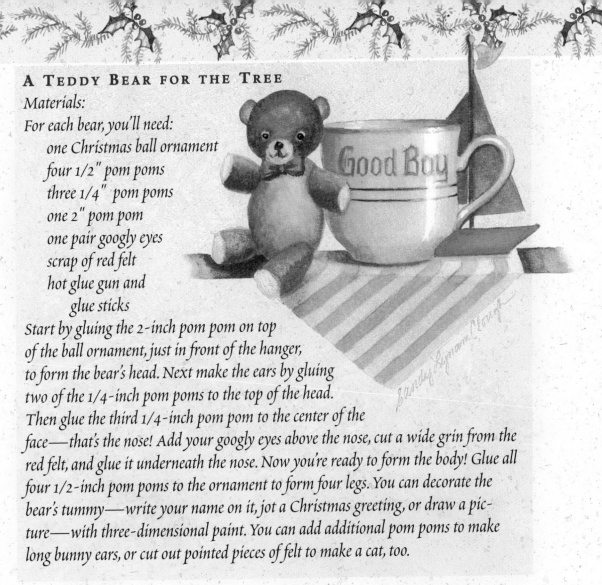

Start by gluing the 2-inch pom pom on top of the ball ornament, just in front of the hanger, to form the bear's head. Next make the ears by gluing two of the 1/4-inch pom poms to the top of the head. Then glue the third 1/4-inch pom pom to the center of the face—that's the nose! Add your googly eyes above the nose, cut a wide grin from the red felt, and glue it underneath the nose. Now you're ready to form the body! Glue all four 1/2-inch pom poms to the ornament to form four legs. You can decorate the bear's tummy—write your name on it, jot a Christmas greeting, or draw a picture—with three-dimensional paint. You can add additional pom poms to make long bunny ears, or cut out pointed pieces of felt to make a cat, too.

1535. According to legend, Luther was walking home through the woods one Christmas Eve under the bright, starry sky, contemplating the wonder and beauty of the evening and wishing he could somehow capture the moment to share with his children. An image of a tall evergreen tree sparkling with candlelight popped into his mind, and on his way home he found a tree just the right size. He cut it down, carried it home, and decorated it. And, just as he'd imagined, his children were overjoyed. In 1841, the custom began in England when Prince Albert had a Christmas tree set up in Windsor Castle especially for his wife, Queen Victoria, and their children. As you can see, the putting up of the

Christmas tree is certainly a family affair!

Evergreens have become a yuletide symbol shared by many cultures. The green branches represent the promises of spring and new life. The candles or lights on the tree reflect the hope and peace of the season. And the Early Americans found in the Christmas tree a traditional holiday decoration from the Old World that could brighten even the bleakest of frontier cabins.

Once you've returned home with the tree, reward yourself with a hearty tea and prepare to begin the trimming. If your tree is already up and decorated, you could take some time to make a few special ornaments or get a roaring fire going while you string popcorn or cranberries. Little ones might have fun stringing styrofoam packaging peanuts instead of popcorn. They're easy to string and not as crumbly as popcorn pieces. To add some variety to your popcorn or peanut chain, randomly add brightly colored buttons to the string for an old-fashioned look.

When trimming the tree, be sure to turn on your family's favorite Christmas music. For a tree rich in memories, display all the ornaments your family has collected over the years. Or perhaps you'd like to do a themed tree this year—an animal tree, a gingerbread tree, a Nativity tree. Remember, everything doesn't have to perfectly match; in fact, it looks best if it doesn't! And be sure to let the children hang some of the ornaments. Mom might want to hang all of the fragile silver balls, or Dad could be in charge of the lights. But certainly let the little ones help. They'll be proud of how they, too, have made the tree pretty!

It goes without saying that once you're finished decorating the tree, you need to turn off all the lights and gather round to admire your family's creation. Pour cups of herbal tea or cocoa, and snuggle up together on the sofa to sing Christmas carols, tell stories, or reminisce about past Christmases as you celebrate the warmth of togetherness. You might decide to come together to admire the tree *every* evening of December!

CUSTOMS OF CHRISTMAS

A Christmas tradition I've long cherished is the tradition of the Advent calendar. Advent is the four-week period prior to Christmas that serves as a time of preparing the heart and the spirit for the coming of the Christ child. Many people celebrate Advent by purchasing or making an Advent calendar—a calendar that contains a door for each of the twenty-four days before Christmas that, when opened, reveals a picture or a small treat. On the twenty-fifth day, the door generally opens to reveal a Nativity scene. Others celebrate the season of Advent by lighting the candles of the Advent wreath each night and saying a prayer. The evergreens in the Advent wreath symbolize life and growth; the shape of the wreath, a circle, is a sign of eternity without end; and the lighted candles stand for the presence of God.

Your family might choose to celebrate Advent by doing a special Christmas activity every day. At the beginning of the month, write down twenty-four ways to celebrate the season on small slips of paper. Then place the slips into a decorated jar. Each day, take turns drawing an idea from your Advent jar. By thinking of the activities and doing them together, you're sure to create even more family traditions!

The rooms were very still while the pages were softly turned and the winter sunshine crept in to touch the bright heads and serious faces with a Christmas greeting.

—LOUISA MAY ALCOTT
Little Women

THE THIRD TEA OF CHRISTMAS

A Celebration of Joy

Pampering guests with traditional good cheer

*Please come and join me
for a proper afternoon tea
in celebration of Christmas.*

If this Christmas you're longing to escape back to a time of romance and gentility, an era of propriety and luxury, consider putting on a traditional Victorian high tea. This is the tea party where you pull out all the stops, dress your home—and yourself—to the hilt, serve an abundance of delectable sweets, and pretend like you're back in that era of waltzes, petticoats, and horsedrawn carriages. You get to play the part of the gracious hostess, and your friends the part of the pampered guests.

DID YOU KNOW...?

We have Anna, the Duchess of Bedford, to thank for the delightful tradition of a proper afternoon tea—tea served with miniature sandwiches, small cakes, and other such delicacies. In her day, the English people typically ate a large breakfast and a late dinner, without much in between. By the middle of the afternoon, the Duchess always experienced a "sinking feeling," which she staved off by dining on tea, cakes, tarts, and biscuits at four o'clock in the afternoon. Thus was born the custom of taking afternoon tea.

It's a wonderful way to share the spirit of Christmas and express your love and appreciation for those who have made your year so special.

My tradition is to put on a formal tea every Christmas, and I love to go all out and create a celebration that everyone will remember long after the party is over. Yet as I scan the many tasks on my holiday "to-do" list, my heart starts beating more quickly when I think of all that I still need to accomplish. Surprisingly, I've found that hosting my Christmas tea helps me keep everything in perspective and reminds me what it is that I'm celebrating. My tea party helps warm up my holiday and reminds me how I find the meaning of the season in the giving. And I encourage you to do the same.

A Celebration of Joy tea party helps spread traditional good cheer and gives those you care about something to look forward to year after year. It's your love expressed in your preparations—the tea table standing at attention next to the Christmas tree, outfitted in snowy white linens and pearly china. The platters of freshly baked cakes and cookies. The strains of a string quartet playing familiar Christmas songs. A picture of joy.

A WORD ABOUT TEA

To prepare your tea in the proper way, steep instead of boiling it. Tea leaves release their flavor in hot water, and the taste is more pleasant in the beverage that has been steeped. The hotter the water, the faster the tea will steep. Three to five minutes is sufficient steeping time for most teas. The term "the agony of the leaves" refers to the process of the leaves uncurling when the hot water is poured over them.

Menu for a Celebration of Joy tea party—

Traditional Tea Sandwiches
Trifle Fit for a Queen
Scones with Lemon Curd

RECIPES

Traditional Tea Sandwiches

Afternoon tea sandwiches are made from very thinly sliced bread with crusts removed. Try these delicious ideas for filling:

- Thinly sliced chicken breast or smoked salmon with watercress and mayonnaise on white bread.
- Stilton cheese crumbled over apples on pumpernickel bread.
- Cream cheese mixed with chutney, a dash of curry, and lemon juice on white bread.
- Paper-thin slices of red radish on white bread with unsalted butter.
- Tomato slices sprinkled with freshly chopped basil on rye bread spread with mayonnaise.

Trifle Fit for a Queen

    5 peaches, peeled and
       sliced

2/3 cup + 2 tablespoons peach schnapps
1 5 x 9-inch pound cake
fresh berries for garnish
10 ladyfingers
1 recipe peach cream
   (recipe follows)
1 cup whipping cream
2 tablespoons sugar

Brush flat sides of ladyfingers with 1/3 cup of peach schnapps and line the sides and bottom of a glass serving bowl with 8-10 cup capacity. Spoon half of the peach cream over the ladyfingers lining the bottom of the dish. Arrange half of the peaches on top of the peach cream. Slice cake lengthwise into 1/2-inch slices and brush cake slices on both sides with 1/3 cup peach schnapps. Arrange half of the cake slices on top of peaches. Repeat layers of peach cream, peaches, and cake slices. Whip cream until medium-soft peaks form. Add sugar and 2 tablespoons schnapps and continue beating until blended. Spread cream mixture over the top of trifle and garnish with fresh berries. Wrap tightly with plastic wrap and refrigerate overnight.

Peach Cream
   8 egg yolks
   2 1/4 cups half-and-half
   3 tablespoons peach
      schnapps

CHRISTMAS TIMELINE
1660: Record of a tree lit with candles in Germany.
1800: Tree ornaments being manufactured in Europe.

6 tablespoons sugar
4 teaspoons cornstarch

In a medium bowl, beat egg yolks until thick-ened. Gradually add sugar and beat until mixture is thick and lemon-colored. Pour into a saucepan and beat in 2 cups half-and-half. Mix cornstarch with remaining half-and-half and beat into egg mixture. Cook over medi-um-low heat and stir constantly until mix-ture thickens (6-8 minutes). Do not let mix-ture boil. Remove from heat and stir in the peach schnapps. Cool to room temperature and then chill. Mixture will thicken more as it cools.

Basic Scones
2 cups flour
1 tablespoon baking powder
2 tablespoons sugar
1/2 teaspoon salt
6 tablespoons butter
1/2 cup buttermilk
1 egg, lightly beaten

Mix dry ingredients. Cut in 6 tablespoons butter until mixture resembles coarse corn-meal. Make a well in the center and pour in buttermilk. If you don't have buttermilk, you can use regular milk. Mix until dough clings together and is a bit sticky; do not overmix. Turn out dough onto a floured surface and shape into a 6-to-8-inch round about 1 1/2 inches thick. Quickly cut into pie wedges or use a large biscuit cutter to cut circles. The secret of tender scones is a minimum of handling. Place on ungreased cookie sheet, making sure the sides of scones don't touch each other. Brush with egg for a shiny, beautiful brown scone. Bake at 425 degrees for 10-20 minutes, or until lightly browned.

Lemon Curd
grated peel of 4 lemons
juice of 4 lemons (about 1 cup)
4 eggs, beaten
1/2 cup butter, cut into small
   pieces
2 cups sugar

In the top of a large double boiler, combine lemon peel, lemon juice, eggs, butter, and sugar. Place over simmering water and stir until sugar is dissolved. Continue to cook, stirring occasionally, until thickened and smooth. While still hot, pour into hot, sterilized 1/2-pint canning jars, leaving about 1/8 inch for headspace. Run a narrow spatula down between lemon curd and side of jar to release air. Top with sterilized lids; firmly screw on bands. Place in a draft-free area to cool and store in a cool, dry place. (I keep mine in the refrigerator.) Lemon curd doesn't keep indefinitely, so make only as much as you will use in a couple of weeks. Makes about 1 pint.

> There are few hours in life more agreeable than the hour dedicated to the ceremony known as afternoon tea.
>
> HENRY JAMES
> Portrait of a Lady

READYING THE ROOMS

As you prepare to decorate your rooms for the holidays as well as for your Celebration of Joy tea, consider bringing the beauty of nature indoors as the Victorians did with ornately decorated trees, abundant fruit and floral displays, and piles upon piles of greens. Check in a local nursery to see what's available in your area during the wintertime, then choose a variety of flowers and greenery sure to bring visual pleasures as well as the delightful fragrance of the winter outdoors into the home—holly, ivy, mistletoe, poinsettias, Christmas rose, juniper, pepperberries, paperwhites, pine, rosemary, and eucalyptus. If you have pets or small children, limit your selection to non-toxic materials and keep anything else out of reach.

Decorate mantels and staircase banisters with an array of fresh garlands, and pile armfuls of greenery on top of cabinets and bookcases. You can even twine some white lights through the greens to make an elegant display. Fill large wicker baskets and wooden boxes with holiday greens, gathering them up with silver or gold organdy ribbon. Plant greens in crystal or ceramic bowls, display them on every stairstep accompanied by fragrant candles in sparkling holders, peek them out of the tops of stockings, and even arrange them around place settings!

With their delightful color, scent, and texture, evergreens have long been a part of wintertime celebrations around the world. While other plants lost their leaves and appeared to hide for the winter, the evergreens met the season boldly, retaining their fresh color as a reminder of life and hope. The hanging of greens, holly and ivy in particular, has long been a winter tradition in Great Britain. The verdant color helped warm those who had been out in the cold, reminding them that spring and warmth were just around the corner. For primitive European tribes, branches hung above doorways promised good fortune and good health through the chilly months. The Romans exchanged evergreen branches with friends as tokens of good wishes. And many all over the world have regarded the red berries and green branches of wintertime plants as a symbol of the love and hope brought by the Christ child.

Think of delighting all of your guests' senses as they arrive at your Celebration of Joy tea party. After all, you do want to make this an occasion to remember, don't you? Now that the greens have been placed throughout the house and the seasonal flowers—poinsettias and paperwhites, for instance, create a beautiful red-and-white effect—have been put on display, put the fragrance of Christmas in the air even more with the scents of the season.

You can purchase potpourri bags of Christmas herbs, pinecones, twigs, and dried flowers in craft stores, or make your own. To make the potpourri smell extra fragrant for your guests, evenly spread a generous amount in a large bowl. Place a few scented votives securely atop the potpourri. The heat from the candles will warm up the potpourri, and the delicious scent will be released all throughout your home. You can also fill a big punchbowl with cloved oranges, evergreen branches,

apples, and cinnamon sticks. For a really quick and easy pick-me-up, sprinkle

An Invitation to Tea

A PROPER INVITATION TO TEA

I suppose you could call and invite your friends to afternoon tea, or send them an email. But to make your celebration proper in all ways, you really should send them an invitation via the post office. Victorian invitations to tea were works of art in themselves, extravagantly engraved on white paper. You don't have to go that far, but hand lettering (calligraphy, if you know it) looks very pretty and personal in this age of computers. Choose Christmas-themed stationery, or design your own notecards with stencils, rubber stamps, or free-hand with pens. You can add glitter, Christmas confetti, or other festive touches. The wording, however, should be simple and clear:

Emilie Barnes
requests the pleasure of your company for a Celebration of Joy Christmas tea.
Saturday, December 6
between four and six o'clock.
R.S.V.P.

powdered cinnamon in an aluminum pie plate and let it warm slowly in your oven. A holiday baking smell will fill the air in no time!

Choose candles, potpourri, and those little aromatic lightbulb rings in your favorite holiday scents. Think of the mood you wish to create. If holiday baking comes to mind, consider the fragrances of cinnamon, apple, vanilla, gingerbread, or nutmeg. Pine, juniper, and other outdoorsy scents bring the fresh smell of nature into the rooms of your home. For bedrooms, bathrooms, and other private areas, consider light floral or fruity aromas such as lavender, honeysuckle, tea rose, or gardenia—or, appropriately, tea-inspired smells like chamomile or mint.

Just a few more touches inside and out will guarantee that every guest is in the holiday spirit the minute he or she walks through the front door—a Christmas doormat that brightens your front step; a fragrant wreath of evergreen branches, berries, pine cones, and a fancy big bow; lots of little white lights outdoors, lining rooftops and windows and wound through branches and bushes; jingle bells tied to the front door; and, most of all, a hearty hug or handshake that welcomes everyone to your tea party, the celebration you've planned just for them.

CUSTOMS OF CHRISTMAS

If you'd like to put on a traditional tea with a capital "T," consider spreading your tea table with standard fare from the 1700s and 1800s—capons and turkeys, geese and sirloins of beef, plum puddings and mincemeat pies. (Your guests will forgive you for leaving out the boar's head and the lampry eel pie, I'm sure.) Though most households today do not have the luxury of a hired cook, it might be fun to let your guests know what English gentlemen of the 15th and 16th centuries did to *their* cooks during their Christmas morning open houses. If everything was not ready when the first guest arrived, the cook was taken by the household's men and run through the marketplace as the men announced the cook's laziness. Your guests, however, will probably be happy to help add the finishing touches to a near-completed meal!

The Scandinavians celebrated Christmas with a bevy of traditional foods—animal-shaped *julkuse* bread and *limpa*, a bread made with orange peel and molasses. In addition to the classic *lutfish*, a great variety of sweets were served—seven different kinds of cookies, including almond-flavored *sandbakelse*, ginger-flavored *pepparkaker*, and *strutar*, a cookie filled with jam and whipped

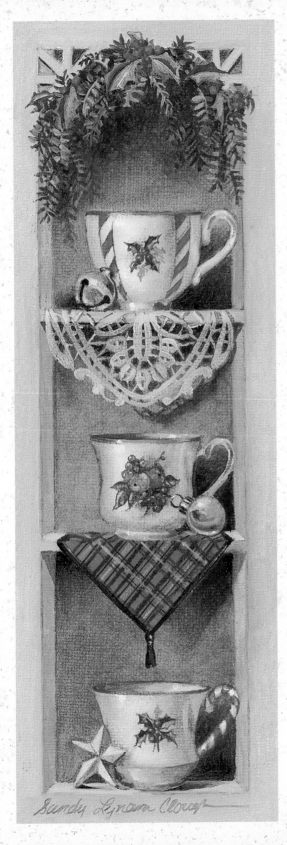

cream. A Christmas Eve rice pudding called *risgrynsgrot* was always fun to serve, for hidden in the pudding was a single almond. If you found the almond, luck and marriage were sure to soon follow.

Fanciful desserts hailed from Germany—*marzipan, lebkuchen, springerle, stollen,* and a mouthwatering collection of spiced cookies. In America, the Pennsylvania Germans made sure to eat their daily seven sweets and seven sours along with black walnut cake, fruit dumplings, macaroons, and a concoction of popped corn, nuts, and taffy syrup.

A Mexican Christmas tradition is a special hot chocolate, made with a Mexican chocolate which is composed of sugar, almond, and cinnamon. The drink is whipped with a wooden stick called a *molinillo* that is rolled back and forth in your hand.

Think about where your family comes from, and the heritages of your guests. It's fun to bake these traditions right into your holiday celebration with a variety of customary treats. Stories, sharing, and laughter are sure to follow, making for a joyous time together and many wonderful memories.

27

A Celebration of Warmth

Letting the lights of the season fill the heart with coziness

You're invited to a fun sleepover—a sleepover tea party!
Please join me for games and goodies,
and maybe even cookies at midnight!

Slumber parties are always fun. Children plan them for weeks, figuring out what games to play and what to eat if they are hosting, or thinking of toys to pack and a small gift to bring if they're the fortunate one who has been invited. This holiday season, try holding a whole new kind of sleepover—a tea party sleepover! You can invite your children's best friends, your nieces and nephews, your grandchildren, or your best friend's children.

You have lots of options for a slumber party tea, but the most important rule is that teatime must happen when it's dark outside. After all, this is a Celebration of Warmth tea party! And only when it's dark do all of the holiday lights shine in all their glory, warming cold little hands and feet and making everyone's heart happy.

Before you take your tea, go for a drive around the neighborhood and look at all the holiday lights. Everyone can even wear their pajamas for this trip and bring blankets and teddy bears in the car. Or bundle up and walk up and down your block, admiring the glow of Christmas. Afterwards, gather inside and warm yourself up with tea and treats.

If you've mixed up some cookie dough beforehand, you and your little guests can have a cookie-making party. Let the children roll the dough, cut out shapes with holiday cookie cutters, and decorate the treats with colored sprinkles. Then, if you have the luxury of sleeping in the next morning, you can even wake everyone up for a cookies-at-midnight kitchen raid! Grab some cookies and a warm glass of milk. Then bundle up in warm clothes and sit in the backyard. Look at the stars and talk about the Star of Bethlehem—the light that led the wise men to the true source of warmth at Christmas.

DID YOU KNOW...?

Many people place a five-pointed star on their treetop, but do you know why? The star's appearance can be found in the Christmas story in the Bible. The New Testament says that a star appeared over Bethlehem and served as a light to guide the wise men from the East to the Christ child. The child, Jesus, is sometimes referred to as "the bright and morning star."

Menu for a Celebration of Warmth tea party—

*Peanut Butter and Jelly Sandwiches Cut
into Shapes
Gumdrop Bread
Grandma's Strawberry Bread
Strawberries and Pineapples Dipped in
Orange Chocolate Sauce*

RECIPES

Gumdrop Bread

    2 1/2 cups flour
    1 1/4 cups buttermilk
    1/2 cup white sugar
    1/2 cup brown sugar
    1 teaspoon salt
    1 teaspoon vanilla
    1/2 teaspoon baking soda
    1/4 cup shortening
    2 eggs
    3 tablespoons baking powder
    1 cup small gumdrops,
       cut into halves
    1/2 cup chopped nuts, if desired

*Heat oven to 350 degrees. Grease bottom
only of 9 x 5 x 3-inch loaf pan. Beat all
ingredients except gumdrops and nuts in
large mixing bowl on low speed for 15 seconds. Beat on medium speed, scraping bowl
constantly, for 30 seconds. Stir in gumdrops
and nuts; pour into pan. Bake until wooden
pick inserted in center comes out clean, 60-
65 minutes. Loosen sides of loaf from pan;
remove from pan. Cool completely on wire
rack. Store bread at least 24 hours before
slicing. To store, wrap and refrigerate no
longer than 1 week.*

Grandma's Strawberry Bread

    2 cups sugar
    3 cups flour
    1 teaspoon cinnamon
    1 teaspoon baking soda
    1/2 teaspoon salt
    2 cups frozen strawberries, thawed
    1 cup pecans
    4 eggs
    1 1/4 cups cooking oil

*Mix all ingredients together in mixing
bowl. Grease and flour three 8 x 4 x 2-inch
loaf pans. Bake one hour at 350 degrees.*

Orange Chocolate Sauce

    12 ounces semi-sweet chocolate
       chips
    2/3 cup heavy cream
    2 tablespoons orange flavoring

*Melt chocolate and cream over low heat
until chips melt. Stir in flavoring. Keep
warm over low heat. Enjoy!*

CHRISTMAS TIMELINE
*1819: Popular sketch by Krimmel
released depicting an American family
with a Christmas tree on the table.*

READYING THE ROOMS

When you're decorating for your Celebration of Warmth tea party, think of light as a major element in your decor. Get out all your candles, hurricane lamps, oil lamps, and strings of Christmas lights. If you're concerned about wax dripping, use natural beeswax candles. They have a delicate scent, and they burn cheerily minus the drips. Of course, be very careful when you mix candles with children. Put the candles out of the reach of little hands, and never leave candles burning unattended.

To get the outside of your house warm and welcoming, line your driveways and sidewalks with paper lanterns. You can make these luminaries with ordinary brown paper lunch sacks. Cut snowflakes, stars, or other shapes in the bags so that the light will shine through. You can also glue colored tissue paper on the inside of the bags, covering your cutout shapes, for a stained-glass look.

MAKE A CHRISTMAS CANDLE HOLDER

Materials:
4-ounce juice glass with straight sides
tea light
glue
water-based craft paint
paintbrush
craft knife
heavy, black paper

Paint the outside surface of the glass, covering it entirely. You can use red or green paint, or even a shimmery color. Cut out a piece of black paper that fits around the outside of the glass. Next, cut Christmas shapes—trees, stars, bells—out of the paper. Now you'll glue the paper, making sure the black is facing out, to the outside of the glass so it covers the paint, except where you've cut out the shapes. Place the tea light inside the glass. When you light the wick, your original cut-outs will shine through the black paper.

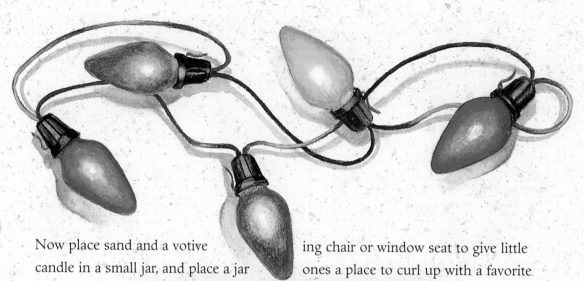

Now place sand and a votive candle in a small jar, and place a jar in each bag. You'll have a glowing path that welcomes all to your home!

Now it's time to come inside and get the guest quarters prepared! Think comfortable and cozy—it's okay to leave a pile of children's books scattered on the bedside table or a stack of blankets at the foot of the bed. Add a quilt and pillows to a rock-ing chair or window seat to give little ones a place to curl up with a favorite

AN OLD-FASHIONED LIGHT OF WELCOME

You and your little guests can spend part of your tea party making old-fashioned lights of welcome for the windows. You'll need sturdy cardboard, heavy aluminum foil (aluminum pie tins work well, too), a long bread-type twistie, and a single plastic candle with an electric cord and a bulb (found at a craft store). Cut out a five-to-six-inch star from the cardboard and punch two holes in one of the points. Cover the star completely with aluminum foil (or you can just cut the star out of the pie tin). Now secure the star to the plastic base of the candle, right below and in front of the bulb. When you plug in your light of welcome and place it in your window, those outside will see a star surrounded by a halo of light.

story. Pillows filled with lavender promote a good night's sleep, as does a soft teddy bear or rag doll. A reading light, nightlight, and alarm clock are thoughtful touches, too.

You can even put decorated miniature trees in the guest rooms, or drape a swag of greenery over the bed. Plant a poinsettia in a

cheery basket, and tie a bright red ribbon around the handle. Just before your guests head for bed, sneak into the room to turn down the covers and place a small chocolate truffle or mint on the pillow for a cute bed-and-breakfast touch. For a midnight snack, keep small bowls of fresh fruit in the rooms. You can also stash sandwiches and juice in the fridge, and make sure the cookie jar

is filled for those cookies at midnight! Another fun thing to do is to keep a blank journal and pen on a bedside table so your guests can journal their thoughts. It makes a great memory book of all the wonderful people who have stayed in your home.

Finish up your preparations by making sure the bathroom is stocked with sweet-smelling soaps, shampoos, and

A Word about Tea

Tea parties don't always have to happen with tea! You can serve hot chocolate, spiced cider, or even a glass of warm milk and have the same enjoyable experience. In fact, many children prefer something a bit sweeter than tea with sugar. Here are some good tea replacements for your Celebration of Warmth tea party—

Cranberry Punch

4 cups cranberry juice

1 1/2 cups sugar

4 cups pineapple juice

1 tablespoon almond extract

2 quarts ginger ale

Mix all ingredients. Chill or add ice cubes.

Old-Fashioned Egg Nog

6 eggs

1 cup whipping cream, whipped

4 cups milk

1/4 cup sugar

1/4 teaspoon salt

1 teaspoon vanilla

Blend together eggs, milk, sugar, and salt. Fold in whipping cream and vanilla. Pour into bowl or pitcher. Cover and chill thoroughly, several hours or overnight. Sprinkle with nutmeg, if desired.

Spiced Mocha Mix

1/2 cup sugar

1/4 cup freeze-dried coffee

1/4 cup cocoa

1 teaspoon nutmeg

1/2 teaspoon cinnamon

Place all ingredients in blender. Cover and blend on high speed 15 seconds; stir. Cover and blend until completely mixed (15 seconds). Store in tightly-covered container. For each serving, place 2-3 teaspoons of mix into cup. Fill with boiling water; stir. Top with whipped cream if desired.

• Cranberry/raspberry juice mixed in equal parts with ginger ale, with raspberry sherbet floating on top tastes delicious, and looks festive when set out in a large crystal punchbowl.

conditioners. Think of the things your guests might forget—a toothbrush or toothpaste, a hair dryer, a brush—and keep extras of those items on hand.

As you're setting the table for the morning's meal, make individual bouquets out of seasonal plants—pansies, tiny sprigs of holly, small evergreen cuttings, lingonberries—and arrange them in bud vases next to the place settings. You can even design tiny placecards to go next to each person's vase.

CUSTOMS OF CHRISTMAS

There's just something about light at Christmastime—candlelight, firelight, starlight, strings of Christmas lights. Long ago in the northernmost parts of Europe, people burned yule logs to give off warmth during the season of darkness. The Yule log, which was actually an entire tree, was carefully chosen to last the entire Yule season. ("Yuletide" means "the turning of the sun.") The people would place one end of the tree in the fire, leaving the rest of it jutting out into the room, and slowly burn a bit of the log each day. You probably won't want to fully adapt this tradition, but do make sure to take advantage of the fireplace or woodstove if you have one!

Candles have long been popular at Christmas, perhaps as representations of the star that guided the wise men to Bethlehem. In Scandinavia and Germany, people set out candles on Christmas Eve to light the way for *Kristkind,* or Christ child. In other European countries, including France, Belgium, and Holland, processions of children followed illuminated stars through the village streets. A door propped open and a candle shining in the window welcomed all visitors to homes in Ireland on the holy night. And in northern Germany, people kept lights burning throughout the night along with a table laden with food for the Virgin Mary and an angel who passed by while everyone slept.

I encourage you to make this Christmas a season of warmth and light, full of welcome to all who stop by. Reward them with a hearty dose of friendship and caring at this enchanting time of the year.

> *"Ain't it nice," old Anna was saying, "dat it shust go on and on—Christmas lights and Christmas trees and Christmas spirit? All over town, no matter who lives in 'em, de nice Christmas candles burn on. In yours; in mine."*
>
> BESS STREETER ALDRICH

A Celebration of Sharing

Spreading the message of the season through song

*Here we come a-caroling!
We'll stroll through the neighborhood singing,
then return to my house for food and conversation.*

A cheery group of Christmas carolers at my door always brings a smile to my face and joy to my heart. Caroling is such an old-fashioned, homey way of spreading the good news of the season. In modern-day America, a group of Christmas carolers serenading your home is a fairly uncommon occurrence. Most of us rely on our CD players and radios to provide us with holiday music. But there's just something about a group of carolers that outshines even the best recording of "Silent Night" or "The Coventry Carol." Dressed in warm coats and scarves, making their way from house to house with laughter and conversation, these groups of singing angels

DID YOU KNOW...?

The custom of Christmas caroling began in England around 1660. Many of our favorite carols today, such as "Joy to the World," "Silent Night," and "O Come All Ye Faithful," were not composed until the 1800s.

lend a neighborly caring to big city streets and country roads alike.

You don't have to be a great singer to take part in a caroling party. When you join your voice with the voices of ten or fifteen others, something wonderful happens. Voices young and old, high and low, blend together in a familiar chorus to bring a touch of neighborly kindness and caring to the evening. When you're preparing for your Celebration of Sharing tea party, be sure to prepare enough extra food to go around. A caroling party is the sort of event where a few additional people show up and join the festivities. And they're always welcome to do so! After all, this tea party is about sharing—sharing your time and your happiness and your home with others.

In your invitations, encourage all the carolers to bring lanterns or flash-lights and to bundle up, especially if snow or cold weather is in the forecast. Depending on what time you decide to carol, you can serve tea either before or after the singing. A party around dinnertime calls for an early, hearty tea so your carolers will be well-fortified to sing their best. And a celebration later in the evening can conclude with hot tea and cookies or cakes. Because your guests will be giving to others, you can reward them by giving something to them!

Christmas Eve was a night of song that wrapped itself about you like a shawl. But it warmed more than your body. It warmed your heart...filled it, too, with a melody that would last forever.

BESS STREETER ALDRICH

Menu for a Celebration of Sharing tea party—

Seafood Butter on Mini Pumpernickel Loaf
Sweet Poppyseed Bread
Nut Gem Cookies
Peanut Brittle

RECIPES

Seafood Butter

1 cup cooked shrimp or lobster
1/4 pound butter
1/2 teaspoon lemon juice
pepper to taste

Combine all ingredients into blender. Blend on high until spreadable. Chill before serving.

Sweet Poppyseed Bread

1 box yellow cake mix
small box vanilla pudding mix
5 eggs
1/2 cup oil
1/2 cup water
1/2 cup orange juice
1 tablespoon almond extract
1/2 cup poppy seeds

Combine all ingredients. Bake at 325 degrees for 50 minutes in greased loaf pan. Makes two loaves.

Nut Gems

1 cup butter
4 tablespoons sugar
2 tablespoons milk
2 teaspoons rum extract
2 cups flour
1 cup chopped walnuts

Mix, chill, and roll into small balls. Bake at 300 degrees for 15 minutes. Roll in powdered sugar after balls are slightly cooled.

Peanut Brittle

1 cup peanuts
1 cup sugar
1/8 teaspoon salt
1/2 cup white corn syrup
1 teaspoon butter
1 teaspoon vanilla
1 teaspoon baking soda

Stir peanuts, sugar, and salt; add syrup in 1 1/2-quart glass bowl. Microwave on high 7-8 minutes; stir well after 4 minutes. At end of 7-8 minutes, add butter and vanilla. Blend well. Return to microwave and cook on high 1-2 minutes more. Remove from oven and add baking soda. Stir until light and foamy. Pour immediately onto greased cookie sheet. Cool 30-60 minutes. Break into pieces and store in airtight container.

CHRISTMAS TIMELINE

1822: Clement Clarke Moore, an American, writes "A Visit from Saint Nicholas" for his family (now known as "Twas the Night Before Christmas")— published in 1848.

1822: German merchants living in England display decorated trees in their homes.

Readying the Rooms

To prepare your home for a caroling party, make sure it's cozy and clean inside, with the tea table set, chairs and sofas plumped up and made inviting with plush pillows and festive throws. The majority of your party, however, will be held out of doors. In essence, you're bringing the celebration to the homes at which you carol. While some of your neighbors might invite you in to warm your hands and have something toasty to drink, for the most part you and your guests will be sharing your hospitality with them. So think of yourself as having two sets of guests—the guests you invite to go caroling with you and the guests to whom you sing!

You can purchase inexpensive songbooks or pages of sheet music at a local music store to prepare for the caroling. Another good idea is to borrow some hymn books from your church, or print pages of Christmas carols off the Internet. And ask your guests to bring favorite music of their own. If you've found a few pages of elaborately decorated sheet music, display them in shiny silver frames tied with red or green ribbon on your piano or mantel. You might even want to run through a few songs with everyone before you leave the house.

Once your home is warm, cozy, and filled with the sound of music, you can turn your focus to bringing that same Christmas cheer to your neighborhood.

Along with the gift of song, it's fun to give away other presents at a caroling party. Bake and decorate your favorite sugar or shortbread cookies, then arrange them on colorful paper plates and wrap them up in cheery cellophane. Add a bow and a Christmas greeting on top. You can even make up a name for your caroling group and sign it that way!

If your caroling group includes several other bakers, invite them to contribute a plateful or two of cookies to the celebration. Divide up the cookies, placing some on plates for the neighbors and bagging up some for your guests to take home. This way, you've combined a cookie exchange and a neighborhood gift-giving party all into one event! By delivering the cookies personally, you'll get to visit elderly people who often stay indoors and neighbors who aren't at home very much.

Another quick and easy holiday gift is my "beanbag" soup mix. It's a simple mixture of soup beans that I love to give along with a recipe card and a holiday greeting. You can hand out the gift-wrapped mixes to your neighbors and guests, and perhaps even have a big pot of soup simmering for a hearty pre- or post-caroling meal. To make the bean soup mixture, I tuck a generous combination of dry beans into a zip-lock bag and include my favorite bean soup recipe. To make enough soup mix for eight bags with 2 1/2 cups of

EMILIE'S YUMMY BEAN SOUP

This is the recipe I like to include with my gifts of "beanbag" soup—

1 package of gift beans

1 large onion, chopped

1 29-ounce can crushed tomatoes

1 clove crushed garlic

juice of 1 lemon

salt and pepper to taste

Wash beans thoroughly and place in large pot. Add enough water to cover beans by two inches. Boil two minutes and let stand one hour. Drain and add two quarts of water and 1/2 pound of ham or ham hocks and simmer 1 1/2 to 2 hours, covered. Add the rest of the ingredients and simmer 30 minutes or until beans are tender. Makes 10 to 12 big servings.

beans for each gift, I combine 2 cups of each of the following types of beans in a large container—black beans, pinto beans, pearl barley, lima beans, lentils, butter beans or large limas, navy beans, split green peas, red beans, and Great Northern beans. You may use any combination, though. Divide it up, add a cute tag and a recipe card, and your thoughtful gift is sure to feed many others!

Here's a few more ideas for a successful Celebration of Sharing tea party—

- *Type out the words to a selection of carols,* both traditional and fun, and paste them into bright red and green folders.
- *Tell your guests to come wearing brightly colored hats and scarves, coats and gloves, sweaters and skirts. If you have access to top hats or hoop skirts, wear those for a real Dickens-style caroling party.*
- *Wear bells on your shoelaces and carry strings of jingle bells.*
- *Bring along candles, flashlights, or lanterns.*
- *Serve hot cocoa when you come home, and use candy canes as stirring sticks.*

Most of all, sing loudly, put a smile on your face, and wish everyone you pass a spirited "Merry Christmas!"

CAROLERS' WASSAIL BOWL

My Christmas wassail recipe is sure to reward an enthusiastic group of carolers!

1 gallon apple cider
1 large can pineapple juice
1 cup orange spice herb tea
1 tablespoon whole cloves
1 tablespoon whole allspice
2 cinnamon sticks
square piece of muslin cloth
small piece of string

Mix the juices together in a big pot or crockery pot. Put the spices in the middle of a small square of muslin cloth and tie with a string into a little bundle. Put the spice bag in the pot and let the whole thing simmer 4 to 8 hours. Add water if the wassail gets too strong.

CUSTOMS OF CHRISTMAS

Did you know that not all songs we sing at Christmastime are truly carols? (It's still okay to call them that, though.) Most sacred songs, or songs that we sing in church, are actually called hymns. Many centuries ago, a carol was a dance accompanied by a merry song. The meaning gradually changed to include the song itself—a joyful tune that anyone could sing. The world "caroling" means "celebrating in song." It's an appropriate name, isn't it?

During the Middle Ages, groups of men and boys roamed the streets of

41

Suddenly, the angel was joined by a vast host of others—the armies of heaven—praising God: "Glory to God in the highest heaven," they sang.

THE GOSPEL OF LUKE

London, in search of food or money. The groups traveled from house to house, singing ancient carols and spreading holiday spirit in exchange for a bit of food or a few coins. If one of the members of the group had dark hair, he would attempt to be the "first foot" across someone's threshold on Christmas morning to bring good luck to the house along with a reward for his efforts. Later in the day, the "waits" would make their rounds. They were carolers, generally children, who sang and danced.

Perhaps the very first carols were those sung by the angels to announce the birth of the Christ child in Bethlehem. Many ancient carols were composed to retell the Christmas story, long before people had access to books or sheets of music. Years later, great musicians and theologians composed some of the carols we now consider classics. Martin Luther penned the words to "Away in a Manger," Mendelssohn composed "Hark! The Herald Angels Sing," and Handel wrote "Joy to the World" along with what is widely regarded as his masterpiece, "Messiah."

In Australia, a popular custom is "Carols by Candlelight," a communal outdoor singalong. When darkness falls, groups as small as five or as large as fifty thousand join together to sing Christmas songs while holding candles or torches. Norman Banks of Melbourne is credited with beginning this tradition in 1937. He came up with the idea of an entire community caroling together after he saw an old widow holding a single candle and singing along with her radio. It's a joyous tradition, sharing the uplifting message of the season through favorite melodies.

THE STORY OF "SILENT NIGHT"

There's a charming story behind the favorite carol "Silent Night." It was December 23, 1818, and the setting was the village of Oberndorf, Austria. Franz Gruber, a church organist, and Father Mohr, the priest, discovered a hole gnawed by a mouse in the leather bellows of the church organ. The thought of a Christmas service with no music saddened them both, but there was no way to fix the organ. Franz, thinking quickly, handed the priest a simple poem he had written and asked Father Mohr to set the words to music. On Christmas Eve, Father Mohr strummed his guitar while a choir of twelve boys and girls sang in clear, innocent voices the words to "Silent Night," filling the air with quiet reverence.

A Celebration of Merriment

Opening heart and home to those around us

All around us Christmas bells are ringing!
Please come to my home for
teatime, crafts, games, and singing!

Can you recall a Christmas scene from a cherished book or favorite film that included a big, merry gathering of family and friends? Perhaps you remember the winter reunion of aunts, uncles, cousins, and grandparents in Laura Ingalls Wilder's *Little House in the Big Woods.* Or you might dream of attending a traditional Christmas ball, like the heroine did in Jane Austen's *Emma.* Maybe you'd like to bring the spirit of the season to your neighbors, as the March girls did in Louisa May Alcott's *Little Women.* Whatever your preference, you too can have a big gathering of friends, family, and neighbors. It takes just a little bit of work and a lot of excitement— and the rewards in memories and strengthened friendships will last a lifetime!

A Celebration of Merriment tea party could take several forms—a big open house that brings

> **DID YOU KNOW...?**
> *In the 19th century, it was common for children to have their own small tables set with cakes and candies on Christmas Day.*

many different groups of friends, a tea for the extended family, or a large party given in honor of all the neighborhood children (parents are encouraged to come too, of course). This type of tea party is a great way for you to meet your neighbors, your children's friends, or reconnect with people you haven't seen in awhile. Food and music are musts for this gathering. If your supply of either is limited, turn the party into a potluck and encourage guests to bring along their favorite Christmas music. Many people enjoy baking and preparing goodies around the holidays anyway, and a delicious recipe is always a sure conversation starter! You and your family can provide the tea, the hospitality, and the setting for a Christmas party that is every bit as memorable as your favorite literary gathering!

A Word about Tea

There are many folk stories that accompany tea drinking. If you find bubbles on the surface of your cup, it is said that you will soon receive money. If a few loose leaves float to the top of your teacup, it is rumored that an intriguing stranger will come to visit. And did you realize that if you stir the tea in the teapot, you could be stirring up trouble? Here's one more—if two ladies pour tea from the same pot, one of them supposedly will give birth to a child with red hair within the year. These are just stories of course, but they might be amusing to share with your guests. You could even come up with a few folk stories of your own!

Menu for a Celebration of Merriment tea party—

Shrimp Crescents
Garlic Cheddar Biscuits
Pistachio Bread
Sliced Apples with Apple Dip

RECIPES

Shrimp Crescents

3 ounces cream cheese, softened
2 tablespoons mayonnaise
1 tablespoon catsup
1 teaspoon prepared mustard
1 cup finely chopped shrimp, cooked and cleaned
1/3 cup chopped celery
1 1/2 teaspoons finely chopped onion
10 crescent rolls

Blend cheese with mayonnaise; mix in catsup and mustard. Stir in shrimp, celery, and onion. Use as a filling in sliced crescent rolls.

Garlic Cheddar Biscuits

2 cups Bisquick
2/3 cup milk
1/2 cup shredded cheddar cheese
1/4 cup butter
1/4 teaspoon garlic powder

Mix first 3 ingredients vigorously for 30 seconds. Drop by spoonfuls onto ungreased cookie sheet. Bake at 350 degrees for 8-10 minutes. Mix butter and garlic powder; brush on hot biscuits.

Pistachio Bread

1 box butter recipe cake mix
1 box instant pistachio pudding
1 cup sour cream
4 eggs
1/4 cup oil
1/4 cup water

Mix above ingredients together.

TOPPING:
4 tablespoons brown sugar
chopped nuts
2 teaspoons cinnamon

Grease two bread pans or line with parchment paper. Fill pans with half of the batter. Sprinkle with topping and then add remaining batter. Bake at 350 degrees for 45 minutes or until done. Cool on wire rack for 10 minutes, then remove from pans and let cool completely.

Apple Dip

12 ounces cream cheese, softened
1/2 cup brown sugar
1/2 tablespoon vanilla

Mix well with hand mixer.

READYING THE ROOMS

To create an instant feeling of Christmas at your Celebration of Merriment tea, think of a familiar sound of Christmas—bells ringing! You can find jingle bells and ribbon at your local craft store. Choose ribbon to match your decor—silver and gold for an elegant appearance, plaids and raffia for a country feel, or red and green velvet for a traditional look. Tie a few bells to the end of each piece of ribbon, and fasten the ribbons around your doorknobs. Every time someone opens a door, you'll hear the sounds of Christmas.

Another fun thing to do with bells is to make a wreath with them. You'll need two sizes of wire (16-gauge and 24-gauge), jingle bells, and ribbon. First, twist the 16-gauge wire into a circle, making a closed loop at one end with a pair of pliers. Thread the jingle bells onto the open end until the wire is filled. Then form the unlooped ends into a

CREATE A CANDY WREATH CENTERPIECE

A candy wreath centerpiece is fun and functional at a big gathering. Encourage your guests to sneak candies throughout the evening—that's why you made the centerpiece!

Materials—

    1 styrofoam ring
    2 pounds of assorted cellophane-
        wrapped candies
    box of straight pins
    1 large candle or several smaller ones
        to fit in the center of the wreath

Take the straight pins and attach the candies to the styrofoam ring, covering it completely. Place the wreath in the center of the table, and set the candle or candles inside. Remind your guests that they simply have to unpin the candies to eat them!

hook and fasten the hook onto the closed loop. You can use the 24-gauge wire to fasten ribbon bows onto the wreath. Hang it on the door and listen for the bells.

Make sure you include your children in the party! If you don't have children, ask some nieces and nephews or neighborhood children to be party hosts and hostesses. They'll be happy to help with the festivities. Assign each child a task—greeting guests, taking coats and hats, passing out hors d'oeuvres and pouring water, clearing the table, serving dessert. You can even tell them to come wearing a certain color combination—red and white, or green and red. To really get into it, the kids can wear official party helper nametags. Reward them with a thank-you note and a small gift. Your guests will enjoy their delightful helpers, and the children will feel like they've really put on the party.

Think of fun and easy ways to serve your food—colorful paper plates, cups, and plasticware, veggies for dipping and Christmas cookies displayed in paper bags that are rolled down and tied with ribbon (try crushing the bags and then unfolding them for an old-fashioned, textured look), dips and dressings in hollowed-out gourds. The table will look festive, and you won't spend hours in the kitchen cleaning up everything.

Your punchbowl can double as a container for a delicious beverage and a cheery centerpiece. Make colored ice cubes with juice, or create big blocks of fruited ice. Freeze slices of fruit and berries along with water or light-colored juice in plastic containers. To ease the blocks out of the containers, soak them in a tub of warm water for about fifteen minutes. They'll slide out just fine and add a

SQUISHY AND NATURAL HOLIDAY PLAYDOUGH

Kids and adults alike will enjoy whipping up a batch of this preservative-free playdough. Be sure to store your supply in an airtight container in the fridge.

Materials:

2 cups flour

1 cup salt

4 teaspoons cream of tartar

4 tablespoons oil

2 cups water

food coloring

Combine flour and salt in a large bowl. Add cream of tartar and oil, mixing each separately. Now add the water and food coloring of your choice. You're ready to play!

bright touch to your punchbowl.

Let the decorations for your Celebration of Merriment tea party be dictated by the activities you plan. You can focus on arts and crafts, music and drama, or sports and games. For an arts and crafts party, designate an art room somewhere in the house. You can set out pens and paints, paper and ribbon, rubber stamps and glitter for creating cards and giftwrap. A table filled with oranges, cloves, toothpicks, ribbon, and scissors serves as a Christmas pomander-making station. Or make terra-cotta tree ornaments with terra-cotta modeling clay, fabric paint, Christmas cookie cutters, ribbon, and paperclips (for the hooks). Make sure the art room is

staffed at all times with an adult or teenager. In fact, you'll probably have no shortage of parents "helping" with the crafts!

If your group is talented at acting or music, you might want to dedicate a portion of your program to a Christmas variety show. Let your guests know about the show ahead of time so they can practice. You can even put a written program together if you know what everyone will be doing. Participation is optional, but encouraged. Create a "stage" area with plenty of chairs for the audience. Choose an older child with a flair for drama to be the master of ceremonies.

If snow is on the ground, kids won't need to be told to head outside for sledding fun and games. Get a snowman-building contest going, or have everyone come together to construct an igloo or snow fort. If the ground is dry and the sun is shining, take advantage of the nice weather to play the children's favorite outdoor games.

If you live in a friendly neighborhood and your neighbors are just as into hosting a Christmas party as you are, consider a progressive dinner tea—appetizers at one home, soup and salad at another, the main course next door, dessert down the street. No matter what you choose to do, your Celebration of Merriment tea party will assure that happiness and good cheer will ring well into the coming year.

CUSTOMS OF CHRISTMAS

When you're celebrating with a large group of people, it's fun to discuss everyone's favorite Christmas traditions. I come from a Jewish background, so I might want to share about how Christmas is celebrated in Israel. In Bethlehem, Christians mark their homes by painting a cross over the door and displaying a homemade manger scene. On the other side of the world in Mexico, the poinsettia is a very important part of the season. Legend has it that a little boy named Pablo was walking to the Nativity scene in his village one day when it dawned on him that he had nothing to give the Christ child. Noticing some green branches growing along the roadside, he picked them up and brought them to the manger. At first the other children laughed at Pablo, but their laughter turned to wonder when a brilliant red star-shaped flower appeared on each branch.

All throughout the world, children are an important part of the Christmas celebration. Youngsters in Brazil prepare breakfast on Christmas morning, then find gifts in their shoes and hunt for presents hidden all around the house. In Greece, children travel in groups from house to house offering good wishes and singing *kalanda,* or carols, while playing metal triangles and clay drums. Rumanian children also parade through the village, singing carols and reciting poetry and legends. Kids in Iran are given new clothes for Christmas, which they wear proudly for the celebration.

With just a little bit of research, you can discover some wonderful, long-lasting traditions that you can incorporate into your holiday celebration. Or borrow from several cultures to create your own unique customs. Ask your guests to share their favorite traditions at your Celebration of Merriment tea party. You'll learn some new things about your friends and family, and you'll have some fresh ideas of how to celebrate the Christmas season.

The air broke into a mist with bells.

ROBERT
BROWNING

51

A Celebration of Peace

Hosting a very special mother/daughter angel tea

Tis the season for angels!
Please come to a mother-and-daughter
angel tea party for a memorable time together.

In the midst of all the holiday hustle and bustle, it is important to take some time to remember that Christmas is a season of peace. The Christmas story in the Bible helps remind us of this when we read about the angels telling the shepherds, "Glory to God in the highest, and on earth peace, good will to men." Peace is something that all of the world hopes for—peace among nations, peace within families, and peace in each of our hearts. In that spirit of peace and good will, why not put on a Celebration of Peace tea party this season? An angel theme works beautifully for this type of tea party.

DID YOU KNOW...?

Many Christmas carols feature lines about angels. Do you know what songs these lines come from?

"Angels from the realms of glory..."

"Angels we have heard on high..."

"Lord, with the angels we, too, would rejoice..."

"Hark! the herald angels sing..."

"Sing, choirs of angels..."

Another wonderful touch is to make your celebration a mother-and-daughter tea party. Women are also welcome to bring grand-daughters, nieces, or little friends. Find stationery or note cards with angels on them, or make your own angel invitations, letting your guests know that this is an angel tea. They're sure to be excited because angels are such a beautiful, hopeful part of the holidays.

A Celebration of Peace tea party has many options for food and activities. Angel food cake with whipped cream and strawberries is a lovely touch, and dressing in white provides a festive mood, also. A mother-and-daughter fashion show is another idea to consider. Mothers and daughters can come dressed in similar attire and model their holiday outfits. You can also ask your guest to bring their favorite stories or poems about angels to read out loud. As you can see, the possibilities for an angel tea party stretch as high as the heavens!

A WORD ABOUT TEA

Do you know all of your teatime manners? You probably know that elbows stay off the table and that the napkin goes in your lap, but can you remember if it is the tea or the cream that goes into the teacup first? Actually, that one is up to you. Each way is respectable, and each has its advantages and disadvantages. If you choose cream first, the hot tea might scald the cream. If you choose tea first, the cream might cool off the tea too much. Sugar, however, should be put in after the tea is poured. And let your hostess offer you the sugar cubes. If you are the hostess, be sure to ask your guests, "One lump or two?"

Menu for a Celebration of Peace tea party—

Almond Chicken Tea Sandwiches
Shortcake Biscuits with Assorted Jellies
Peppermint Candy Cane Cookies

RECIPES

Almond Chicken Tea Sandwiches

3 boneless, skinless chicken
    breasts, cooked and chopped
    coarsely
1/2 cup slivered, blanched almonds
1/2 cup mayonnaise
butter
white or wheat bread

Mix chicken, almonds, and mayonnaise.
Butter each slice of bread well. On half the
slices, spoon about 3 tablespoons of almond
chicken mixture. Top with remaining slices.
Stack three sandwiches tall. Wrap in waxed

CHRISTMAS TIMELINE

1843: Charles Dickens writes "A
    Christmas Carol."
1846: Illustrated London News publishes a
    picture of the Royal Family
    gathered around a Christmas tree.
    The picture helps popularize the
    tabletop Christmas tree.

paper and again in a slightly dampened
kitchen towel. Let set for at least an hour.
Unwrap, cut off crust, and cut into triangles.

Shortcake Biscuits

2 cups flour
1 1/2 tablespoons sugar
1 tablespoon baking powder
1 1/2 teaspoons salt
1/4 cup unsalted sweet butter, cut
    in 1 1/2-teaspoon-sized pieces
    and frozen
1 1/2 cup + 1 tablespoon heavy
    cream
1 egg yolk
1 1/2 teaspoons vanilla
2 tablespoons powdered sugar

Preheat oven to 375 degrees. Mix together
flour, sugar, baking powder, and salt. Add
butter and blend in quickly, just until butter
is broken into small pieces. Add 1 cup of the
cream and combine until moistened.
Immediately turn out dough onto a lightly
floured board and knead ten times. Roll out
to 3/4-inch thickness, keeping the dough in
a square shape. Cut into 6 squares and
transfer to an ungreased cookie sheet. Mix
the egg yolk with a tablespoon of cream and
brush on biscuits. Make a cream glaze by
whipping the remaining cream, vanilla, and
1 1/2 tablespoons of powdered sugar. Brush
this over the yolk glaze. Sprinkle with
remaining powdered sugar and bake 15-20
minutes, until golden brown.

Peppermint Candy Cane Cookies

1 cup sugar
1 cup butter
1/2 cup milk
1 egg
1 teaspoon vanilla
1 teaspoon peppermint extract
3 1/2 cups flour
1 teaspoon baking powder
1/4 teaspoon salt
1/2 teaspoon red food coloring

Mix sugar, butter, milk, egg, and vanilla. Add peppermint. Stir in flour, baking powder, and salt. Divide dough into halves, tint 1 half with red food coloring. Cover and refrigerate at least 4 hours. Heat oven to 350 degrees. Roll ropes of each color of dough on floured surface and spiral one of each color together for candy cane effect. After placing it on the cookie sheet, curve the top of the cookie to form the handle of the cane. Bake until set and very light brown, 9-12 minutes. After baked, immediately sprinkle cookie with a mixture of 2 tablespoons crushed peppermint candy and 2 tablespoons sugar.

ANGEL TREE PLACE CARDS

When you're setting the table for your angel tea, remember the place cards! It might be fun to mix up the seating to encourage people to make new friends. To make the angel tree place cards, gather some branches that are a little larger than the size you'd use for kindling. Carefully cut the branches crosswise into thin circles, then drill a small hole in the center of each circle. This will be your tree base. Now insert a bit of greenery into each hole to form your tree. Next cut angels out of construction paper (either trace one from a pattern or draw them freehand) that will fit in the top of your tree. Write each guest's name on an angel, arrange the trees on the table, and let each angel find her place.

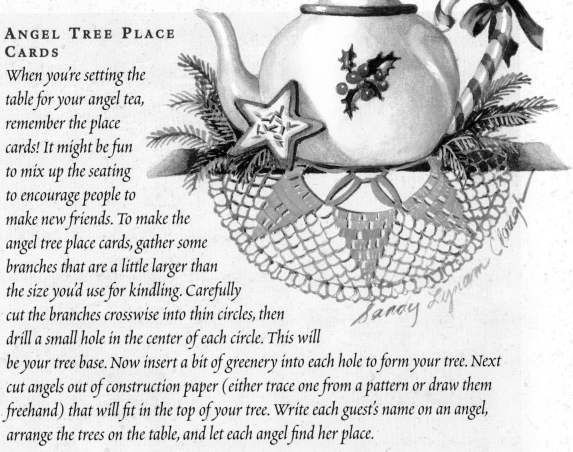

READYING THE ROOMS

When you're dressing up the house for the party, think of using serene colors and fabrics, such as white, silver, and pale blue, and organdy, silk, and tulle. Wrap up your table with silver, tying silverware and napkins together with French-wired satin ribbon and a frothy bow. Place each silverware-napkin combination across each guest's place so it looks like a little gift. And be sure to use lots of candles on the table! Use old-fashioned candle holders (silver, if possible) and tie bows down low on long tapers.

If you're planning to have a mother-and-daughter fashion show, set up chairs on either side of the living room and mark off a runway with rows of potted poinsettias. Your guests can take them home as favors when the party's over. Find some instrumental Christmas music to play as the "models" show off their holiday fashions, and be sure to give standing ovations to each participant! You'll also want a camera or video camera for this event. Another fun idea is to take classy black-and-white pictures of each set of models, then mail the best photo to each of your guests. They'll appreciate the memory and be thrilled to have a pretty picture to display.

If you haven't yet decorated your tree, you might want to consider an angel theme this year. If you already have an angel ornament collection, you'll be off to a great start. Clothespin angels are also easy to make. Purchase some wooden clothespins and silver- or gold-colored muffin cups. The clothespins will be the angel bodies, and the muffin cups their wings. Draw faces on the round end of the clothespins, attach cotton hair, and place the wings on the back. You can also add fabric clothing or paint the rest of the clothespin. Another fun type of angel to make is a pasta angel. You'll need a supply of different shapes of pasta, silver or gold spray paint, ribbon, and glue. Use a thick piece of pasta for the body, bow-tie pasta for wings, macaroni pieces for arms, and little curly or round pieces for the hair. Once you've formed the body, spray paint the entire angel, then draw a face using pens or paints. Tie a little ribbon onto the wings for a hanger.

Have you ever had a Christmas cookie exchange? It's a great way to sample many types of cookies and get some favorite new recipes. On your invitations, ask your guests to bring several dozen homemade cookies. (That's another fun activity for mothers and daughters to do together *before* the party!) Ask them to please bring a copy of the recipe, too. Set aside a special cookie table, and display each guest's cookies along with the recipe. A nice touch is to include a stack of recipe cards and some colored pens in a basket. Your guests can write down any recipes they'd like to make on their own. When everyone is ready to head home, hand out paper gift bags or boxes and let guests package up an assortment of the left-over goodies. To make the cookie exchange extra fun, request that each guest to come up with her own creative name for the cookie. The one catch is that each name must include the word "angel" somewhere in it!

After you're finished with your crafts and cookies and modeling, take a few quiet moments around the fireplace to talk about the peace and joy of the season. Perhaps you'd like to take turns reading the Christmas story out loud from the Bible. Or you could go around the room and share what you think it means to be an angel in someone's life. Maybe you could tell about a time when someone was an angel to *you* in the past year. You could even share about the angel or star atop your Christmas tree and the story behind it. Then sing a few carols quietly,

MAKE AN ANGEL COOKIE GARLAND

Here's an easy way to make a decorative, mouthwatering garland to hang on the tree, the mantle, or above a mirror.

Materials—

   one unbaked batch of gingerbread or other rolled cookie dough
   several feet of satin ribbon (1/2" width works well)
   angel cookie cutters

Roll cookie dough as directed in recipe, and cut into angel shapes. Place the shapes on a cookie sheet. Using a toothpick, poke two holes near the top, making sure the holes are evenly spaced and are large enough to string ribbon through. Now bake the cookies as directed and let them cool before you decorate them with icing and sprinkles. (You can also leave them undecorated.) Thread the ribbon through the cookies to make a garland. Starting at the back of the cookie, push a ribbon through the first hole. Then push it, from front to back, through the second hole. Continue until you have completed the garland.

letting your voices blend together in a joyous medley.

CUSTOMS OF CHRISTMAS

Angels are one of the most popular Christmas decorations around. Angel ornaments abound on trees, angel figurines are set up during the holidays, and lighted angel silhouettes adorn outdoor light displays. In addition, many Christmas carols contain lyrics about angels, and artists throughout the world have linked angels and Christmastime together in breathtaking depictions.

If you look at the Christmas story, you'll realize that it's no surprise how angels came to be such an important part of the season. The Bible relates many stories in which angels announced events connected with the very first Christmas. An angel appeared to Zachariah, the husband of Elizabeth (Mary's cousin), and told him of the coming birth of John the Baptist. After that, the angel Gabriel came to Mary and told her the good news that she would give birth to the baby Jesus. Joseph, too, was visited by an angel. The angel told him not to be afraid, and to take Mary as his wife. After Jesus was born, an angel appeared to a group of shepherds. The angel told them that he brought "good news of great joy," and soon a multitude of angels appeared, praising God and proclaiming peace on earth.

"You're an angel," we like to say to someone who has done us a favor, helped us out when times were tough, or offered a sympathetic ear. This Christmas, take a bit of time to reflect on the angelic element of the season. You'll find yourself renewed and ready to enter into the celebration with a heart full of peace and love.

...The cheery warmth of the blazing fireplace sets the tone, and the evergreen smell of the decorated Christmas tree fills the air along with the music. We can almost hear the angels singing!

EMILIE BARNES
If Teacups Could Talk

A Celebration of Dreams

Imagining winter wonderlands and snowy surprises

Come to a party where snowflakes sparkle,
where sugarplum dreams and the romance of the season
come to life with a tea served in your honor.

For many people, attending a ballet production of the *Nutcracker* or going to a local theater presentation of *A Christmas Carol* are holiday traditions. If you and those dear to you enjoy the wonderful world of dress-up and make-believe, why not hold a Celebration of Dreams tea party? This party gives you a chance to go all out decorating your home with enough sparkle and glitter to impress even the Sugar Plum Fairy!

DID YOU KNOW...?

Now a Christmas classic, Tchaikovsky's Nutcracker premiered on December 18, 1892 to less-than-favorable reviews. Poor casting and the audience's unfamiliarity with the plot kept the performance from being considered a success. Happily, the music and the story have endured, and audiences worldwide now look forward to this beloved ballet every holiday season.

To really get everyone in the spirit of things, encourage guests to come dressed up as characters from a favorite holiday story. A *Nutcracker* theme leaves the door wide open to many costumes—Clara or Fritz, the Mouse King, the Nutcracker, Arabian or Chinese dancers, or one of the many supporting characters. If you're thinking along the lines of *A Christmas Carol*, traditional Victorian costumes will do for the villagers, with the most dramatic guests perhaps showing up as Ebenezer Scrooge, Bob Cratchit, or Tiny Tim. Another option is to have your guests come dressed as a character from their favorite Christmas story. Everyone will have great fun trying to identify the costumes, and friends might discover some shared interests that draw them even closer together!

Tchaikovsky's *Nutcracker*, of course, is a logical choice for music. Brass quintets also sound delightful, as do classical choirs. With a fantastical setting, a table filled with sweet treats, the strains of delightful Christmas music, and captivating costumes, dreams will certainly come true at this tea party that celebrates the romance of the season.

Menu for a Celebration of Dreams tea party—

Antipasto Squares
Orange Slices
Emilie's Triple Chocolate Fudge Cake
Cream Cheese Mints

RECIPES

Antipasto Squares

2 packages crescent rolls
14-ounce jar roasted red peppers, drained
1/4 pound pepperoni, sliced
wafer-thin
1/4 pound ham, sliced thin
1/4 pound Genoa salami, sliced thin
1/4 pound Provolone cheese
1/4 pound Swiss cheese
3 eggs
9 tablespoons grated parmesan or romano cheese

Take one package of crescent rolls, spread, flatten, and press into bottom of 9 x 13-inch baking pan. Layer ham, Swiss, Genoa, Provolone, and pepperoni over crescent roll bottom. Spread out well-drained peppers over top of cold cuts.

Beat the egg and cheese together and pour over the top of peppers. Open second package of crescent rolls and spread over top, pressing seams of triangles together. Cover with foil. Bake at 350 degrees for 25 minutes. Remove foil and bake for an additional 15 minutes until golden brown. Cool before cutting.

Emilie's Triple Chocolate Fudge Cake

1 small package chocolate pudding (not instant)
1 box chocolate cake mix
1/2 cup semi-sweet chocolate pieces
1/2 cup chopped nuts
whipped cream

Cook pudding as directed on package and blend dry cake mix into hot pudding. Pour into prepared oblong pan (13 x 9 x 2 inches) and sprinkle with chocolate pieces and nuts. Bake 30-35 minutes at 350 degrees. Cool 5 minutes; cut into 2-inch squares. Top with whipped cream.

Cream Cheese Mints

2 1/4 cups powdered sugar
3 ounces cream cheese, softened
peppermint flavoring to taste
food coloring
granulated sugar
candy molds (optional)

> ### CHRISTMAS TIMELINE
> *1880: German glass ornaments sold at Woolworths.*
> *1882: First electric Christmas tree lights sold in New York.*

Mash cheese and mix in sugar. If you will be using more than one color, divide mixture and place in separate bowls. Add flavoring and coloring sparingly; you want soft pastels with a delicate flavor. Stir together until mixture resembles pie dough. Roll into small balls. Roll each ball in granulated sugar. Press balls into patties with glass dipped in granulated sugar or press them into candy molds and unmold at once. (Shake sugar into mold, if necessary, to prevent sticking.)

A WORD ABOUT TEA

Like a giant, flaky, slightly sweet biscuit, scones are the staple of a proper tea. The proper pronunciation of "scone" rhymes with "lawn," not "cone." Traditionally, scones are served with clotted cream or Devonshire cream instead of butter. You cannot find the same kind of cream in the United States, but there are many good substitutes—a cream made with heavy cream and buttermilk, or another type made from softened cream cheese, powdered sugar, and sour cream. You can also add fruit preserves, lemon curd, or other delicious toppings. Fresh strawberries on the side taste wonderful, too!

READYING THE ROOMS

Lights, sparkle, and glitter—these elements will help transform your home into a winter wonderland. Drape curtains and tables in layers of tulle, an affordable yet elegant fabric commonly used on wedding dresses. It comes in a variety of shades and is very easy to work with. Because tulle is transparent, you can add gold and silver confetti—choose Christmas shapes like stars, trees, or angels—between the layers.

Get the rooms scented for the season by making simple velvet sachet bags in crimson, hunter green, or black. Fill the bags with Christmas-scented potpourri and tie them with gold or silver ribbons. Put sachet bags all throughout the house—in bathrooms, coat closets, the living room—anywhere guests will enjoy their delightful aroma.

Remember that food can play a major part in your Celebration of Dreams tea party! Look through your cookbooks for sweet treats with fanciful names such as petits fours and marzipan. If you don't have time to cook, gourmet food shops are usually stocked with these goodies during the holidays. Or take a simple recipe for sugar cookies and dress them up with pastel frosting, sprinkles, silver balls, and other trimmings. Magazines provide you with lots of good ideas for the decorations! To make cakes glitter for the holidays, frost them with pale-colored icing, then tie gauzy Christmas ribbon around them for a fancy effect.

This display isn't edible, but it does make a pretty arrangement. Dust pears

A SUGARPLUM CENTERPIECE

To get visions of sugarplums dancing in heads of both children and grown-ups, create an easy yet elegant centerpiece using a variety of fruits (think different shapes and sizes), pasteurized egg white (found in most supermarkets), and granulated sugar. Brush the fruits lightly with the egg white, then roll them in granulated sugar. Your centerpiece will look especially fanciful displayed in ornate cut glass dishes. Sprinkle iridescent confetti at the base for a true fairyland feel.

and apples in gold or silver spray paint, then display them on the mantel or arrange them on a platter. Add ribbons, bows, greenery, and lights for a spectacular effect.

If you're fortunate enough to have a banister, you can dress it up with a fancy garland. Gather up long lengths of greenery (either fresh or silk) and wind them tightly around the banister, fastening them with florist's wire. You can swathe the outside of the banister with more swags, and add gold, silver, or pastel-colored ribbon. To really make the display sparkle, set baskets filled with pinecones, lemons, oranges, pears, eucalyptus branches, and other natural materials on each stairstep.

Tiny trees all throughout the house also add to the spirit of anticipation at your Celebration of Dreams tea party. Display them on bookshelves, in children's rooms, on a hutch or sideboard, or atop a piano. You can decorate them

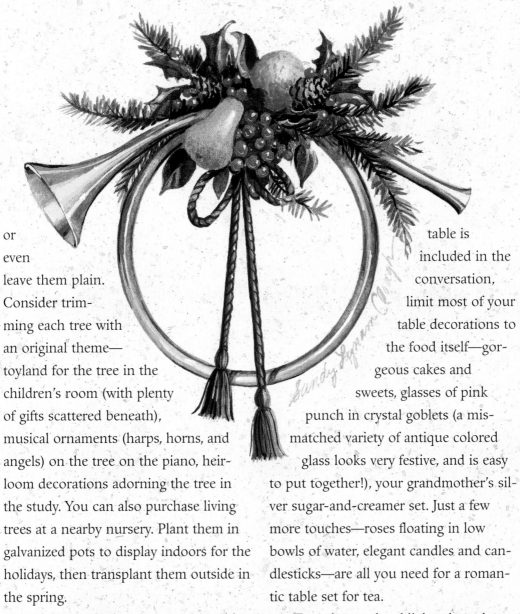

or even leave them plain. Consider trimming each tree with an original theme— toyland for the tree in the children's room (with plenty of gifts scattered beneath), musical ornaments (harps, horns, and angels) on the tree on the piano, heirloom decorations adorning the tree in the study. You can also purchase living trees at a nearby nursery. Plant them in galvanized pots to display indoors for the holidays, then transplant them outside in the spring.

When you're dressing up your table, keep in mind that experts suggest limiting the height of centerpieces to about one foot. Why? Anything higher will hide guests across the table from each other. To ensure that everyone at the table is included in the conversation, limit most of your table decorations to the food itself—gorgeous cakes and sweets, glasses of pink punch in crystal goblets (a mismatched variety of antique colored glass looks very festive, and is easy to put together!), your grandmother's silver sugar-and-creamer set. Just a few more touches—roses floating in low bowls of water, elegant candles and candlesticks—are all you need for a romantic table set for tea.

Turn the overhead lights down low, relying on the old-fashioned look of lamplight, candlelight, and firelight for a cozy glow. If you have children or friends who are talented musicians, perhaps you could make the evening extra special with

PRETTY PAPER CREATIONS

After the printing press was invented in 1436, paper became affordable to nearly everyone. It took on a variety of uses— paper table coverings instead of fabric tablecloths, edgings for shelves, paper dolls, makeshift curtains, even Christmas tree ornaments (including the still-popular paper chains). The Victorians, however, really immersed themselves in the paper craze. As photography had not yet been invented, they cut out paper silhouettes of each other that functioned as pictures. Paper doilies became extremely common, and at Christmastime entire families sat down together to create stacks upon stacks of paper decorations—snowflakes, boxes, fans, trees, pinwheels, and stockings. With so many interesting colors and textures of paper available now, why not try your hand at making some Victorian Christmas decorations? Browse through a few antique shops to get ideas, then head to your local art supply store to pick out different kinds of paper. At home, sit down at the table, put on some classical Christmas music, and start creating!

live music played by a string quartet, a piano-and-flute duo, or a brass quintet. You could even put some musical entertainment on the agenda, encouraging everyone to retreat to the "parlor" for group songs and individual performances after teatime. Anything is possible when you let your imagination carry you away at a Celebration of Dreams tea party.

CUSTOMS OF CHRISTMAS

Mistletoe is a favorite symbol associated with Christmas and romance. The tradition of kissing under the mistletoe began with a mythical Scandinavian woman named Frigga. According to the story, Frigga's son, Balder, was shot with an arrow of mistletoe. Hearing about her son's fate, Frigga cried tears that became the white berries on the plant. Meanwhile, her loyal friends were able to save Balder's life. That day, Frigga declared that mistletoe would never again be used to harm people. It would instead become a symbol of love and forgiveness, and people who passed under it were required to kiss each other.

Other cultures have put their own

spin on the legend of mistletoe. Romans believed mistletoe was a symbol of peace and good will. Our modern custom that an unmarried woman passing under the mistletoe will be kissed by her future husband evolved from this tale. In Yorkshire, a sprig fed to the first cow was supposed to bring good health to the entire herd. And in Worcester, it is said to be bad luck to cut mistletoe in an apple orchard, except on Christmas Eve.

In modern-day England, the custom of the "kissing ball" is still widely celebrated. To make your own kissing ball, hang a large sprig of mistletoe above an interior doorway, then surround the sprig with a framework ball of evergreens. Kissing balls are every bit as essential as Christmas trees for the British.

Hang your mistletoe up high this Christmas, then wait and see what happens during this season of dreams!

WHAT TO WEAR FOR A DRESS~UP PARTY

Planning to have your guests come in costume? You could specify a theme such as the Nutcracker or A Christmas Carol, and ask your guests to come appropriately dressed. Be sure to include suggestions of what to wear. Here are some ideas for a Dickens-style party—

- ***Men**—warm woolen coats, scarves, top hats, old-fashioned round spectacles, big bow ties, tweeds and herringbone patterns*
- ***Women**—bonnets and caps, gingham dresses, frilly aprons, stockings, fancy dresses with bustles and hoops, vintage jewelry, lace-up boots, elaborate hairstyles*

A Celebration of Tradition

Enjoying best-loved rituals and old-fashioned holiday fun

*Step back in time and celebrate
Christmas the old-fashioned way
with traditional food, games, and fun!*

Perhaps the one word we link with Christmas more than any other is *tradition*. We carry boxes full of holiday decorations down from the attic or in from the garage, unpacking them with glee and exclaiming over forgotten ornaments or favorite table runners. That's tradition. Many of us bring our Christmas CDs to the forefront on the first day of Christmas, playing exclusively seasonal music to warm our days. That's tradition. We outline our rooftops with glittering lights, get out our most festive

DID YOU KNOW...?

According to legend, the candy cane was invented by an English candy maker in the 17th century. The government did not let the people celebrate Christmas at that time, so the candy maker fashioned a sweet, hard candy shaped like a shepherd's crook as a secret symbol of the Christmas story. The white represented purity and the red represented life. Now, of course, Christmas is celebrated throughout the world, and candy canes are a familiar part of the holidays.

cookie cutters, or head downtown for an evening of holiday shopping. Those, too, are traditions.

Traditions make us feel good, giving us a sense of belonging to our family and to our community, and anchoring us in anticipation for the days of joy to come. One fun way to celebrate the customs of Christmas is to hold a Celebration of Tradition tea party, one with an Old World flair. Focus on the rustic, the simple, and the homemade. You'll not only create a quaint, old-fashioned feel, but you'll also find pleasure in the simple things of the season.

Read some historical novels or American classics to put you in the spirit of things. Laura Ingalls Wilder's *Little House* books are highly recommended, as is anything by midwestern writer Willa Cather. If you have school-age daughters, they probably enjoy the American Girls books, a series of fun and educational stories about girls from different ethnic backgrounds living long ago in the United States. You can also search specialty music stores for regional recordings of traditional music. Take advantage of the opportunity to learn a little more about the area in which you live or the part of the country where your ancestors settled. And then host a tea party that highlights what you discovered.

Menu for a Celebration of Tradition tea party—

Watercress Sandwiches
Date-Nut Bars
Christmas Clover Cookies
Mixed Fruit Medley

RECIPES

Watercress Sandwiches
Butter white or rye bread and fill with watercress leaves. Cut into squares, arrange on a plate, and garnish with watercress.

Date-Nut Bars
    1 cup butter, melted
    1 cup white sugar
    1 cup brown sugar
    4 eggs
    1 teaspoon vanilla
    15 ounces chopped dates
    2 cups chopped walnuts
    1 1/2 cups flour, sifted
    1 teaspoon baking powder

Mix butter and sugar. Add eggs and vanilla. Stir in dates and nuts. Fold in flour and baking powder. Spread on greased 9 x 13-inch pan. Bake at 350 degrees for 30 minutes. Cool and cut into squares. Roll in powdered sugar.

Christmas Clover Cookies
    1 cup shortening
    2 2/3 cups flour
    1/2 cup white sugar
    2 teaspoons cream of tartar
    1/2 cup brown sugar
    1 teaspoon baking soda
    1 egg
    food coloring
    3 teaspoons milk
    raisins or nuts
    2 teaspoons vanilla

Mix shortening, sugars, eggs, milk, and vanilla. Add sifted dry ingredients. Divide dough into 3 parts and put into separate bowls. Add green food coloring to one bowl, red to another, and leave the third plain.

Chill dough 1 hour. With each color, roll small amount of dough in hand and lay one of each color together on a cookie sheet in the form of a cloverleaf. Put raisins or nuts in center. Bake in preheated oven at 350 degrees until done.

CHRISTMAS TIMELINE
1892: Wire hook for hanging tree ornaments is patented in the United States.

A Word about Tea

Did you know that the teabag was once a source of controversy? Teabags were invented quite by accident in 1904 by a New York tea merchant. Instead of sending samples of tea to his customers in standard tea tins, the innovative merchant came up with the idea of packaging them in handsewn silk bags. Soon he was overwhelmed with orders for tea in bags. Many tea lovers, however, looked down their nose at teabags, claiming that simmering loose leaves was the only proper way to brew tea. Others, however, enjoyed the convenience of teabags. Because the tea particles in the bags were small, the tea brewed faster. Teabag aficionados had to be careful not to leave the bag in the water too long, lest the tea take on a bitter taste. Today, most people agree that teabags do make an acceptable cup of tea.

Readying the Rooms

In Early American times, holiday decorating was much simpler than it is today. Families did not have department stores or mail order catalogs—not to mention Internet shopping! Even oranges were considered a luxury in wintertime. When you're decorating for your Celebration of Tradition tea party, use the simplest of items that can readily be found in nature. Gather up an armful of pine branches to line a mantel, and add some color with just a few oranges tucked into the greenery.

To decorate your tree, weave strings of popcorn and cranberries throughout the branches. It takes awhile to make a garland this way, so you can pass the time by telling stories by the fire or taking turns writing Christmas cards and making the popcorn and cranberry strings. Children will enjoy making paper chains out of colorful construction paper. Did you know that popcorn strings have long been used in the United States? When the European settlers arrived on the continent, they found people adorning statues and even themselves with strands of popcorn! You don't have to go that far, of course. Your tree will do just fine.

If you suddenly found yourself celebrating Christmas in a frontier cabin in the Northeastern Woods, you might find decorations of bayberry and pine boughs accented with rose hips all throughout the house. Your family would have brought a Christmas tree home from the woods on a sled. The tree would be trimmed with strings of popcorn and cranberries, popcorn balls (to be eaten later), little presents, and candles in tin holders (our electric lights are thankfully much safer). The table would be laden with traditional food, but it would be limited to what was available—a goose or a roasted raccoon served with browned sweet potatoes, mincemeat and apple pies, an apple pudding that had been steamed in a tin lard bucket, and a fruitcake that had been gathering flavor for a month or two in the pantry. The table would be simply decorated with a plain cloth made of muslin or paper, several candles in sturdy pewter candlesticks,

and a few branches of greenery.

Proper entertainment is another consideration when you're planning your Celebration of Tradition tea party. Remember that the early Americans didn't watch television programs or rent movies! Activities that involve everyone and promote conversation are more fun, anyway. Old-time games include hide the thimble, blind man's bluff, and definitions (similar to the current dictionary board game, *Balderdash*). You can play some of these games, or get out your favorite board games and chess and checkers sets. If your gathering is large, set out several card tables around the house and encourage your guests to sit down and partake in some friendly competition.

If you were a child growing up in the woods of the American frontier, a winter storm blowing fiercely outside was typical on Christmas Eve. While the wind whistled and fat snowflakes piled up on the ground, families stayed warm and cozy indoors by the fire. The air was filled with anticipation, not just for the Christmas Day but for the arrival of the *Belsnickel,* a character of German origins who was rumored to come check out each home and make sure the children had been good that year doing their

73

chores, obeying their parents, being quiet and respectful, and paying attention in school and in church. Although older children were told that the *Belsnickel* was just a neighbor, they still couldn't completely calm their fluttering nerves as they waited for the cabin door to burst open.

The *Belsnickel* announced his arrival by banging on the door and shouting to be let inside. Dressed in a bearskin cap, a pantherskin cape, and layers upon layers of hides and furs, he cut an imposing figure. Yet although his manner and appearance were a bit intimidating, he did engage in a bit of teasing and laughter. Before departing, he told the children to hang up their stockings and head for bed. He went out into the storm with a hearty "Merry Christmas!" and traveled through inclement weather on to the next family who was eagerly awaiting his visit. When the children awakened on Christmas morning, they rushed to their stockings and exclaimed over gifts of apples, oranges, nuts, small cakes made of maple sugar, and perhaps a homemade toy.

Like the tradition of the *Belsnickel*, most holiday celebrations in frontier cabins were a blend of Old World customs and New World creativity. What traditions of your own can you invent to make Christmas extra special in your household? Perhaps you can dream up an original character who comes to visit at your Celebration of Tradition tea. Maybe Dad gets up on the roof and imitates the sound of reindeer hooves for all to hear. Or a mysterious visitor knocks on the door just before teatime and deposits a load of Christmas cookies and candy canes at the front doorstep. With just a little bit of imagination, you too can have your own version of the beloved *Belsnickel*.

All you need for an evening of traditional good cheer is a simple yet abundant supply of goodies, plenty of hot chocolate, eggnog, and tea, a few modest games and ideas, and a heart full of welcome. Your Celebration of Tradition tea party will become something that all of your guests look forward to year after year.

CUSTOMS OF CHRISTMAS

Of all traditional holiday foods, gingerbread is among the most delightful. Stories like *Hansel and Gretel* and *The Gingerbread Man* lend a whimsical touch to the easy-to-make cookie, and ornate gingerbread houses give it an air of elegance. Gingerbread has a long history. Its origins go all the way back to the eleventh century, when Crusaders returning from the Middle East came back with a new spice called ginger. Shortly afterward, many different types of gingerbread sprung up throughout Western Europe—some light and some dark, some sweet and some spiced, some moist and some dry.

Gingerbread was actually not called gingerbread until the fifteenth century, when it got its name from the Latin word for ginger, *zingebar*. By that time gingerbread had become so popular that French and German bakers formed their own guilds, giving them the exclusive right to make the bread. However, they were not allowed to bake gingerbread on Christmas or Easter. Later that law was overturned, and Christmas markets became the rage all throughout Europe, featuring bakers making fresh gingerbread in their stalls.

Nuremberg, Germany, became known as the gingerbread capital of the world, and Germans made the first gingerbread houses, or *hexenhaeusle*, which were launched into prominence in the nineteenth century with the publication of *Hansel and Gretel*. Sometimes thought of as an old-fashioned cookie and sometimes thought of as an elaborate dessert, the two reputations of gingerbread are equally deserved. Gingerbread was once so precious that it was gilded and considered a treat fit for the king. In fact, a common saying was, "The gilding is off the gingerbread." Early Americans contributed to the countrified view of gingerbread, adapting the recipe to fit with available ingredients. New Englanders used maple syrup in place of sugar, and Southerners added molasses to their recipe. Popular trimmings for gingerbread today include colored icing, sugar sprinkles, red hots, silver dragees, chocolate chips, gumdrops, chocolate candies, dried cherries, raisins and currants, and nonpareils.

A Celebration of Giving

Focusing upon the true meaning of the season

*Christmas is a season of giving.
Please come to my tea party
and let me share the gift of friendship with you.*

Most of our favorite Christmas stories and poems contain a not-so-small lesson about the importance of giving. In O. Henry's short story *The Gift of the Magi,* a poor yet devoted husband and wife sacrifice their most prized possessions in order to give each other a meaningful gift on Christmas. Charles Dickens' short novel *A Christmas Carol* tells the tale of the miserly Ebenezer Scrooge, who, through seeing vignettes of his own life pass by—past, present, and future—discovers that the richest rewards are in the giving. Even the humorous children's book *The Best Christmas Pageant Ever* contains an important message about how we should treat other people.

Going all the way back to the very first

DID YOU KNOW...?
The Victorian rule of thumb for filling a Christmas stocking was "Something to eat, something to read, something to play with, and something they need!"

Christmas in Bethlehem, the holiday season has long been celebrated as a time of giving. Unfortunately, today's emphasis on purchasing impressive and expensive presents for friends, family members, and coworkers often swings too far to the side of materialism. What was originally intended as a joyous act that brought a smile to the heart of both giver and receiver has become a major cause of stress in some of our lives. And that's not how it was meant to be. While it's wonderful to give what we can, we should definitely embrace the old adage that "it's the thought that counts."

fun in flexibility. Invite your children's best friends to come over after school for tea, or ask a few families to join you for a party after the church Christmas pageant. You can invite people you are close to, but you can also add to the

This Christmas, focus on the true meaning of the season with a Celebration of Giving tea party. It doesn't have to be fancy, nor does everything have to go perfectly according to schedule. There are elements of surprise and

guest list someone you'd like to get to know better. Come together over simple food and an easy craft for the kids, then engage in some good, rich visiting. Everyone will be renewed and refreshed by the time spent together.

Menu for a Celebration of Giving tea party—

Sweet Tea Spread on Brown Bread
Cucumber Sandwiches
Pumpkin Pie Cake
Sugar Cookies

RECIPES

Sweet Tea Spread on Brown Bread
   3 ounces soft cream cheese
   grated rind of 1 orange or lemon or
     2 tablespoons orange, lemon,
     or ginger marmalade
   1/8 teaspoon paprika

Combine all ingredients with hand mixer on low speed. Spread on your favorite brown bread.

Cucumber Sandwiches

Peel cucumbers and slice very thin. Sprinkle slices with salt and drain on paper towel. Spread white bread with unsalted butter and a thin layer of cream cheese. Layer cucumbers no more than 1/4 inch high. Cut into desired shapes.

Pumpkin Pie Cake
CRUST:
   1 cup yellow cake mix
   2 eggs

   1/2 cup melted margarine

FILLING:
   1 29-oz. can pumpkin
   1/2 cup white sugar
   1/2 cup brown sugar
   1 cup evaporated milk
   1 tablespoon cinnamon
   3 eggs

TOPPING:
   1/2 cup margarine
   1/2 cup sugar
   1 cup yellow cake
     mix
   chopped pecans.

Layer in 9 x 13 greased glass pan and bake at 350 degrees for 1 hour.

Sugar Cookies
   1 cup butter
   2 cups sugar
   4 eggs
   2 teaspoons vanilla
   5 cups flour
   4 teaspoons baking powder
   1/2 cup sugar (for rolling)

Cream butter and sugar. Add eggs and vanilla. Mix flour and baking powder into mixture. Chill. Roll and cut out Nativity shapes (see "Bake Me a Story" in this chapter). Sprinkle with colored sugar. Bake at 350 degrees for approximately 12 minutes.

> **CHRISTMAS TIMELINE**
>
> *1896: The T. Eaton Company produces its first Christmas catalog.*
>
> *1905: Santa Claus arrives by wagon at the T. Eaton Company store in Toronto.*

Readying the Rooms

The most basic of decorations can instantly transform your living room into a cozy Christmas tea room. A tree lit and hung with ornaments is a must, of course. Try to have some of your gifts wrapped in time for the party. A gathering of presents under the tree adds to the spirit of anticipation, and children will be drawn to the cheery packages. For a homespun feel, wrap this year's packages in plain brown paper and string, then tie in just a bit of plaid ribbon and raffia. It's a very inexpensive yet attractive way to giftwrap.

Add candles glowing throughout the room, a tea table on wheels (or you can substitute an ottoman), and a few crimson poinsettias. And be sure to hang up your stockings! According to legend, the custom of hanging stockings comes from St. Nicholas, a real person who lived long ago. The three daughters of a poor man in St. Nicholas' village did not have a suitable dowry, which severely limited their marriage prospects. One cold evening in December, the eldest daughter discovered a stocking-shaped purse filled with gold lying on the floor. The next night, the middle daughter also discovered a

A Word about Tea

In 1904, visitors to the Louisiana Purchase Exposition in St. Louis sweltered in a heat wave and declined the hot brew offered by Indian tea growers. An Englishman named Richard Blechynden, who represented the tea growers, tried pouring the tea over ice in order to please his visitors. The result was iced tea, which now accounts for 80 percent of the tea consumed in the United States. If you live in a warm climate, iced tea might be your ideal Christmas beverage.

gold-filled stocking. And on the third night, the father caught St. Nicholas tossing a third stocking into the window, which was intended for the youngest daughter. Children ever since have hung stockings on the mantel or the bedpost, hoping that St. Nicholas will fill them with surprises on Christmas morning.

Do you know why we hang stockings on the mantel? This tradition comes to us from the English, who claim that Father Christmas (their version of St. Nicholas) dropped some gold coins while he was making his way down the chimney. A stocking hung out to dry on the mantel caught the coins and prevented them from being lost in the ash grate.

In the olden days, the Christmas stocking—not the tree—was the main source of gifts for children. For farming families, a successful harvest meant a well-filled stocking. Edible treats such as gingerbread cookies, fruit-juice flavored hard candies, and apples bulged from stockings. Oranges were always a very special treat. Homemade toys such as dolls, wooden animals, and puzzles often found their way inside the stockings of little ones. Warm clothes were always hoped-for gifts. And sometimes there would be a big gift for all the children to share sitting by the fire—a Noah's ark or a sled, perhaps.

If you have children coming to visit for your Celebration of Giving tea party, ask them to bring a stocking from home to hang on the mantel. Sometime during the evening, have all the young ones retreat to another room to sing some carols, read a Christmas story, or eat a few freshly baked cookies. If snow is on the ground, a quick sledding trip is the perfect diversion. While they're gone, you or another adult can stuff a few oranges, candy canes, and cookies into the stockings. The gifts are simple, but the looks on the children's faces are guaranteed to warm the heart. Everyone loves a surprise!

CUSTOMS OF CHRISTMAS

Most people today equate gift-giving with Santa Claus, but aren't aware that

there is a special story about who Santa Claus really was. He was a dear Christian man named Nicholas, and we call him St. Nicholas. In his town lived many poor children who didn't have enough food, clothes, or toys. St. Nicholas used his own money to buy them what they needed. He didn't want the children to be embarrassed by his gifts, so he gave them secretly. St. Nick always gave in the spirit of helping and sharing, and we follow his example when we take part in gift-giving. All the gifts he gave and all of the gifts we give remind us that it's better to give than to receive.

You've probably heard of a holiday called Boxing Day, but might not be familiar with the custom. Boxing Day falls on December 26 and is celebrated by the British. The tradition began in the Middle Ages when the churches opened their "alms boxe"—boxes filled with gifts or money that people had donated throughout the year. The contents of the alms boxe were distributed to the poor and needy on the day after Christmas. Today, Boxing Day gifts are also given to delivery workers and children who carry newspapers.

Prior to the Victorian era, gifts were generally exchanged on New Year's Day or Twelfth Night, the evening of Epiphany. The Victorians popularized the custom of giving gifts on Christmas Day. Today, some families open gifts on Christmas Eve and others on Christmas Day, and some even do a little opening on both days.

I love Christmas, don't you? All the decorations and the food and the excitement...and of course, the Christmas tree. Let's use our tree cookie cutter to cut out some delicious trees **(Cookie Cutter #1: Tree).**

First we cut them out...then we decorate them with pretty colored sugar...then we pop them in the oven. While they're baking, who can tell me what we put under our tree? That's right. Presents! Everybody likes to get presents, and it's fun to give them, too. But can you tell me who gave the very first Christmas presents? You don't know? Well, I'll tell you...

A long time ago, there were three very wise men who knew a lot about stars. They knew every star in the sky! But one night they looked up and saw a new star—all bright and shining and bigger than the rest. And every night that star was in a different place. It was moving! "Let's follow it!" the wise men said. So they got on their camels and traveled west, toward the beautiful, shining star. We can make some stars with our star cutter to help us remember those wise men **(Cookie Cutter #2: Star).**

And do you know what the wise men brought with them? Presents! You see, because they were wise, they knew that the new star meant something special had happened—the birth of a new king. They were following the star because they wanted to bring him special gifts. One present was a bag of gold. They also brought him a jar of frankincense. (That's a little like the sweet-smelling potpourri your mother uses to make the house smell nice.) And they brought him a special box of myrrh, a spicy, strong-smelling perfume.

But while the wise men were making their long journey, something was going on in faraway Judah. A group of sleepy, cold shepherds were out on a hillside, taking care of their sheep. Then something wonderful happened. An angel appeared and talked to them, then more

angels sang to them. Here's an angel cookie cutter so we can cut out some pretty angel cookies **(Cookie Cutter #3: Angel).**

The angel told the shepherds the same thing the star had told the wise men—that someone special had been born. The new baby was going to be the savior of the world, and he had been born in a stable in Bethlehem. The shepherds couldn't believe their ears. Bethlehem was their town! Quickly they jumped to their feet and herded their sheep down the hillside. They wanted to see if it was all true!

Well, you know what the shepherds and the wise men found when they finally got to Bethlehem, don't you? That's right. They found a little baby—baby Jesus. But he wasn't just any baby! Look at this cookie cutter and see what they really found **(Cookie Cutter #4: Heart).** That's right. A heart stands for love, and that's why that baby was there. Jesus was God's loving Christmas present to the wise men and the shepherds and to you and me. He gave us His only Son...because He loves us so much!

And here's another cookie cutter that helps us understand about the special Christmas present God gave the world. This cutter is a beautiful, graceful bird, a dove **(Cookie Cutter #5: Dove).** The dove stands for peace, and that's

what the angels were singing about. They sang, "Glory to God in the highest, and on earth...Peace." But the dove stands for something else special, too. It's also a sign that God is here with us and lives in our hearts. And that's a very important thing to know at Christmastime!

And now, who knows what this last cookie cutter is? You see them everywhere at Christmastime. That's right, it's a candle **(Cookie Cutter #6: Candle).** What do candles do? They give light! It can be really dark in a room, but if we light a candle we can see. The yellow flame also gives us a welcome, warm, peaceful feeling. And do you know what? We're supposed to be like that, too—like candles shining in the darkness. We can tell people the story about Jesus, and we can give them that warm, peaceful feeling by being kind and helping them and sharing God's love with them.

And that's exactly what we're going to do when all our cookies are baked and cooled. First, we're going to enjoy eating some of the cookies with a cold cup of milk—yum! And then we're going to put one of each pattern into these plastic bags and tie them with a pretty bow to give to our friends. They may not know the meaning of each cookie shape, but you do—and you can tell them!

A Celebration of Creation

Laughing and playing in the wonderful winter outdoors

*Come to a celebration of snowflakes
and sledding and laughing and playing
in the winter wonderland!*

"The weather outside is frightful, but the fire is so delightful..." The beloved Christmas song "Let It Snow" echoes our sentiments during this snuggle-up time of year. And although it's warm and cozy inside, most of us like to venture out every now and then for wintertime walks and hikes, trips to the mountains, and outdoor fun such as skating and sledding, grateful for the warmth that embraces us when we step back indoors.

I live in Southern California, so of course I don't expect to have a white Christmas. But I can travel to the mountains to see snow-covered fields, and the temperature does drop a bit during winter in my hometown. We all adjust to what we know, and the weather outside gives us yet another hint that

DID YOU KNOW...?

Fairy tales in Germany and Holland explain snowflakes as feathers that Holle, the Queen of Winter, is shaking out of her mattress.

Christmas is coming.

If you're an outdoor enthusiast who loves going on nature walks and cross-country ski trips with friends, delighting in the magnificence of the great winter outdoors, then a Celebration of Creation tea party is just for you. With lively activities and a bounty of healthy snacks, this tea party is sure to put a touch of pink in your cheeks and a deep appreciation of creation in your heart. If you live in a town that regularly gets snow in the winter, check in the phone book for companies that offer sleigh rides. If the ground is dry and the sun is shining, an old-fashioned horsedrawn carriage gives you a similar effect. Long walks through the wintertime woods, an ice skating party at a nearby pond, or your standard snowman-and-sledding party are all sure to be hits with enthusiastic guests. If you're inviting a mixture of nature lovers and homebodies, plan on some indoor and outdoor activities. Those who like to stay warm and dry inside can bring reading or knitting and enjoy some spirited conversation by the fireplace while the rest of the group frolics outdoors.

A Word about Tea

Tea leaves are very delicate and easily absorb moisture. Therefore, you should always store your tea in airtight containers. The tea's life and fragrance will keep indefinitely this way, whereas tea left open in the kitchen will pick up undesirable odors. Tea is also affected by strong light and heat, so make sure you keep it in a cool place. If you are using a tea ball, fill it only halfway to allow the leaves room to expand in the hot water. If you love the taste of cloves or cinnamon, store them with your sugar cubes. The sugar will absorb the spicy flavors.

Cream Cheese, Celery, and Walnut Sandwiches
Bunches o' Grapes
Mrs. B's Whole-Wheat Carrot Cake
Assorted Store Bought Cookies

RECIPES

Cream Cheese, Celery, and Walnut Sandwiches

    4 ounces cream cheese, room
        temperature
    1/4 celery heart, very finely
        chopped
    1/4 cup diced walnuts
    white or whole wheat bread
    parsley sprigs, for garnish

In small bowl, beat cream cheese until smooth. Mix in celery and walnuts. Make sandwiches with cheese mixture. Trim off crust of bread and cut sandwiches into rectangles or triangles. Garnish with sprigs of parsley.

Mrs. B's Whole-Wheat Carrot Cake

    2 cups whole wheat flour
    1 tablespoon toasted wheat germ
    1 teaspoon baking powder
    1 teaspoon baking soda
    1 teaspoon salt
    1 teaspoon ground cinnamon
    1 1/4 cups honey
    1/4 cup brown sugar
    1 1/2 cups unsalted sweet butter,
        melted
    1 teaspoon molasses
    1 teaspoon vanilla
    4 eggs
    3 cups carrots, finely shredded
    1 cup chopped pecans or walnuts

Preheat oven to 350 degrees. Grease and flour two 10-inch or 9-inch round baking pans. Combine flour, wheat germ, baking powder, baking soda, salt, and cinnamon. Add honey, sugar, butter, molasses, and vanilla; beat on low until combined. Add eggs one at a time, beating well after each egg. Stir in carrots and nuts. Pour batter into pans and bake 30-35 minutes, or until toothpick comes out clean. Cool for 10 minutes, remove from pans, and cool completely before frosting with cream cheese frosting.

Cream Cheese Frosting

    8 ounces cream cheese, softened
    1 1/2 cups unsalted sweet butter
    2 cups sifted confectioner's sugar
    1 teaspoon vanilla
    1 1/2 teaspoons honey or molasses
    1/4 cup chopped pecans (optional)

Beat together cream cheese and butter until very fluffy. Beat in remaining ingredients and chill to spreading consistency.

READYING THE ROOMS

A child's sled makes a great focal point for your Celebration of Creation tea party. The old-fashioned kind with a metal blade works best. Lean the sled up against the house on the front porch or nestle it in a corner in the tea room. You can trim it with garlands of pine, sprigs of holly, bright plaid or velvet ribbons, and even a string of white lights. It's sure to put everyone in a playful spirit.

Decorate styrofoam hanging balls with objects from the outdoors, such as miniature pinecones, assorted nuts and berries, feathers, and small twigs. Hang the balls on the tree, from the mantel, or even dangle them from the ceiling. You can add a bit of mistletoe if you'd like. Instead of purchasing flowers for a traditional arrangement, head for the woods and gather up seasonal materials by the armful—evergreen branches, eucalyptus, holly berries, and juniper. Arrange them in vases, then tie ribbons around these original—not to mention affordable—displays.

If it's too warm for icicles to be hanging from the eaves, you can dangle a collection of clear ornaments, shaped as icicles or in other holiday motifs, from curtain rods. Tie them on with pale blue ribbons for a frosty outdoor glow. And you can always make paper snowflakes! Sit down with the children and

CHRISTMAS TIMELINE
1917: J.C. Hall (of Hallmark) imports fancy decorated envelope linings from France to sell as "gift dressing."

teach them how to cut snowflakes from white tissue paper. Soon you'll have enough for a blizzard covering your workspace. Display the snowflakes in the windows of your house, then wait in anticipation for the real thing.

Poinsettias, a plant native to Mexico, are also known as the "flower of the Nativity" because the crimson flower resembles the star of Bethlehem. Set groupings of poinsettias throughout the room, on mantels, and tucked around the Christmas tree. To continue with the plant-and-floral theme, you can set your table using natural materials. Tuck sprigs of greenery beneath each plate for festive "placemats." The greenery looks particularly fresh against a white tablecloth. For an interesting centerpiece, head to your grocery store to gather up some fresh herbs like rosemary, basil, and sage. Display them in bud vases and add a few

blossoms of freesia or white roses. Another simple yet refreshing display is a terra-cotta garden pot filled with beeswax candles (anchor them in florist's foam) and sprigs of holly and greenery. You can also use low terra-cotta pots and planter bottoms as unique serving dishes for cookies, breads, veggies, and other treats.

And remember to prepare the outdoors for your party! An abundance of Christmas lights, both on the house, wound through trees and bushes, or marching along a fence, instantly transforms your home into an enchanted cottage. Go with all-white lights for a starry, elegant look, or choose colors for a gingerbread village feel. A wreath or swag on the front door is another essential, along with the happy sound of jingle bells.

If you have access to a wheelbarrow, set it on your front porch or in the yard to welcome guests as they arrive at the tea party. Fill the wheelbarrow with greenery—pine, juniper, western cedar, Douglas fir, whatever is readily available in your area. Now add a galvanized watering can filled with twigs and tied with a ribbon, large pinecones, sprigs of holly, huckleberry, or lingonberry, apples and pears, abandoned bird's nests, and whatever other objects strike your fancy. If plenty of snow is on the ground, head outside with the kids and make a cheery snowman to welcome your guests. Use all the old standards—round pieces of coal for the eyes, a carrot nose, a frayed scarf, twigs for the arms, a funny hat.

Once the party begins, more snowmen and snow angels are sure to spring up as temporary but charming lawn decorations. When those at play come back inside, reward the snowman makers and sledders with steaming mugs of peppermint-flavored hot chocolate or aromatic cups of orange spice tea. Then sit by the window and gaze at the beauty of the wintertime outdoors.

CUSTOMS OF CHRISTMAS

Ice skating has long been a wintertime tradition for people who lived in rural parts of the United States. The sport gained popularity in the mid-1800s when city folk took to ice skating in the countryside as an invigorating way to relax, exercise, and enjoy the wintertime woods. Ice skating also provided people with a sense of community, as it was an activity that appealed to men and women, parents and children. In fact, an 1866 issue of *Frank Leslie's Illustrated Newspaper* deemed ice skating as "our national winter exercise."

Any sort of lake or pond that had frozen solidly drew a number of skaters, among them young men and women who enjoyed the social and romantic aspects of the sport. They could skate together free of a designated chaperon, but parents were comfortable knowing that the entire community kept an eye on the happy couples gliding across the ice. In later years, indoor skating rings sprung up across the country. They were originally meant to be used when the weather outside was particularly gloomy, and their design was certainly not as awe-inspiring as their outdoor counterparts. The indoor rinks were simply cavernous, unheated structures, certainly lacking the romance of a natural setting. The era of early ice skating fell at a time when playing music was very popular in the home. Songs like "Skating Rink Waltz," "Skating Polka," and "Gliding on the Ice," were printed on sheets of music and played on pianos everywhere, accompanying dreams of snowy woods and frozen ponds.

A Celebration of Stillness

Reflecting upon the past year and preparing for the season ahead

*Come for tea,
just you and me,
and the stillness of the season.*

The stockings have been emptied, the gifts under the tree unwrapped, the cookies baked and delivered, the cards long sent and received, and the Christmas dinner exclaimed over and eaten. Christmas is over for the year, and some people can't help but feel somewhat of a letdown at this time. After so much preparation and anticipation, we've come to expect the next big holiday event or happening. And the truth is that things quiet down significantly the day after Christmas. We can welcome this quietness, though, as something to look forward to, viewing it as a time to celebrate yet another aspect of the holidays—the gift of stillness.

Actually, in some countries, such as

DID YOU KNOW...?

Besides providing a yummy peppermint taste, candy canes are related to the Nativity. The cane is symbolic of the shepherds' staffs. Red stands for giving, and white stands for purity. Peppermint, a member of the hyssop family, is an herb renowned for its cleansing properties.

England, the Christmas season doesn't officially get started until December 25. You've probably heard the song "The Twelve Days of Christmas," but did you know what those twelve days are all about? They are the days leading up to Epiphany (January 6), which is the day the three wise men arrived in Bethlehem with gifts for the baby Jesus. Some people today still give gifts on Epiphany instead of Christmas Day. To stretch your holiday season out a little longer and enjoy a time of catching up, reflecting, and winding down, celebrate the twelve days of Christmas this year.

And somewhere in your twelve-day celebration, schedule a Celebration of Stillness tea party. Remember to make it restful and simple. Invite just one or two people—your spouse, your best friend, your mother, your grandmother, your sisters, your daughters, your granddaughters. Choose a free afternoon or evening, and take some time to sip tea and nibble on treats, engage in some real heart-to-heart talk, and perhaps even laugh and cry together as you share your thoughts about the year that has passed and your dreams for the year to come.

A Word about Tea

Did you know that tea can be used for beauty treatments? To refresh your skin, add a handful of rose petals to a pot of black tea. Let the roses and tea steep for about fifteen minutes, then strain the tea and store the liquid in the refrigerator. Splash rose-scented tea on your face for an instant pick-me-up.

Menu for a Celebration of Stillness tea party—

Egg Salad Sandwiches
Eggnog Holiday Bread
Scones
Mock Devonshire Cream

RECIPES

Egg Salad Sandwiches

4 hard-boiled eggs, finely chopped
1/4 cup mayonnaise
3 tablespoons sweet pickles, finely chopped
1 tablespoon mustard
salt and pepper to taste

Combine all ingredients in a mixing bowl until well blended. Chill until ready to make sandwiches. Spread on bread. Sandwiches can be cut into tree shapes for a more festive look.

Eggnog Holiday Bread

3 cups flour, sifted
3/4 cup sugar
1 tablespoon baking powder
1 teaspoon salt
1/2 teaspoon nutmeg
1 1/2 cups dairy eggnog
1 egg, beaten
1/4 cup butter, melted
3/4 cup pecans, chopped
3/4 cup candied fruit

In a large bowl, sift together flour, sugar, baking powder, salt, and nutmeg. In a separate bowl, mix eggnog, egg, and butter. Add wet ingredients to dry, stirring well. Add pecans and fruit. Bake in greased loaf pan at 350 degrees for 60 to 70 minutes. Cool on a wire rack.

Scones

The secret of tender scones is a minimum of handling.

2 cups flour
1 tablespoon baking powder
1/4 teaspoon salt
4 tablespoons sugar
6 tablespoons butter
2 eggs, beaten
1/3 cup cream, milk, or half-and-half

In a mixing bowl, combine dry ingredients. With a pastry blender or two knives, cut in butter until mixture resembles coarse crumbs. In a separate bowl, combine eggs and cream until well-blended. Stir cream mixture into dry ingredients until they are moistened. Do not mix the dough for too long or the scones will be

CHRISTMAS TIMELINE
1923: Pink poinsettias produced.
1939: Rudolph the Red-Nosed Reindeer created by Robert May for an American department store as a Christmas promotion.

hard. Divide the dough into two 8-inch rounds on a greased baking sheet. Cut the dough with a sharp knife into 8 wedges. Brush the top with milk and sprinkle on sugar. Bake at 400 degrees for 10 to 15 minutes or until the scones are golden brown.

TASTY ADDITIONS FOR SCONES:

2 teaspoons lemon or orange rind
1/2 cup semi-sweet chocolate chips
1/2 cup finely chopped nuts
1/4 cup cranberries or currants

Mock Devonshire Cream

This is a lovely substitute for English clotted cream. In a pinch, commercial whipped topping may be used.

1/2 cup heavy cream or 8 ounces softened cream cheese
2 tablespoons powdered sugar
1/2 cup sour cream

Using a chilled bowl, beat cream until medium-stiff peaks form. Add the sugar in the last few minutes of beating. (If using cream cheese, just mix in sugar.) Fold in sour cream and blend. Makes 1 1/2 cups.

READYING THE ROOMS

Soothe the senses by preparing a relaxing and restful tea environment. Think of all the little touches that make a difference—your favorite china cups and saucers, dainty lace-and-cotton serviettes, silver demitasse spoons, a beautiful teapot and serving tray. Turn the lights down low, bring out the candles, put on some soft music, fluff up the cushions, and get a roaring fire going in the fireplace. You can hold a Celebration of Stillness party wherever you feel the most comfortable and refreshed—in the living room, in your study, or, if your special guest is your spouse, you can even serve tea in the bedroom.

Wherever you choose to be, use this time to foster an atmosphere of caring and sharing. One thing I like to do is to choose two "companion" flowers—two roses, two carnations, two daffodils—and arrange them in a vase with ferns or baby's breath. I also spread a lovely tea cloth on a table or tray, and bring out the very nicest pots and cups I have. Then I light a candle and set a little gift—a card, a book, a tape, an ornament

for next year's Christmas tree, something I've made by hand—at my guest's place. I play some of our favorite music, dress up, and tell my guest to wear one of his or her favorite outfits. And the setting draws us closer together, encouraging us to share things we may not have shared before. That's the wonderful spirit of a Celebration of Stillness tea party.

One idea for a snug setting is an open attic or loft, someplace cozy with a low roof overhead. If you don't have such a room, add curtains to a four-poster bed to create a delightfully private sitting area. You can also mount curtain rods on the ceiling and frame any bed with some airy fabric. Rooms filled with books, ticking clocks, and flowers also put you in a contemplative mood, ready to spend some one-on-one time together with a cherished friend.

Once you've set the scene, you can plan a few simple activities for your tea party. Quiet conversation and a time of praying or sharing are wonderful if that's what you and your guest enjoy. If both of you like to write, give your friend a journal and spend some time together writing down your memories of

THE CHRISTMAS STORY AS TOLD IN THE GOSPEL OF LUKE

And there were shepherds living out in the fields nearby, keeping watch over their flocks at night. An angel of the Lord appeared to them, and the glory of the Lord shone around them, and they were terrified. But the angel said to them, "Do not be afraid. I bring you good news of great joy that will be for all the people. Today in the town of David a Savior has been born to you; he is Christ the Lord. This will be a sign to you: You will find a baby wrapped in cloths and lying in a manger."

Suddenly a great company of the heavenly host appeared with the angel, praising God and saying, "Glory to God in the highest, and on earth peace to men on whom his favor rests."

When the angels had left them and gone into heaven, the shepherds said to one another, "Let's go to Bethlehem and see this thing that has happened, which the Lord told us about."

So they hurried off and found Mary and Joseph, and the baby, who was lying in the manger. When they had seen him, they spread word concerning what had been told them about this child, and all who heard it were amazed at what the shepherds said to them. But Mary treasured up all these things and pondered them in her heart. The shepherds returned, glorifying and praising God for all the things they had heard and seen, which were just as they had been told.

the season—special gifts given or received, memorable family outings, the trip to visit the grandparents, reflections upon past Christmases, your ideas about the coming year. When you're writing, a good rule of thumb is to keep all the senses in mind. That way, you'll create some vivid memories that let future generations experience your holidays as if they, too, were there.

Another fun and meaningful activity is to make a living herbal wreath. It does take a bit of effort, but you can talk as you work and the end result will be stunning. Start with a base of florist's foam, or secure the herbs in damp sphagnum moss tucked inside a three-dimensional wire frame (the moss will encourage the herbs to put forth roots, making it very long-lasting). If you're using florist's foam, fashion a cage of plastic-coated chicken wire around it, then soak it until the foam is completely wet. Now, gather up an assortment of herbs from a grocery store or garden and insert sprigs into the base. You might want to choose herbs with significant meaning, such as thyme (friendship) or rosemary (remembrance). You can also add some dried roses or blossoms of myrtle, which symbolize love, peace, and restfulness. Your

living herbal wreath will be a fragrant reminder of the delightful time spent together with your very special friend.

If you're planning to share your Celebration of Stillness tea party with an elderly friend or relative or someone who has small children at home, be innovative and bring the party to them. Tea is a portable feast and a wonderful vehicle for sharing. Pack up the goodies and the following items in a large picnic basket with a handle—tea cloth and serviettes, teacups and saucers, tea plates, dessert forks, a small dish for butter or other spread, several small serving plates, a four-cup teapot, tea in a thermos, a tea strainer, a butter knife, teaspoons, cream, lemon wedges, and lumps of sugar, a candleholder and a candle, matches, a small vase and some silk flowers, and several tea towels (wrap breakable items in these). Pack the tea cloth last, and use it to cover the top of the basket. Now your tea party is ready to go!

CUSTOMS OF CHRISTMAS

The Nativity scene is perhaps the most common symbol of Christmas throughout the world. The earliest known depiction of the Nativity dates back to the fourth century, when a mural showing Christ's birth in a manger was discovered on the wall of a Christian tomb. In thirteenth century Italy, St. Francis of Assisi put on the first Nativity play as a part of a midnight mass. In the play, men and animals acted out the very first Christmas. Shortly after, churches all throughout Italy began recreating the Nativity scene during the holiday season. During the Middle Ages, Christmas plays told the story of the Christ child's birth to the people, most of whom could not read. In order to hold the attention of the audience, those putting on the plays encouraged audience participation and created eye-catching props.

Early American Pennsylvania German households fashioned their own carved wooden Nativity scenes, called *putzes,* to take the place of the elaborate pageants and plays that had been performed in the streets and homes of their native land. During Christmas week, neighbors would travel from one house to another, admiring each other's Nativity scenes and sharing traditional holiday food with each other. Today, many families display Nativity scenes, also called *creches*, in their homes or yards, and some churches have outdoor Nativity performances that feature live animals and wonderful costumes. Children enjoy learning about the Christmas story in this imaginative and interactive way.

There's more, much more, to Christmas
Than candlelight and cheer;
It's the spirit of sweet friendship
That brightens all the year.
It's thoughtfulness and kindness,
It's hope reborn again,
For peace, for understanding,
And for goodwill to men!

AUTHOR UNKNOWN

HIDDEN
EVIDENCE

HIDDEN
EVIDENCE

40 TRUE CRIMES AND HOW FORENSIC SCIENCE HELPED SOLVE THEM

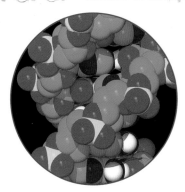

DAVID OWEN

FIREFLY BOOKS

A FIREFLY BOOK

Published by Firefly Books Ltd

Fifth Printing, 2003

Canadian Cataloguing-in-Publication Data
Owen, David, 1939-
    Hidden Evidence : 40 true crimes and how forensic science helped solve
them
Includes index.
ISBN 1-55209-483-9
1. Forensic sciences. 2. Criminal investigation. 3. Crime. I. Title.
HV8073.O93 2000   363.25   C00-930002-3

U.S. Cataloging-in-Publication Data
Owen, David
    Hidden evidence : 40 true crimes and how forensic
science helped solve them / David Owen. ——1st ed.
[240] p. : col. ill. ; cm..
Includes bibliographic resources and index.
Summary: the development of forensic science in
solving crimes, with real-life case examples.
ISBN 1-55209-483-9
1. Forensic sciences. 2. Criminal investigation.
3. Criminal psychology. I. Title.
363.25 –dc21   2000   CIP

Published in Canada in 2000 by
Firefly Books Ltd
3680 Victoria Park Avenue
Willowdale, Ontario
M2H 3K1

Published in the United States in 2000 by
Firefly Books (U.S.) Inc.
P.O. Box 1338, Ellicott Station
Buffalo, New York
14205

This book was designed and produced by
Quintet Publishing Limited
6 Blundell Street
London N7 7BH

Creative Director: Richard Dewing
Art Director: Simon Daley
Designer: James Lawrence
Senior Project Editor: Toria Leitch
Editor: Diane Pengelly
Picture Editor: Veneta Bullen

Typeset in Great Britain by
Central Southern Typesetters, Eastbourne

Manufactured in Hong Kong by Regent Publishing Services Ltd
Printed in Hong Kong by Midas Printing

Contents

Foreword

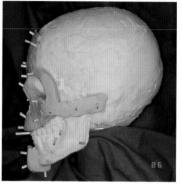

Hidden Evidence is a fascinating book. It focuses on the development and evolution of the techniques and technologies used in forensic criminal investigation, from the recognition of the uniqueness of fingerprints some 3,000 years ago in ancient China, to the present-day use of computerized DNA analysis. Each forensic subject is illustrated with synoptic examples using famous or infamous cases that will be familiar, to some degree, to most readers. Some of the cases cited occurred here in Los Angeles, where I have lived and worked since 1952. As I was reading, I reminisced of the days when I was involved in the investigations surrounding the deaths of Marilyn Monroe, Robert F. Kennedy, Sharon Tate, Janis Joplin, William Holden, Natalie Wood, John Belushi, and other lesser known cases. The history of the development of the technology and advances in criminal investigation is very interesting for me, because in my 50-year forensic career, I have witnessed many of the remarkable technological changes outlined in this book.

Chapter 1 begins with a reference to a T'ang Dynasty Magistrate, Ti Jen-Chieh, who is reputed to have used forensic evidence and logic to solve crimes. Using the facts of various cases to illustrate, the chapter goes on to describe the early history of forensic investigations and I found the discussions of some of these now-discarded theories fascinating, such as the identification of criminal types by facial structure. Subsequent chapters are well-organized into selected topics covering investigation, individual identification, weapons, knives and blunt instruments, strangulation and suffocation, and more. Each chapter starts with an informative discussion of the various elements of specific

investigative techniques, followed by factual presentation of illustrative cases, with a minimum of speculative analysis and conclusions.

Author David Owen has written for investigative-type publications since graduating from the University of Manchester, England, in 1961 with a B.Sc. in Engineering. His writing experience includes TV scripts based on fact, articles for engineering magazines, and an encyclopedia of technology and air-accident investigation.

The book is strictly factual, and easy reading for those who would like to have an introduction to the various fields of the forensic sciences, and for readers interested in the true facts of old and more current, well-known cases, some of which have been fictionalized in earlier publications.

I found, among the cases cited, some that I was either a part of the investigation or have heard and seen the scientific presentations at professional meetings, such as the annual meetings of the American Academy of Forensic Sciences (AAFS) and/or the National Association of Medical Examiners (NAME). I recall that at an AAFS meeting one year, I was a part of the speaker panel of the unique, annual scientific session called "The Last Word Society", where well-recognized forensic scientists are asked to review and give definitive thoughts or conclusions on well-known, unsolved cases. I was assigned to analyze the case of "Jack the Ripper." The author's introduction is entitled "The Trail of the Ripper" and covers this famous, and still unsolved, case.

I like *Hidden Evidence* very much for its factual, non-controversial presentation of the events with only the key issues cited. The book will be of interest to first-time readers of forensic topics, as well as long-time forensic investigators who want a synoptic, historical overview of their profession. For those interested in a quick reference to past cases with key scientific issues addressed, this is the book: an excellent mini-encyclopedia of widely discussed, high-profile cases.

I would recommend this book for every library as a quick reference to the forensic science professions. It may be of interest to science-oriented students, history majors, journalists (particularly those covering crime), and criminal investigators. *Hidden Evidence* offers testimony to the centuries of progress in forensic medicine and sciences, and criminal investigation.

Thomas T. Noguchi, M.D.

Chief Medical Examiner-Coroner (ret), and USC Professor Emeritus of Forensic Pathology

March 2000

Los Angeles, California

"Whenever you have excluded the impossible, whatever remains, however improbable, must be the truth."

Sir Arthur Conan Doyle, The Adventures of Sherlock Holmes; *The Adventure of Beryl Coronet.*

Stated differently, "The truth is out There." That assertion, made at the opening of each episode of the television series, *The X Files*, is the premise upon which forensic investigation is based. The truth is present and discoverable at every crime scene. To find it, according to Sherlock Holmes, one must follow the rules of scientific inquiry, gathering, observing, and testing data, then formulating, modifying, and rejecting hypotheses, until only one remains.

Polymerase chain reaction; Neutron activation; Microspectrophotometry; Gas chromatography; Gel electrophoresis; Mass spectrometry; Scanning electron microscopy. Today's techniques are far different from those employed by Sir Arthur Conan Doyle's fictional sleuth but the goals of police science remain the same.

The men who murdered Tsar Nicholas II and his family and servants thought their crime would never be discovered, but bones eventually came to light. Theodore Bundy was convicted by his own bitemark. DNA brought Colin Pitchfork's killing spree to an end. For the "Nightstalker," Richard Ramirez, it was a fingerprint, for Clifford Irving, a voiceprint.

Modern crime and medical examiner/coroner laboratories use a vast array of scientific specialities to exonerate the innocent and send murderers, rapists, burglars, and swindlers to jail. Bones tell stories of identity, trauma, and postmortem mutilation. The forensic anthropologist reads them. The odontologist analyzes teeth and the marks they make. People constantly exchange bits of themselves with their surroundings.

The trace evidence specialist studies hairs, fibers, pollen, paint, soil, and glass to determine who was present at a crime scene. The ballistics expert looks at tools and weapons. The biologist analyzes blood, saliva, and semen to tie perpetrators to victims or locations.

When people ask how I ended up in forensic anthropology I tell them it was accidental. In graduate school I studied archaeology and human skeletal biology, intending to focus on the ancient dead. But early in my career, when I did the occasional coroner case, I experienced an excitement I hadn't felt with prehistoric bones. The cases that came to me in body bags, or transported by sheriff's deputies, had immediacy lacking in my archaeological work. I found forensic investigation both fascinating and rewarding. I could use my science to solve a puzzle. I could provide a family with closure. I could contribute to law enforcement's effort to take criminals off the streets.

That is the purpose of forensic science, and that is what this book describes. *Hidden Evidence* takes you from crime scene to crime lab, and demonstrates how science has been used to untangle lies, both modern and historic. Commingled bones in a septic tank. Fibers in a car trunk. Paint chips on a mangled bike. Fingerprints on a bloody bat. By the use of sophisticated technology, expanded databases, and complex global linking, scientists now probe these bits and pieces, this hidden evidence, to exclude the impossible, find the truth, and sort the guilty from the innocent.

Kathy Reichs

The Trail of the Ripper...

In the late 1880s the East End of London was a grim and dangerous place to be. Grinding poverty trapped many hundreds of people in the dark and depressing jumble of the Whitechapel slums. Criminals of all kinds, from robbers and pickpockets to burglars and prostitutes, plied their trades among the poorly-lit streets, and violence was an unfortunate fact of everyday life.

One morning in November, 1888, a year in which two women had already been murdered in the area, an assistant to a local landlord called at 13 Miller's Court to collect rent owed by a twenty-four-year-old prostitute named Mary Jane Kelly. He knocked on the door and, since there was no response, peered through a broken window pane. To his horror he saw a human corpse, cut to pieces; the floor of the

room was awash with blood.

When the police arrived, they found that the woman's body had been dismantled: both breasts removed, the liver placed between the victim's feet and one hand placed in her stomach. The fireplace contained ashes of burned women's clothing.

Witnesses reported having seen the victim earlier with a man who had a mustache and was wearing a type of bowler hat known as a Derby. Two witnesses claimed they had heard a cry of "Oh, murder!" coming from the corner of Miller's Court just before four in the morning, and a neighbor had heard footsteps leaving the area some two hours later.

ABOVE 13 Miller's Court, Whitechapel, London 1888 where the mutilated body of the hapless Mary Jane Kelly was found.

LEFT Illustrated periodicals of the time fed the public appetite for details of the Ripper's murders.

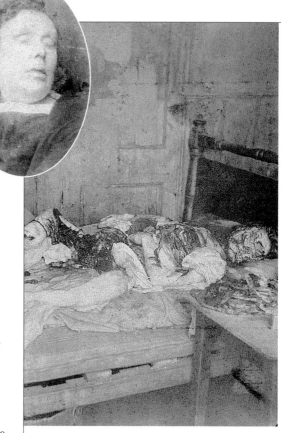

This horrific killing was the last in the series of extraordinarily savage attacks known to have been carried out by a shadowy figure nicknamed Jack the Ripper. Other brutal murders were committed during the late 1880s: some of the victims were women and some had had their throats cut, but differences in the way in which the fatal injuries had been inflicted made it unlikely that the Ripper had been involved.

In spite of the witness accounts and a tantalizing stock of forensic evidence, no credible suspect was identified in the Ripper case, though contemporary speculation was understandably rife. Over a century later, theories regarding the motives and identity of this most notorious of killers are still being published by writers, researchers and police officers. Suspects were traced and charged in connection with the later attacks, but no one with a real, provable connection to the genuine Ripper murders was ever found.

The Ripper case illustrates both the potential and the limitations of forensic science. During the twentieth century, forensic evidence has played an increasingly important role in a wide range of cases but, just as with this greatest and best-known of unsolved crimes, forensic evidence cannot find and convict the criminal unaided. It does, however, provide an additional weapon in the detective's armory; a weapon that can be used in two principal ways. It can offer clues to help detectives track down the criminal and it can help detectives prove a suspect was present at the crime scene or committed a particular act of violence. In some cases, it can even do both. By using powerful weapons such as fingerprinting and ballistics, DNA comparison, and trace-element analysis, the modern forensic scientist can uncover facts, expose crucial details, and confirm or discount theories with a certainty that would have startled previous generations.

TOP AND ABOVE RIGHT Mary Jane Kelly and Annie Chapman—both victims of the Ripper.

BELOW *The Illustrated Police News* highlighted every development.

But, spectacular as the results may be, the power of this exacting science can be fully brought to bear only once a recognizable target has been identified. Finding that target depends on solid and reliable police work.

Forensic science is not infallible. Even now there are cases where the evidence it isolates seems confusing or incomplete, or is open to more than one interpretation. Sometimes expert opinion differs over the significance of a particular finding. In other cases, techniques used to locate the tiniest traces of a particular substance have become so sensitive that a trifling weakness in laboratory hygiene or the simplest human error can lead to mistaken conclusions or inadvertent tampering with the evidence. As forensic science becomes more powerful, it must be handled with greater and more scrupulous care, if the guilty are to be convicted and the innocent exonerated.

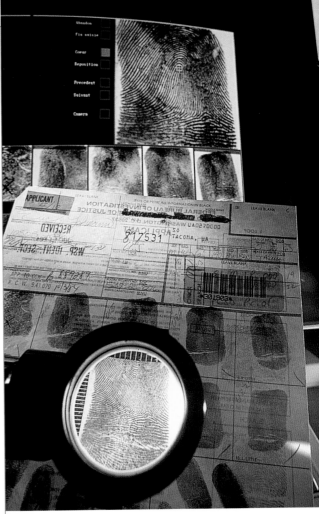

RIGHT Fingerprints provided the first reliable proof of a person's presence at the scene of a crime and are still vital today.

BELOW Taking samples from blood-stained cloth to determine through DNA fingerprinting whether the blood was from the victim or the attacker.

In the Beginning

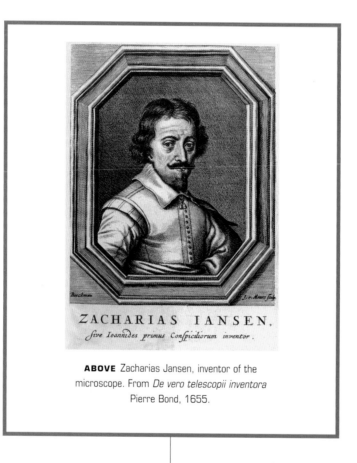

ZACHARIAS IANSEN,
five Ioannides primus Conspiciliorum inventor.

ABOVE Zacharias Jansen, inventor of the microscope. From *De vero telescopii inventora* Pierre Bond, 1655.

The dawn of forensic science as we understand it today took place in the civilization of ancient China. Documents found in Chinese archives dating back to the seventeenth century refer to a magistrate who lived a thousand years before in the remote age of the T'ang dynasty. Ti Jen-Chieh is reputed to have used both logic and forensic evidence to help solve a wide range of crimes in the late seventh century AD. Ti used a team of investigators, studied the crime scene, examined physical evidence, and interviewed witnesses and suspects. Though his methods and tools bore little resemblance to their sophisticated modern counterparts, Ti's attitude to his work and his careful investigation of the evidence would not be out of place today.

The development of forensic science owes much to the ages of scientific discovery in the sixteenth, seventeenth, and eighteenth centuries. The compound microscope was invented by Zacharias Jansen in 1590. It used a combination of lenses to produce an image much larger than that provided by the conventional magnifying glass: just two or three lenses produced a magnification of some ten times. This technique eventually allowed details of a single fingerprint to be examined

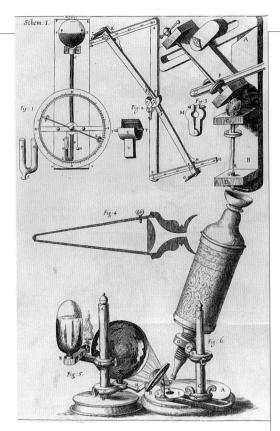

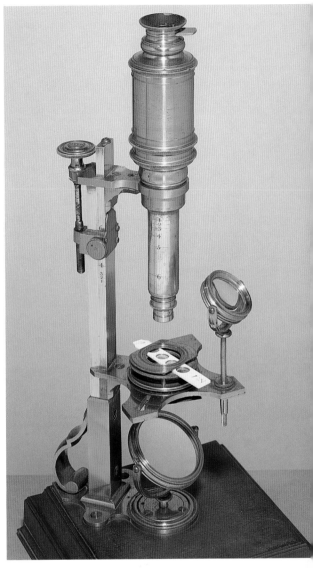

LEFT Robert Hooke's compound microscope 1665, from his book *Micrographia*.

BELOW Cuff compound microscope, 1905, photographed in the Science Museum, London.

much more closely and so compared more precisely with other prints on record cards or at a crime scene, for example.

Complex combinations of more accurately ground lenses were developed in the seventeenth century to produce a magnification of up to three hundred times. Such power enabled forensic scientists to examine hairs and fibers, blood samples, or scraps of cloth or other material, and to make informed decisions as to whether or not one sample matched another.

By the 1880s, optical microscopes with magnifications of up to two thousand times had been developed, as had other variations on the theme which were particularly useful in this field. These included the stereoscopic microscope, which has double eyepieces and double lens systems and works through prisms to provide a three-dimensional image. Stereoscopic microscopes are useful for comparing soil samples or viewing paint fragments to, for example, help identify a particular location or vehicle.

The comparison microscope, like the stereo microscope, has two lens systems, but these are combined with prisms to bring two images side by side for direct comparison, instead of superimposing them to create a third dimension. This makes it ideal for comparing the marks on two bullets to check whether or not they were fired from the same gun, or comparing samples of fabric or hair to check

13

for a match. The comparison microscope was originally developed by Philip Gravelle and Calvin Goddard in the 1920s in New York's Bureau of Forensic Ballistics. There is now also an adaptation of the optical microscope that can be used with infrared light to show whether or not documents have been tampered with.

Photographs cannot lie?

The principle behind photographic film was first discovered in 1724 by a German inventor named Johann Heinrich Schultze. He noticed that silver salts darkened when exposed to light, at a rate that varied with the intensity of the light. Although this was the basic principle of photographic film, the image could not be fixed until 1826, when a retired French army officer named Joseph Nicéphore Niepce succeeded in focusing a beam of light on a pewter plate covered with a light-sensitive bitumen solution. In his initial experiments it took eight hours to complete the exposure, but within another thirteen years Niepce had gone into partnership with Louis Daguerre. By using a copper plate coated with silver iodide and then developing the image on the exposed plate with mercury vapor, the first photograph,

or "daguerrotype," was developed.

The method was limited to producing just one picture for each exposure, but when William Fox Talbot invented the negative, which could then be used for making any number of positive prints, the technique became much more useful. In 1850 the wet-plate enabled photographs to be taken more quickly and cheaply, and in 1871 the process became easier still with the invention of dry-plate photography. By then, photographs were being used routinely to record shots of evidence at crime scenes, details of victims and/or their injuries, and shots of subjects arrested on suspicion of committing a crime. The "Rogues' Galleries," books of full-face and profile portraits of known criminals, were important to many criminal enquiries. In 1886, New York detective Thomas Byrnes had his collection of "mug-shots" published to help the public recognize criminals who might attack or attempt to rob them.

ABOVE French physicist and inventor Joseph Neipce (1765–1833).

LEFT English photography pioneer William Henry Fox Talbot (right) at work, with device to keep sitter's head still during long exposure.

BELOW Police identification table, based upon Bertillon's system (see p. 21).

ABOVE Replica of Fox Talbot's Mousetrap, forerunner of the box camera.

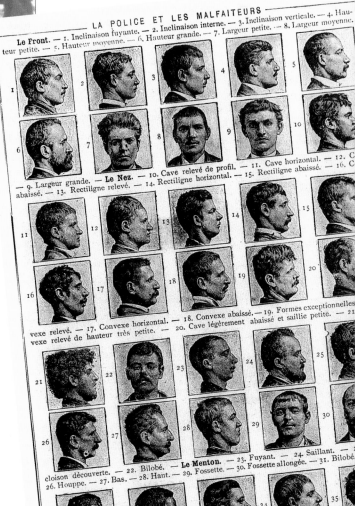

375

LA POLICE ET LES MALFAITEURS

Le Front. — 1. Inclinaison fuyante. — 2. Inclinaison interne. — 3. Inclinaison verticale. — 4. Hauteur petite. — 5. Hauteur moyenne. — 6. Hauteur grande. — 7. Largeur petite. — 8. Largeur moyenne.

9. Largeur grande. **Le Nez.** — 10. Cave relevé de profil. — 11. Cave horizontal. — 12. Convexe abaissé. — 13. Rectiligne relevé. — 14. Rectiligne horizontal. — 15. Rectiligne abaissé. — 16. Convexe relevé. — 17. Convexe horizontal. — 18. Convexe abaissé. — 19. Formes exceptionnelles vexe relevé de hauteur très petite. — 20. Cave légèrement abaissé et saillie petite. — 21. cloison découverte. — 22. Bilobé. **Le Menton.** — 23. Fuyant. — 24. Saillant. 26. Houppe. — 27. Bas. — 28. Haut. — 29. Fossette. — 30. Fossette allongée. — 31. Bilobé.

RIGHT Exhibits from the Maybrick case, where Florence Maybrick was found guilty of poisoning her husband, Liverpool merchant James Maybrick.

Pure Poison

For hundreds if not thousands of years, poison of one sort or another has been the weapon of choice among dispassionate murderers. Avoiding the drama and mess often generated by an overtly violent death, a carefully chosen poison could be relied upon to work slowly, stealthily, and ultimately surely. With the advantage of a little background knowledge and access to the right materials, a murderer might even tailor his weapon to confuse the victim and any subsequent enquiry by using it to produce symptoms resembling those of natural killers such as heart disease or pneumonia.

But modern scientific methods make it increasingly difficult for poison to remain undetected. As long ago as 1814 Matthieu Orfila earned the title of "the father of toxicology" by publishing his book *Traité des Poisons*, which classified the common poisons favored by criminals. In 1836 another pioneer, Alfred Swaine Taylor, published a monumental textbook called *Elements of Medical Jurisprudence*, which became a classic of forensic medicine.

In October that year, English chemist James Marsh, working at the Royal Arsenal at Woolwich, south London, developed an accurate technique for revealing traces of arsenic. This poison was favored by criminals because arsenic actually already exists in small traces in the healthy human body. A victim of arsenic poisoning, however, has traces of the

ABOVE Matthieu Joseph Bonaventura Orfila, expert chemist, in 1847.

chemical in almost every part of the body as opposed to concentrations in particular organs such as the stomach or liver; these remain in the bones and hair even after death, whereas other poisons may be broken down by body chemistry. Marsh's test could reveal a trace as small as one-fiftieth of a milligram in a sample taken from the body of a victim of a suspicious death, and the principles of his technique are still in use today.

The telltale bullet

Before the mid-1830s, little could be done to link a particular weapon to a particular crime—unless of course the criminal was found at the scene clutching the still-smoking gun. In 1835, however, a policeman named Henry Goddard succeeded for the first time in tracing a bullet to the weapon that had fired it. Goddard had been a member of the Bow Street Runners, London's first police force, which had been formed in the eighteenth century as a group of "professional thieftakers."

In those days, bullets were often still molded individually by the owner of the firearm.

Goddard was called in to investigate a burglary in Southampton, and was told that the household's butler had been shot at by the intruders. He found the bullet buried in the butler's bed headboard and compared it carefully with the butler's own pistol and bullet mold. He found a raised mark on the bullet that matched a defect in the mold, proving that the shot had been fired from the butler's own weapon. Faced with the evidence, the butler admitted that it was he who had attempted to rob his employer, and that he had fired the shot in an attempt to divert suspicion from himself.

By 1869, a French investigator was able to analyze the chemical composition of a bullet found in the head of a murder victim and compare his findings with an analysis of bullets found on the chief suspect. The results proved beyond reasonable doubt that all the bullets had been molded in one batch, which strongly suggested that the suspect had made and fired the fatal bullet.

The science of ballistics developed more fully with the advent of rifled weapons and mass-produced ammunition. In 1889 Professor Alexandre Lacassagne showed that a bullet

BELOW George III (1738–1820), King of Great Britain, guarded by Bow Street Runners, forefathers of today's police force.

could be matched with the gun that had fired it by comparing the number of rifling grooves in the barrel with the number of grooves carved into the surface of the bullet when it was fired. The Bureau of Forensic Ballistics, founded in New York in 1923, continues to develop this increasingly sophisticated science.

The "criminal face"

Sadly, not all pioneering ideas in forensic science proved to be truly scientific. The surgeon at Toulon prison in southern France developed a theory linking habitual criminality with a particular shape of skull, and took plaster casts of the heads of notorious inmates to reinforce his ideas. In 1876 Cesare Lombroso, a forty-year-old former army surgeon and the medical superintendent of a lunatic asylum at Pesaro in northern Italy, published a treatise on criminal man, *L'Uomo Delinquente*, which claimed that his lifetime study of more than 6000 criminals had shown that they tended to possess certain well-developed physical characteristics.

In Lombroso's view, habitual criminals tended to have wide jaws, high cheekbones, long arms, and large ears (approximately square in shape), as well as an unusually narrow field of vision. He even claimed to be able to point to characteristics that were associated with particular types of criminal activity. Fire-raisers, for example, had small

heads; highwaymen had thick hair; swindlers and conmen were usually heavily built, with wide jaws and strong cheekbones, while pickpockets had usefully long hands and were often tall and dark-haired. At the time his theories were convincing enough to prompt others to invent instruments to measure these essential indications of criminal tendencies. A ball on a string was swung like a pendulum to test a suspect's field of view, for example, and a "craniometer" was developed to trace the shape of a head onto paper. But there has never been any real evidence of anything more than a random connection between physical appearance and criminal behavior.

One of Lombroso's contemporaries, an inventor named Patrizi, designed an early type of lie-detector. Called the "volumetric glove," the device was made of gutta-percha, a tough, grayish-black plastic substance from the latex of various Malayan trees. It was designed to fit over the hand and be tightly sealed at the wrist. The glove was then filled with air and connected to a tube linked to an apparatus for recording changes in pressure caused by the pulse in the veins of the hand. When questions were put to the suspect, an increase in emotional tension was supposedly shown by an increase in the blood flow to the hand, and a consequent increase in the pressure changes caused by the pulse. Sadly, the glove was no more reliable than the "criminal face" as an indicator of criminal tendencies.

OPPOSITE Bertillon's attempts to find a way of recording individual facial details depended on recording these measurements very accurately. Here a 1907 subject is photographed under controlled studio conditions for his details to be recorded (see p. 21).

Bumps of character

Another once-prominent theory was that developed by a Viennese physician, Dr. Franz Josef Gall, in 1796. The theory of phrenology held that a person's character was revealed by the shape of the cranium. Prominent bumps were thought to reveal quirks of the individual's identity: domestic tendencies, for example, were concentrated at the back of the skull, intellectual virtues at the front, moral senses at the top, and selfish centers at the sides, just over the ears. As many as forty-two different faculties were thought to be

ABOVE 19th century caricature of Franz Josef Gall (1758–1828) showing a skull to a group of his followers. The busts and human skulls in the background are arranged according to the type of person they came from.

concentrated in different places on the surface of the skull. The theory became popular during the nineteenth century and its adherents claimed to be able to take measurements of a subject's head and reveal anything from an over-zealous love of food or drink to excessive thrift, an appreciation of music, or a respect for social conventions. Scientific evidence to support the theory was, however, nonexistent.

Bertillon and the "vital measurements"

Scientifically more respectable were the theories of Frenchman Alphonse Bertillon, a clerk at the Préfecture of Police in Paris in 1879, who also happened to be the son of the president of the Paris Anthropological Society. Bertillon had the idea that a criminal's physical measurements could be used, not as an indication of whether or not he or she was a criminal, but simply as an extra aid to precise identification.

Bertillon produced a report to promote his theory, which was based on recording detailed measurements of all convicted criminals, but it was initially rejected by the Préfet de Police and the head of the Sûreté. In December 1882, however, Bertillon was given a chance: he was allowed three months, during which two clerks were put at his disposal, to prove that his ideas could work. After two and a half months, during which the team had carefully measured and recorded details of more than 1500

criminals, no important discoveries had been made by Bertillon.

With just two weeks to go, Bertillon took the measurements of a suspect named Dupont. These measurements exactly matched the recorded details of a thief known as Martin. When challenged, Dupont admitted to being

ABOVE Alphonse Bertillon, 1853–1914.

FAR LEFT Bertillon's anthropometric measuring system used to record the dimensions of a subject's ears.

LEFT The system recorded twelve measurements including the circumference of the skull.

Martin, and it seemed that "Bertillonage," as the scheme was known, was a genuinely useful technique.

Bertillon's system chalked up many hundreds of successful identifications, and its originator was promoted to Director of the Judicial Identification Service and given a large staff to help with record-keeping. However, when experiments with fingerprinting in England resulted in pressure for prints to be added to French criminal records, Bertillon insisted on relegating them to the far less important category of "distinguishing marks." When the *Mona Lisa* was stolen from the Louvre in 1911, incomplete records left detectives with no way of identifying fingerprints found at the scene. The criminal was eventually caught two years later when he tried to take the painting to Italy, and Bertillon and his system of measurements were discredited. When records were checked, it emerged that the thief, an eccentric Italian named Vincenzo Perugia, had been interrogated several times by the Paris police, and Bertillon himself had actually been responsible for taking his measurements.

The "portrait parlé"

One last attempt to resurrect the "Bertillonage" system was based on the *portrait parlé*, or "word portrait." This set out to categorize the description of an individual's appearance by developing a standard set of features and variations with reasonably precise meanings. For example, a man's face could be described with reference to the shape of the forehead, the nose, the chin, the ears, and the eyes. In describing the nose, attention would be paid to the profile, the tip, the nostrils, the base, and the height, together with any particular distinguishing features.

Using this system, officers were able to match a spoken or written description of an individual with an actual face—sometimes with remarkable accuracy—and the technique was practiced by detectives in France and the U.K. until the 1950s. It was finally rendered obsolete by new techniques such as Identikit and Photofit, and by computerized photographic records.

ABOVE Measuring an ear based on the old "Bertillonage" system.

OPPOSITE This drawing by Eugene Francis Vidocq (1775–1857) shows the first fictional character by Edgar Allen Poe, which was based on Auguste Dupont. The visual characteristics are taken from the description in the book, together with the Bertillonage measurements.

RIGHT An identification specialist of the French Gendarmerie National creates a "Portrait Robot" under the direction of a witness. The utility of this system was quickly recognized and spread to police agencies worldwide.

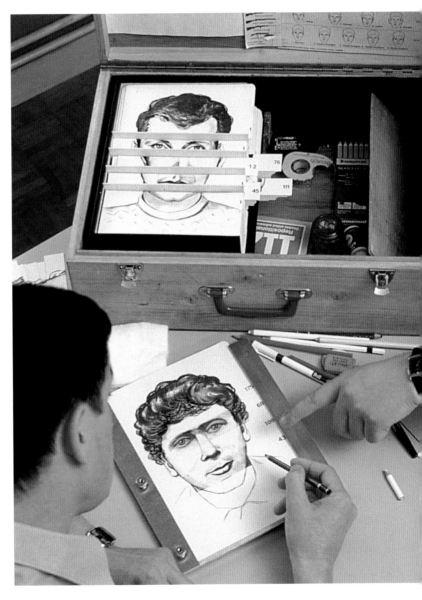

Paul Revere and his Dentures

One of the ways in which modern forensic science can positively identify an individual is through accurate dental records, since teeth not only differ in detail from person to person, but they last longer than other physical elements after death. Although there are subtle changes as the subject ages, the overall pattern of the teeth changes so little that records compiled years before can still be accurate enough to provide positive identification. Moreover, where natural teeth have been replaced by false teeth, the dentures are also a very useful form of record, and in the U.S. in particular they are often marked with both the wearer's name and his or her social security number.

One of the earliest cases of identification by teeth dates back to the mid-1770s. Paul Revere, a coppersmith, silversmith, and engraver, had been taught dentistry by English practitioner John Baker. In 1775 Revere made a set of dentures for his friend, Dr. Joseph Warren. The teeth, held together with silver wire, were supported by a bridge made from the tusk of a hippopotamus. In June of that year, at the battle of Bunker Hill where British forces stormed American entrenchments on a peninsula to the north of Boston, Warren was killed by a shot to the head. Though his body was buried in a mass grave after the battle, his family wished it to be found and brought back to England. Revere was able to identify the body from the dental work and it was subsequently returned to be buried in the family plot at Forest Hill, south London.

ABOVE Paul Revere, 1735–1818.

RIGHT Death of General Joseph Warren at the Bunker Hill battle, June 17, 1775.

Dr. John Webster

r. John Webster was the Professor of Chemistry at Harvard Medical College in 1849 when he borrowed $438 from a fellow doctor, George Parkman. Growing impatient for the repayment of the loan, Parkman called at Webster's rooms on Friday, November 23. Parkman was never seen alive again. Two days later his wife reported him missing, and reward notices were posted all over the area.

The first evidence that murder had been committed was found by a college janitor named Ephraim Littlefield. He had noticed that on the day when Parkman was known to have disappeared, Webster's laboratory door had been locked, but the wall against which the laboratory's assay oven was situated felt hot to the touch. When this was put to Webster, he claimed to have been conducting experiments. He then attracted further suspicion by offering the janitor a Thanksgiving turkey.

Littlefield persuaded his wife to keep watch for Webster while he hammered a hole through the laboratory wall. To his horror, he saw through the hole two parts of a human leg and a pelvis. He alerted the police, whose subsequent search of the laboratory yielded a human torso and more than one hundred and fifty bones and body fragments.

A team of university anthropological experts was called in to solve the anatomical jigsaw puzzle, and they found the pieces belonged to a man roughly five feet ten inches tall and aged between fifty and sixty years old.

Parkman had been sixty years old and six feet tall and further evidence in the shape of a set of dentures was found in the furnace. These were compared with the dental records and a cast kept by Parkman's dentist. The result was a perfect match, and Webster was convicted of murder and sentenced to death.

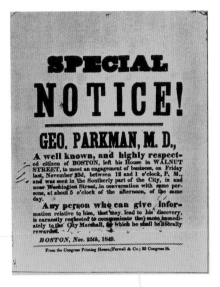

ABOVE A "City Marshal" reward notice for information concerning the disappearance of Dr. George Parkman.

On the Scene

ABOVE Investigator with a bone bag at the scene of the Hilllsville massacre in Virginia.

Wherever possible, forensic investigations start with the examination of the scene where the crime was committed. This is where the first clues are evaluated and the initial impressions formed concerning the nature of the crime, the cause of death of any victims, and the identity of the criminal or criminals involved. The first professional on the scene is usually a police officer, who closes off the site to intruders, checks bodies for signs of life and calls appropriate services. Extra lighting may be needed, and shelter provided over outdoor sites.

Investigating officers search for any evidence beyond the immediate site, and mark the exact position of anything that could conceivably be pertinent to their enquiry. Photographs and, increasingly, videotapes of the scene are taken by professional police operators. If there is a dead body at the scene, it must not be disturbed until the police surgeon or forensic pathologist arrives. More photographs are taken and details noted to show exactly where the body was found in relation to other objects at the scene.

In most cases, this initial search reveals the most important details. But even if there is no obvious evidence immediately visible, modern forensic science can reveal a great deal from the tiniest traces of significant substances as long as they are located, identified, collected, and recorded. This calls for painstaking work: officers may execute a "fingertip search" of the entire area. The search may be organized in an expanding spiral from the center, as a grid pattern, a strip or line search, or a search of one zone after another: whichever systematic, physically practical approach best ensures that the whole area is covered very carefully.

What are the searchers looking for? It may be fingerprints, shoeprints, tire tracks or prints, the tiniest of bloodstains, scratches, paint flakes, hair, fibers... the list is endless. Some evidence can be lifted with tape, or by dusting and brushing. When the actual pieces of evidence are too small for the searcher to spot with the naked eye, areas of the scene are covered with a vacuum cleaner, so the contents can be checked at the forensic laboratory.

When a vehicle is involved in the crime, an equally meticulous search has to be carried out. If a car is suspected of having been involved in a hit-and-run accident, for example, its outside paintwork must be searched for dents, cracks, or scrapes, and the clothing of the victim also has to be screened for matching paint fragments, pieces of broken vehicle glass, or any other evidence that might link vehicle and victim. In cases of abduction or kidnapping, the vehicle's upholstery must be checked for hairs or fibers that may match those belonging to the victim, which can be collected with a special vacuum cleaner.

RIGHT A murder investigation in Eugene, Oregon.

BELOW Irish Police officers using metal detectors.

BELOW An evidence vacuum cleaner.

Finding the time of death

In cases of suspicious deaths, once the anthropologist or pathologist has arrived at the crime scene, a first priority is to establish the time of death. The usual way of doing this with any degree of precision is to take the internal temperature of the body, because the first measurable changes after death occur as the body begins to cool down. The internal temperature is always measured because externally the body feels cold to the touch from a fairly early stage. The temperature of the body falls from its normal level (of around 98.6 degrees Fahrenheit) at a rate of roughly one and a half to two degrees per hour for the first twelve hours, depending on the build of the victim, the amount of clothing or other insulation covering the body, and the ambient temperature. For the next twelve hours the internal temperature falls at about half this rate. If the body has been submerged in water, its temperature can fall much more quickly.

Other signs can cast additional light on the time the victim died. Rigor mortis, a Latin term meaning "the stiffness of death," begins to take effect as the internal chemistry of the body changes from its normal acid state to an alkaline one, usually about two hours after life has become extinct. This causes muscles that were relaxed at the time of death to begin to tense and stiffen. The process begins with the eyelids and progresses to the muscles of the face and jaw, then to the arms, the trunk, and finally the legs.

Rigor mortis is a progressive condition and is usually fully established about twelve hours after death, by which time the body is as stiff and unbending as a block of wood. The body can remain in this condition for anything between twelve and forty-eight hours, until further chemical changes return the body to an acid state, at which point the muscles begin to relax again. This reverse process affects the muscles in the same order in which rigor mortis originally stiffened them: the eyelids first, then the facial muscles... and finally the legs.

Sometimes the picture can be confused by a muscular spasm that initially presents the same symptoms as rigor mortis but is actually brought on immediately by a particularly violent death. The condition is known as cadaveric spasm, and it occurs at the moment of death. If the victim was gripping anything as he or she was killed, the object remains tightly clutched in the hand for several hours. If investigators are lucky, it may provide clues as to the manner of death—or even to the identity of the killer. If, for example, the victim managed to grapple with the murderer, traces of the assailant's hair, skin, or clothes fibers may remain in the victim's hand. Although the spasm renders muscles almost impossible to loosen at first, the condition relaxes within a matter of hours, whereupon the normal pattern of rigor mortis comes into effect.

Another indicator that can help establish the time of death is called livor mortis, or "the bruising of death." When the heart stops beating and the blood stops circulating, the red cells descend by the force of gravity to the parts of the body in contact with the ground. This turns them a bruised color from about two hours after death and, provided the body is not moved, the coloration fixes as the red blood cells break down and separate into the surrounding muscle tissues. In some cases the colors can be particularly vivid, due to the presence of poisons. Victims who have died from carbon monoxide poisoning will show a bright red in the lower parts of the body, while cyanide poisoning produces a pink effect.

In most cases, the best estimate of time of death is based on a compromise between the fairly approximate indications given by these different signs. More recently, however, a quite different indicator was discovered by Dr. John Coe, medical examiner of Hennepin County, Minneapolis. Coe discovered that as the red blood cells break down in the process which produces livor mortis, they release quantities of potassium. This diffuses into the vitreous humor, the fluid that fills the inside of the eyeball, at a slow but consistent rate. Taking a sample of the vitreous humor from the victim's eyeballs and then determining the percentage of potassium present in the liquid may provide the most accurate estimate yet discovered of the time of death.

ABOVE Body of People's Temple Leader, Jim Jones, killed by cyanide poisoning.

LEFT A forensic scientist examines a body at the location of a crime.

Examining the clues

Flies and plants provide evidence of time passing.

TOP The presence of fully-grown blowfly maggots and pupae shows that the body has been buried for at least 10 to 12 days.

BOTTOM Once the coffin flies expose the bones, fungus grows and woodlice establish a colony, grazing on the fungus-coated remains.

Finding the date of death

In cases where the body is not found until some time after death, the processes of decay give a reasonable indication of the length of time the body has laid undiscovered. Normally the action of bacteria breaking down the blood produces green staining on the flanks of the abdomen after two days. In a day or two more the staining spreads to the arms, legs, and neck, and the body begins to swell, and after a week blisters appear on the skin.

In warmer conditions outdoors and at the right time of year, insects can provide another way of establishing, albeit approximately, how much time has elapsed since the victim died. Flies like the bluebottle and greenbottle normally lay their eggs on flesh that is still fresh, and the eggs hatch between eight and fourteen hours later, depending on the temperature of the surroundings. Maggots then develop through three progressive stages, shedding their skin each time, until they are fully grown some ten to twelve days after the eggs were laid. They then leave the body to continue their development elsewhere. The common house-fly follows a similar cycle over a similar period, and forensic entomologists can provide accurate estimates of the date (rather than the precise time) of death by this method, even if a body has been lying undiscovered for several days.

Footprints and tire tracks

In cases where the crime was committed by an intruder, a detailed search of the scene and its surroundings may reveal footprints and possibly tire tracks. Where these are left in the soil, the forensic team uses dental stone, a special variant of gypsum used by dentists to form denture molds, to take a cast of the clearest sample. If footprints or tire tracks are formed in snow, the examiners spray the snow with a special wax to make it hard enough to take a cast.

Shoeprints, even though these are usually incomplete, can provide useful clues as to the identity of the intruder—in addition to indicating the size of his or her feet. Footwear manufacturers cast soles in a bewildering variety of patterns, ostensibly to enhance the grip of the shoe. The diversity of these patterns can help investigators to pinpoint a specific make and model of shoe and, where the shoe is not new, an accurate cast can even reveal patterns of wear dictated by the owner's gait, a characteristic unique to that individual.

Tire tracks can be just as useful. Manufacturers and the police authorities—including the FBI—keep records of different patterns which in turn can be traced to different sizes of tire and often different makes and models of vehicle. Here too any abnormalities of wear or damage to the tire offer the possibility of making a more precise identification.

If shoe prints have been found at the scene, the search is often extended to any nearby vantage points where the criminal might have laid in wait. Cover behind trees or hedges often yields more shoe prints, and perhaps even a cigarette butt or other traces of the person who stood there waiting for the right moment. Any likely approach route is also given special attention.

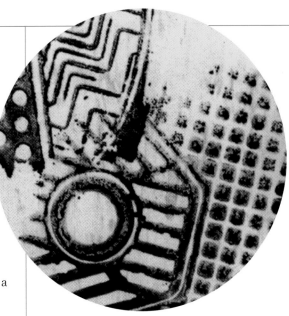

ABOVE Detail of a shoe print.

Some shoe prints cannot be preserved by plaster cast. The criminal may have left his or her mark by having walked in wet paint or spilled blood, or even by treading with wet or muddy shoes on a clean patch of carpet or bare floor. In these cases, photographs are taken to record as much detail as possible. Where prints are clear enough, examiners can tell whether the person who left them was walking or running, carrying a heavy weight, or even limping, all of which helps to build a fuller picture of events.

BELOW Tire print evidence showing impression of a tread in dirt at the crime scene.

Tool marks
and teeth marks

Other telltale signs include marks left by the tools used to gain access. When viewed under powerful magnification, even the sharpest and most standard tool, such as a chisel or a screwdriver, shows peaks and troughs along the cutting edge that produce a characteristic pattern of scratches when it is used to force open a door, a window, or a desk drawer.

Such marks are usually too small for a cast to be useful, so examiners borrow a technique from ballistics specialists. Instead of digging out a spent bullet, they actually remove the wood, metal, or other material that shows the tool marks, and keep it as evidence. If a subsequent search of a suspect's quarters discovers a tool that could have been responsible, the implement is used to produce a mark on a test piece of wood or other material corresponding to that removed from the scene. The test mark and that made at the scene are then viewed alongside each other through a comparison microscope, exactly as a test bullet would be compared with crime-scene evidence for the characteristic pattern of scratches.

There are cases in which criminals have left more personal clues in the shape of bite marks.

These may have been left on food, or there may have been a physical struggle when the victim was bitten by his or her assailant. In either case, clear marks can reveal telling evidence regarding the shape and arrangement of the criminal's teeth, information that might clear or convict a given suspect.

THIS PAGE Evidence from the Linda Peacock murder in Scotland 1967.

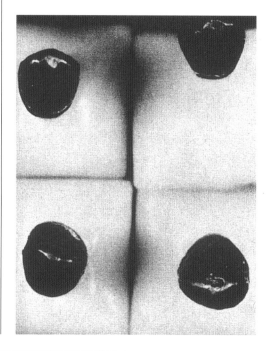

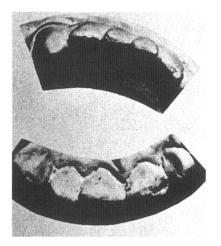

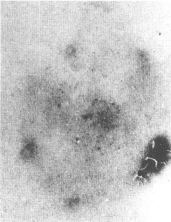

ABOVE Copper-plated models of the killer Gordon Hay's teeth.

FAR LEFT Casts of Hay's front teeth.

LEFT The bite marks on Linda Peacock's body tallied with the individual features of Gordon Hay's teeth.

Soil and mud

Another important source of information for forensic scientists can be the earth around the crime site. Having taken soil samples during the search for other evidence, investigators can use precise techniques to check corresponding traces of soil or mud on a suspect's clothes, or on the tires or bodywork of a suspect vehicle. Conversely, if a person is arrested on suspicion of having committed a crime, but the scene of that crime has not yet been established, traces of soil found on the suspect, or in their living quarters or vehicle, for example, can suggest a particular locality, when unusual soil constituents or vegetation are involved.

One of the most common techniques used to compare soil samples involves a so-called density-gradient tube. This is a long, narrow glass tube, closed at one end, that is filled with mixtures of two chemicals of different density. The mixtures have differing proportions of the two chemicals, and are arranged in the tube so that the mixture with the greatest proportion of the heavier chemical provides the bottom layer. Succeeding layers contain progressively smaller proportions of the heavier chemical, so that the top layer, with the smallest proportion

of the heavier chemical, is the least dense.

When a sample of soil is poured into this density-gradient tube, each particle sinks until it reaches a layer that is of a density equal to its own, where it remains suspended in the liquid. Each soil sample consists of particles of different densities which reveal themselves as dark bands of suspended particles in the tube's different layers. If a second tube is made up of identical density bands of liquid, and a second soil sample is poured into it in the same way, examiners can see whether or not the bands of particles match.

Forensic examiners often take samples at intervals to as far as one hundred yards from the actual location of the crime, for purposes of comparison. The evaluation of samples in this way can also be useful in checking a suspect's alibi.

In vehicles, soil accumulates under fenders and bodywork. In cases where one vehicle impacts against another, lumps of soil can be dislodged, and such samples may be found during the search of the crime scene. They can then be compared with samples taken from the soil still adhering to the underside of the vehicle, and an accurate match may indicate that the vehicle was present at the scene.

Air-crash evidence

Many of the techniques and procedures described previously are used in a similar way by air accident investigators to help them determine the sequence of events leading to an airplane crash. The scene of impact is as crucial to their investigations as the crime scene is to police investigators.

To the lay person, the crash site can be a horrific and bewildering jumble of wreckage, most of which is quite unrecognizable. As a first step toward deciding what went wrong, accident investigators often collect fragments of wreckage—sometimes by the thousands—and piece them together in a rough reconstruction of the aircraft layout.

Just as forensic examiners start by drawing a plan of the crime scene, air accident investigators draw up a record of the wreckage trail, noting the positions of any major sections of the aircraft such as engines, control surfaces, landing gear, and so on. If these are far removed from the main wreckage, it may

indicate that they became detached before the crash, and their absence may have helped to cause the disaster. Examination of the engines can show whether they were running and actually delivering power at the time of the impact.

Air crash investigators work to a routine summarizd by the mnemonic TESTED: the Tips of the wings and tail surfaces; the Engines; the primary and secondary control Surface; the entire Tail assembly; the External devices such as the landing gear and the wing-tip fuel tanks; and the Doors, which also include hatches, canopies and windshields. If any of these are missing from the wreckage, their absence is a powerful clue as to the type of failure that brought down the airplane.

Many of the flight-deck instruments preserve the readings they showed at the time of the crash, which may help in reconstructing events. In cases of fire, the pattern of burning on major components can tell investigators whether the fire started in the air, and possibly helped to bring down the airplane, or whether

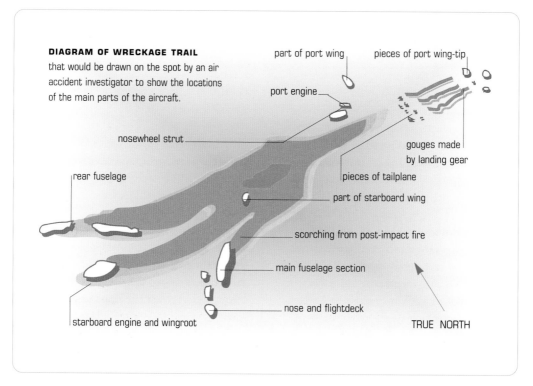

DIAGRAM OF WRECKAGE TRAIL that would be drawn on the spot by an air accident investigator to show the locations of the main parts of the aircraft.

part of port wing

pieces of port wing-tip

port engine

nosewheel strut

gouges made by landing gear

rear fuselage

pieces of tailplane

part of starboard wing

scorching from post-impact fire

main fuselage section

nose and flightdeck

starboard engine and wingroot

TRUE NORTH

The undamaged trees show the aircraft must have stalled, falling to the ground in a horizontal attitude with no forward speed.

Damage to the trees reveals the direction and angle of the aircraft's flight in the seconds leading up to impact.

Damage to aircraft engines shows whether or not they were delivering power at impact.

Aircraft panels showing tears and scratches. If scratches continue across the tear, whatever caused the scratch must have happened before the panel was torn apart.

it broke out after the crash.

Other clues are revealed by the tears and scratches on the airplane skin panels. For example, if a particular section of the skin has been torn apart, and one part shows surface scratches but the other does not, then the scratches were probably made after the panel was torn in two. If scratches can be traced on both parts, then they were made before the panel was split. By drawing up an order of events from careful inspection, investigators can often determine which parts of the aircraft broke up prior to the impact and which were damaged as a result of impact stresses.

In one respect, air accident investigators are luckier than their mainstream forensic equivalents. A criminal may do everything possible to conceal a crime or to deny his or her role in it, but operators of passenger-carrying aircraft are obliged to fit increasingly sophisticated flight data recorders (F.D.Rs) to their aircraft. In addition, cockpit voice recorders (C.V.Rs) monitor the conversation on the flight deck on a continuously recording loop. At air traffic control centers recordings are kept of conversations between pilots and ground controllers and of radar images of other aircraft in the area at the time.

The d'Autremont Brothers

One of the most spectacular examples of successful forensic investigation was that conducted by Edward Heinrich, who was in charge of the forensic laboratory at Berkeley in California after a hold-up gang had attempted to rob a mail train on the Union Pacific Railroad. The crime scene was a remote stretch of track in the mountains of southern Oregon. The mail coach had been blown up with dynamite and the entire train crew murdered in cold blood before the killers panicked and fled with nothing to show for their crimes.

All that was found during a careful search of the spot was a revolver, a battery-powered detonator that had been used to set off the explosives, a pair of shoe-covers made of sacking soaked in creosote to blot out the fugitives' scent in case tracker dogs were used, and a single pair of overalls. Having been unable to trace any useful leads, the police eventually sent the overalls to Heinrich, who examined them in the most minute detail.

Heinrich took samples of the debris from the overall pockets, some of which showed traces of grease. Initially the grease had led investigators to suspect the owner might be a garage mechanic, but Heinrich's analysis showed that the grease came from fir trees. Once he had scrutinized every detail of the overalls under a powerful microscope, he was able to describe in extraordinary detail the characteristics of their owner. Heinrich told astounded officers that they should be looking for a left-handed lumberjack who was about five feet ten inches tall, had light brown hair and weighed around one hundred and sixty-five pounds. This man was in his early twenties, rolled his own cigarettes, was careful with his appearance, and worked in the logging camps of the Pacific Northwest.

BELOW Hugh d'Autremont.

BOTTOM LEFT
Ray d'Autremont.

BOTTOM RIGHT
Roy d'Autremont.

The presence of the greasy pitch from pine trees, and chips of Douglas fir found on the overalls, indicated a lumberjack working in the Pacific Northwest where Douglas firs were plentiful. The pockets on the left-hand side of the overalls showed more wear than those on the right, and the garment had been buttoned from the left, indicating that the wearer was left-handed. A light-brown hair stuck to one of the buttons showed the pigmentation and indicated the subject's age, and the size of the overalls revealed his height and approximate weight.

Strands of tobacco found in the pockets suggested that the wearer rolled his own cigarettes. Nail clippings found in one of the seams suggested someone who cut his nails regularly—an unusual characteristic among lumberjacks. Finally Heinrich found at the bottom of one inaccessible pocket a piece of tightly folded paper which had been almost destroyed by being washed with the overalls. When carefully unpicked and treated with iodine to reveal the printing, it proved to be a U.S. Post Office receipt for a registered mail package sent to a Roy d'Autremont of Eugene, Oregon. When the police checked his last known address, neighbors verified that d'Autremont fitted Heinrich's detailed description in every respect. They also found that he had been missing, together with his twin Ray and brother Hugh, since the day of the robbery. Descriptions were also obtained for Ray and Hugh, and all three were posted as wanted men.

Tracking down the brothers proved more difficult. It was four years before a sergeant in the U.S. Army identified Hugh d'Autremont as a fellow soldier serving with him in the Philippines. He was arrested in Manila, and his brothers were tracked down to an Ohio steel mill where they were working under false names. All three confessed, and were sentenced to life imprisonment.

LEFT Hugh d'Autremont handcuffed to Sheriff Ralph Jennings of Jackson County, Oregon, where he is to stand trial for murder.

The Lindbergh Kidnapping

hen the infant son of well-known aviator Colonel Charles Lindbergh was seized from his bedroom at the family home in New Jersey on March 1, 1932, the kidnapper left few traces at the scene of the crime. A search revealed nothing more than a crude, homemade wooden ladder used to reach the child's bedroom, a chisel, some muddy footprints, and a ransom demand.

The Lindberghs chose to comply with the kidnapper's demands, and an intermediary paid $50,000 to a man with a pronounced German accent who promised the child would be found safe and well aboard a boat moored at the coast.

No trace of the child was found until over two months later, when the body of the Lindberghs' son was discovered in a wood just two miles from his home. The autopsy revealed he had been killed by a heavy blow to the head, probably on the night of the kidnapping. Having little else to help them track down the criminal, the police asked forestry expert Arthur Koehler to make what he could of the ladder, which had almost certainly been constructed by the kidnapper.

Koehler found that four different types of wood had been used in the ladder: Ponderosa and North Carolina pine, birch, and Douglas fir. There were marks on the wood made by the sawmill that originally cut it to size, and nail holes in one of the pieces showed it had been used for something else before being pressed into service to make the ladder. Letters were sent to more than 1500 sawmills over the entire eastern U.S. to track down the source of the North Carolina pine, and it was eventually traced to a company in South Carolina. The mill's planing machine produced marks very similar to those present on pieces of the ladder.

The mill had sent forty-six carloads of one-by-four North Carolina pine to customers in the northeastern U.S. in the three years preceding the kidnapping, and detectives visited every delivery site. At the National Lumber and Millwork Company in the Bronx, they had a much-needed stroke of luck. They found storage bins made from North Carolina pine that perfectly matched the wood used in the ladder.

Unfortunately the company had been selling on a cash-and-carry basis and kept no customer records, so the trail ended

TOP Colonel Charles Lindbergh.

ABOVE CENTER Charles Augustus Lindbergh, son of Colonel Lindbergh.

ABOVE Ransom note.

38

there for the time being. Koehler then traced the Douglas fir to a pair of mills in Bend, Oregon, and Spokane, Washington. Before he could follow these leads further, a suspect was identified in the Bronx area in connection with the ransom note. The note had been traced to a German-born carpenter, Bruno Richard Hauptmann, and when police searched his residence they found $14,000 of the ransom money.

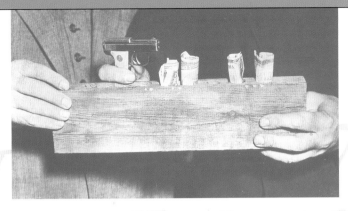

ABOVE Wooden plank with holes for hiding ransom money and a loaded gun.

Hauptmann claimed that he had been minding the cash for a friend who had gone back to Germany and then died of tuberculosis. Nevertheless Koehler was able to show that a plane found in Hauptmann's garage had been used to smooth the ladder, and that a missing floorboard in the man's attic had been used for the ladder rail, since the sawn ends and the nail holes in both ladder rail and attic floor joists matched perfectly. In addition, a detailed analysis of the grain patterns in the wood showed that the ladder rail and the remaining portion of floorboard were originally one single piece of wood. Hauptmann was tried, found guilty, and sent to the electric chair in April 1936, loudly protesting his innocence. Though some aspects of his trial still cause disquiet among students of the case, there is little doubt that Koehler's forensic work provided the strongest basis for the prosecution case.

BELOW Bruno Hauptmann (center) at his trial.

Ghislaine Marchal

BELOW Omar Raddad waits for the start of his trial in Nice on January 24, 1994.

Ghislaine Marchal was found dead in the cellar of her villa, "La Chamade", in the village of Mougins a few kilometers north of Cannes in the Alpes Maritimes in the south of France on June 24, 1991. Pierced by a succession of strikes from her killer's knife, she had apparently managed to write on the wall in her own blood the damning words "Omar m'a tuer" (Omar killed me) and again "Omar m'a T..." as she lay dying. The case seemed brutally simple. Her young Moroccan gardener, Omar Raddad, was missing, as was the sum of 4,000 francs from the villa.

Raddad was charged with her murder and appeared in the departmental courts of the Alpes Maritimes in February 1994. There the prosecution called in two expert graphologists who certified that the way in which the letters had been formed in Ghislaine Marchal's blood was consistent with her own writing, as revealed in newspapers found in the villa where she had filled in crossword puzzles. It seemed as if the prosecution had been able to establish Omar Raddad as the wielder of the fatal knife, and the Moroccan was sentenced to eighteen years in prison.

Since then, an increasing number of doubts has surfaced over the way in which the evidence was collected and presented. Raddad himself proved a model prisoner and was eventually pardoned by President Chirac, but has never ceased to protest his innocence of the crime and his intention to appeal the original verdict and plead for a retrial. In the meantime, he had been offered secure employment working for a fellow Moroccan in Marseilles.

Unfortunately, the appeals procedure is long and difficult, and depends on new evidence being found to cast doubt on the original verdict. Raddad's lawyer, Jacques Vergès, based his case for an appeal on three grounds. Professor Fournier, a specialist in forensic medicine, testified that the murder had actually been committed on the June 24, 1991, a day later than was alleged at the trial, and a day for which Raddad had a solid alibi, having spent the day with friends and relatives in Toulon. Two different graphology experts, one of them the president of their professional association, found inconsistencies between the letters written in blood and those on the crossword puzzles, and furthermore were convinced that the words could not have been written by someone dying from loss of blood. Others have criticized the fact that Madame Marchal's fingertips were not measured, to compare with the blood message, and that her body was cremated.

Finally, two private detectives have criticized the police methods and suggested other suspects who might have written the message to incriminate Raddad and cover up their own role in Ghislaine Marchal's death. One pointed out that the murderer's clothing would have been soaked in blood, but the clothes Raddad was wearing at the time of the murder contained no trace of blood. The other found a car with two Italian men and a woman who had been present at the scene, and that a pair of rubber gloves which could have been used to write the bloody message had been left in the sink of the villa, but then were burned in the fireplace along with Ghislaine Marchal's diary. A case which seemed to be simple and straightforward because of the forensic evidence now seems more complex than ever because of contradictions revealed by additional forensic evidence.

TOP The bloody message, apparently written by Ghislaine Marchal as she lay dying.

ABOVE LEFT Omar Raddad accompanied by his lawyer Jacques Vergès leaving Murel's detention center on September 4, 1998.

ABOVE A smiling Omar Raddad starts his new job in an Islamic Butchery in Marseille on September 14, 1998.

The Kennedy Investigation

ABOVE A detective carries the 7.65 Mannlicher-Carcano rifle believed to have been used to kill the President, which was found on the fifth floor of the Dallas building from which the shots were fired.

BACKGROUND PICTURE
Kennedy slumps after being shot in the open White House car.

n November 1977, fourteen years after the assassination of President John F. Kennedy the persistence of rumors that there had been more than one marksman involved in the shooting led to the fragments recovered from the car being subjected to neutron activation analysis. This involves bombarding an object with neutrons, which renders it radioactive because the neutrons are captured by the atoms that constitute the object's structure. These atoms then begin emitting gamma rays, which can be measured and analyzed to reveal traces of all the elements present.

Some of the bullet fragments recovered from the scene were found in the President's body, others in Governor Connolly's wrist, and the remainder in the car. One complete bullet was found on the governor's stretcher at the hospital. The precise chemical composition of the fragments showed that they were pieces of only two bullets: one had fatally wounded the

President; the other had passed through the governor's wrist. Though the bullets differed slightly in their composition, experts found that they had almost certainly been fired from the same gun. No fragments were found of the bullets that wounded both the President and the governor in the back. Though the evidence fell short of conclusive proof that Lee Harvey Oswald had acted on his own, it offered no support for theories about other marksmen firing from different locations.

Unfortunately, an opportunity for more definite conclusions had been lost at the time. At the autopsy, the specialist photographer detailed to take pictures of the gunshot wounds was refused access by the FBI on security grounds. An FBI photographer was used instead, but the resulting photographs were deficient in that the different entry and exit wounds were not identified, no scale was given to indicate their size, and internal organs were not clearly shown. The evidence was thus inconclusive and, in the absence of hard facts, conspiracy theories continue to flourish.

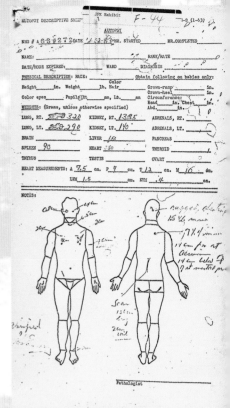

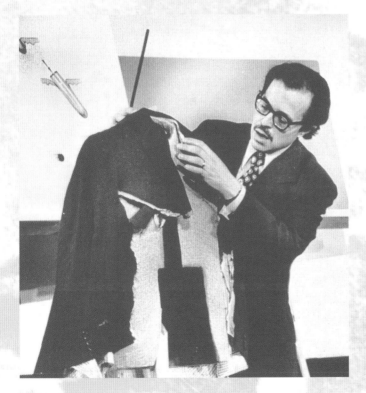

ABOVE The autopsy descriptive sheet, included as an exhibit for the House Assassinations Committee formed in 1976.

LEFT Kennedy's suit coat shown to the House Assassinations Committee by staff physician Dr. Michael Baden.

A Question of Identity

ABOVE Italian crime scene with officers working around the body.

When a body is found at the scene of an accident or a violent crime such as murder, one of the first priorities is to establish the identity of the victim. If the victim died at home or was discovered by family members, friends, or colleagues the procedure is straightforward enough, but otherwise, if no identifying papers are found with the body, the question becomes more problematic. In some cases, bodies are not discovered until some time after death, by which time decomposition may have reduced the remains to little more than a skeleton. In others, killers go to great lengths to destroy the identity of the victim—and so the evidence of their crime—by disposing of the body as thoroughly as possible. However, with more powerful methods and equipment, forensic scientists have been able to trace a corpse's identity through careful and detailed analysis of the evidence that remains.

Illnesses, operations, or injuries leave marks or scars, and particular occupations can be suggested by certain physical characteristics. Even if only the skeleton remains, it can yield valuable information regarding the age and sex of a victim, his or her state of health, physical size, and racial origin, as well as indicating any serious wounds either old or new.

Careful examination of a victim's body to discover the exact causes and circumstances of his or her death is not new. In thirteenth-century China a textbook was published that detailed how signs of drowning or strangulation could be identified, and how particular wounds could reveal the size and type of weapon used.

By the mid-seventeenth century forensic medicine was being taught at several European universities and in Britain, the university of Edinburgh began teaching forensic medicine in 1801. Twelve years later a New York surgeon named James S. Stringham was appointed the United States first Professor of Medical Jurisprudence.

BELOW A body at the scene of a crime in Surrey, England. Forensic scientists search for evidence that may help with identification.

Gleaning the evidence—the autopsy

Whatever the state of the body, in terms of decay or deliberate mutilation, the autopsy follows a set routine. The body is weighed and measured, and the clothing examined for any cuts or holes which may coincide with wounds on the body. The clothes are stored in paper bags, as are scrapings from beneath the fingernails. Swabs for possible DNA analysis are taken, as are saliva samples, which may indicate death by drowning or show symptoms of certain types of poisoning. Stains and dried blood are scraped to produce samples, which are stored separately for later analysis.

The forensic pathologist then checks the body for any other external symptoms of the cause of death, such as color changes associated with carbon monoxide poisoning, needle marks, or any evidence of wounds or physical injuries. The body is then washed and the pathologist plucks and cuts samples of

body hair to be stored in carefully labeled individual bags.

Samples of bodily fluids such as blood, urine, and cerebrospinal fluid are taken and, after removal of the organs involved, samples of the contents of the stomach and intestines are analyzed to determine whether or not the victim was poisoned. In cases of suspected poisoning, the liver is usually removed to be weighed as an indication of how much poison was administered. All these remains and samples are retained by the forensic laboratory, and the pathologist produces a detailed report on his or her findings.

Telltale clues

While carrying out the set autopsy procedure, the pathologist also notes any other abnormalities of the body that might help to identify the victim. Evidence of stomach ulcers, kidney stones or gallstones, degeneration of the joints due to arthritis, constriction of the arteries, and signs of any earlier traumas or surgical procedures such as missing body parts can be checked against

ABOVE Blood samples being used in DNA research at Lifecodes Corporation, Valhalla, NY, U.S.

BELOW Bodies of sacrifice victims.

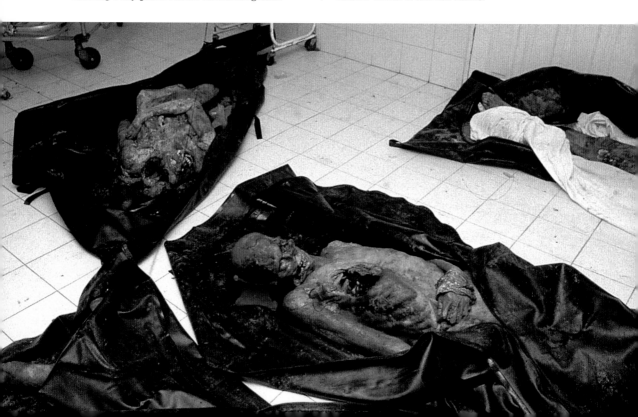

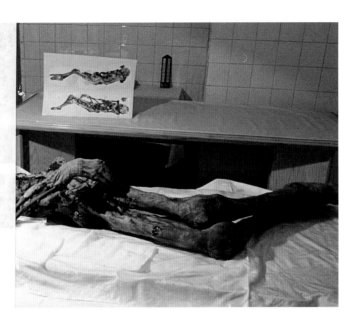

...d reveals
...ell anemia,
...ia.
...usual
...y help to
...an earlier
...sometimes
...wear or
...particular jobs.

Occupational and social status can also be suggested by stains, calluses, or scars on the hands of those used to heavy manual work, to take one example.

Preservation and decay

If the body is not found until some time after the killing, its condition when it is discovered depends to a large extent on the environment in which it has lain or been stored in the meantime. If a corpse has been kept warm and dry, the tissues have a chance to dry out before decay sets in. This has happened in cases where bodies have been concealed under floorboards or inside closets where enough air circulates to complete the drying process quickly. The body shrivels up but the structure

ABOVE Preserved remains of the Prazyryk "Ice Maiden," a young woman found frozen in ice in the Alti mountains of central Asia. The 2500-year-old body is so well preserved (because water seeped into her burial chamber and then froze) that tattoos can still be seen on her skin.

of the face, the hair, and the rest of the individual's distinguishing features can be preserved—in some cases for years.

If a body is buried in a shallow grave or left in the open, however, natural processes aid the breakdown of the tissues. If the environment is moist and warm, bacteria thrive and assist the process of decay. If the body is heavily clothed, or deeply buried in heavy soil, the lack of air circulation prevents bacteria from thriving, delaying the decaying process.

Young people or those who are overweight tend to decay more quickly in most conditions, due to the greater proportion of fat in their bodies, and the decay process is accelerated in victims who die while suffering from an infectious disease. Some poisons, on the other hand, delay decay if they affect organisms that would otherwise carry out the process. The poisons that killed the victim also kill the bacteria that usually break down the body tissues.

LEFT Skeletons from the Middle Ages, leaving only bones to provide information on how the subjects died and the kinds of lives they lived.

The age of a skeleton can be estimated from detailed changes to the teeth in the case of children, except for attrition or radiographic changes, which can be used in the absence of better indicators for adults. At one time the sutures between the bones making up the skull were used to estimate age, but now more accurate estimates are usually made from the condition of the bones joined at the pubic symphysis or from the rib ends of adults, or the fusion of growth centers in the skeletons of younger victims.

Full skeletons can be measured to give the size of the subject, but even when a victim has been dismembered there are formulas to help estimate the height of a person. Once the broad racial group and sex of the unknown victim has been established there are formulas specific to these groups. In the U.S. for example, there is a new formulas provided by the Forensic Anthropological Data Bank at the University of Tennessee and a program called Fordisc 2.0. Previous methods included measuring the length of the femur (thigh bone) or the tibia (shin bone) to calculate the height of the victim, but this method was only accurate to within a couple of inches (a few centimeters).

Dry bones

In cases where the body tissue has decayed leaving only a skeleton, many autopsy procedures are impossible to carry out, but an anthropologist who specializes in this type of problem can infer some clues from the bones alone. The skeleton can be identified as that of a man or a woman by differences in the bone structure; pubic shape, subpubic angle, and the presence of the ventral arc are the most significant areas for assessment. Also, a male for example tends to have a more obvious superorbital crest (the ridge of bone above the eye-sockets) and a more pronounced nuchal crest at the back of the skull than a female.

Ethnic differences

Skeletal characteristics can also indicate differences of ethnic origin. The skull shape, including the width of the jaw, can be useful in giving an indication of race. Furthermore, people of European ancestry, for example, often have teeth crowded closely together on a narrow jaw, while those of Chinese origin may have wider jaws and triple-rooted molars. Native Americans tend to have larger teeth and the incisors (the prominent teeth at the front of the mouth) are often shovel-shaped.

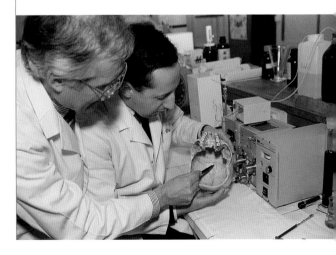

ABOVE The original skull shown alongside the facial reconstruction (see p. 50).

BELOW French pathologists examine the skull of Mozart.

Hair texture and color can also help to identify different ethnic groups. Native American, Chinese, and Japanese subjects tend to have straight black hair. Caucasian hair offers the widest range of possible colors, from blond through reds and browns to black; the particles of pigment in the hair that give it the characteristic color are also more evenly distributed than those in hair of Afro-Caribbean origin. The shape of the cross-section of the hair can also be significant: in Caucasian hair it usually ranges between round and elliptical, while in Afro-Caribbean hair it usually ranges between flat and elliptical.

Dental records

Whenever a patient visits the dentist, surgeons enter or update on a standard form details of the patient's dental abnormalities and the results of procedures, such as extractions and fillings. A full set of adult teeth comprises thirty-two permanent teeth: four upper and four lower incisors (or "biting" teeth), two upper and two lower canines (the pointed or "tearing" teeth), four upper and four lower premolars and six upper and six lower molars (the "grinding" teeth).

The chart used in North America for dental records numbers the teeth in a sequence starting from the outermost (third) molar in the upper right jaw, and moving across to the third molar in the upper left jaw. The sequence is repeated for the lower jaw. A patient's dental chart should show where teeth have been lost through accident or extraction, and where they have been drilled, filled, or crowned. In general, the older the patient, the more detailed and therefore the more individual the dental chart tends to be. The chart should also record details of discoloration, of any missing fillings, and the presence of cracks or chips.

Dental radiography can reveal more specific information such as root canal work, an overbite, and additional, overlapping, or impacted teeth—all of which contribute unique detail to the record. One further record is provided by a technique called rugoscopy. The upper plate of a set of dentures is cast from a mold taken from the patient's own upper jaw and palate, to aid the adhesion of the denture in the mouth. The dentist's mold records the unique pattern of ridges in the palate.

The system for identifying a body from dental records relies on dental charts. It is also sometimes possible to drill out a sample of dental pulp from inside the teeth to provide DNA material for testing (see Chapter Fourteen). While fingerprint and DNA records can provide essential information regarding the identity of a victim or a suspect, dental—

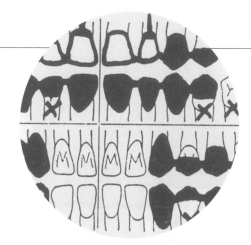

TOP Dental records are often used for identification purposes.

ABOVE Casts of teeth can also help identify bodies and prove whether or not someone was responsible for a bite wound.

and medical—records have one great advantage in that they exist for a far greater proportion of the general population than is ever subject to fingerprint or DNA testing.

Facial reconstruction

Another increasingly common technique used in helping to identify victims where only bones remain is that of facial reconstruction, carried out by forensic anthropologists. It was pioneered more than a century ago by a Swiss anatomist named Wilhelm His, who worked from the bone structure to reconstruct the facial appearance of people as they had been in life. In one case he was presented with a skull which was supposedly that of the composer Johann Sebastian Bach (1685–1750). His reconstruction was subsequently compared with portraits of the composer painted during

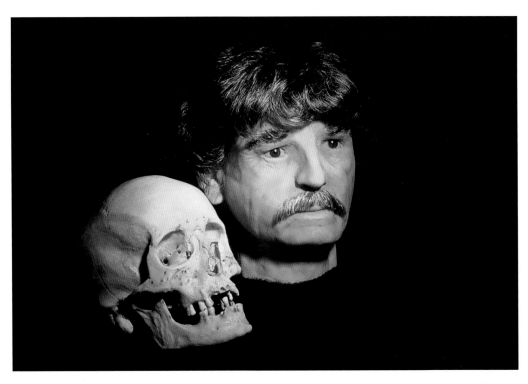

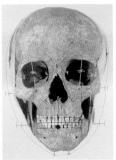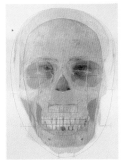

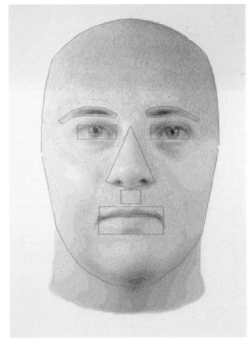

ABOVE AND RIGHT Facial reconstruction of a skull from a man of the Middle Ages carried out on a computer.

TOP The skull is then cast by hand with the final touches of hair added for authenticity.

his lifetime: the likeness was so good that the skull was declared to be definitely that of Bach.

The technique was developed further by Professor Grigoriev, who was a professor of forensic medicine at a medical school in Moscow soon after the October Revolution of 1917. He and his assistant, Mikhail Gerasimov, studied the heads of corpses waiting to be dissected by anatomy classes at the school, and they assembled a great deal of data relating to the thickness of the soft tissues of the face that are overlaid on the framework of the skull.

In 1925 Gerasimov moved to Siberia to work at the museum of the city of Irkutsk, and two years later he was appointed head of the department of archaeology. His work involved re-creating the faces of the earliest men from fossils found in the Siberian tundra. One commission required him to reconstruct the face of Mongol conqueror Tamerlane (1336–1405) from the skull in his tomb.

In Britain the technique was first used in the department of anatomy at Manchester University, initially to provide recognizable faces for historical characters such as Philip of Macedon, father of the conqueror Alexander the Great. However in 1987, a horrific fire at King's Cross station on the London subway system claimed thirty-one victims. All but one had been identified. The police approached the university's medical artist, Richard Neave, to produce a likeness of the unidentified victim's face from the skull, and photographs of the resulting model were widely published. Since then the technique has been used in a number of murder cases where decay or destruction of the body has rendered normal means of identification difficult or impossible.

The process of reconstruction is begun by making a cast of the skull. A series of holes is then drilled into the cast at certain anatomical reference points. A rod is inserted into each hole and secured so that it protrudes to a depth consistent with accepted data on the depth of soft-tissue layers at each point. The eye sockets are filled with plastic "eyeballs" and the muscular structure of the face is built up by applying layers of modeling clay to the surface of the skull until each of the rods is just covered.

The modeling begins with the neck and jaw, and continues upward to the cheeks and eyes. The "tissues" laid over the forehead, the sides, and top of the head are thinner than those

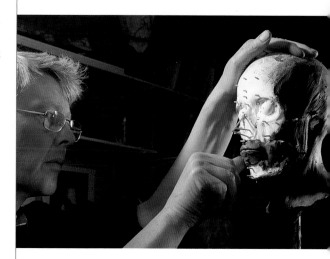

ABOVE Richard Neave, senior medical artist at Manchester University, England, demonstrating his reconstruction techniques.

covering the lower parts of the face where the bones are further below the skin surface. The contours of the cheeks and jaws are then smoothed, as is the whole surface of the clay, to represent human skin.

More superficial touches, added to give the model a more lifelike appearance, are the least reliable area of the reconstruction since the skeleton gives little or no information on the shape or size of the nose or the eyebrows, or the texture, length, and style of the hair. Nevertheless, where skilled anthropologists use a mixture of inspiration and experience, many results have been found to resemble the subject's genuine appearance quite closely, once the identity has been revealed and the models compared with photographs of the individual.

One of the best-known forensic anthropologists in the U.S. is Betty Pat Gatliff, who uses pencil eraser heads instead of the toothpick wooden rods used by Neave to establish the depth of soft tissue at different points on the face. Gatliff was commissioned to produce facial reconstructions of nine unidentified victims of serial killer John Wayne Gacy in Illinois in 1978, but appeals to the public to help identify the models provided only one inconclusive response. Two sisters claimed to have recognized their missing brother, but refused to proceed further because they wished to spare their parents' feelings.

In 1989, Philadelphia forensic anthropolologist Frank A. Bender was asked to prepare a bust of a fugitive suspect in a quadruple family murder who had not been seen for eighteen years. The purpose of the commission was to give investigating officers an indication of how the man's appearance might have changed. Bender was assisted by computer software that was programmed to add signs of age to an existing image. In this case the program even took into account the subject's known dislike of regular exercise. Bender used the resulting image as a start-point for his three-dimensional life-size model.

Some of the alterations of features were necessarily speculative, the heavier jowls, for example, a receding hairline, gray hair, and a pale complexion; but others were based on known details. The subject had worn spectacles eighteen years before, so Bender gave his subject a prominent pair with thicker lenses.

The final result was photographed in the standard full-face and profile attitudes used for criminal records, and pictures were broadcast on a nationwide crime-fighting television program. They prompted more than two hundred and fifty people to call. One was a woman who recognized the face of her neighbor in Richmond, Virginia. The fugitive was tracked down and identified, then tried and imprisoned, having evaded justice for almost twenty years.

Facial reconstruction

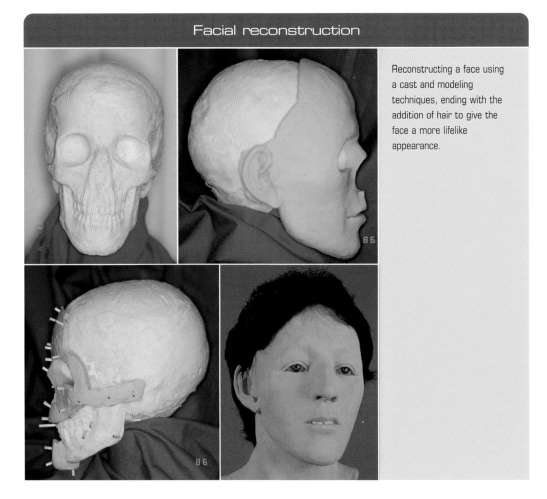

Reconstructing a face using a cast and modeling techniques, ending with the addition of hair to give the face a more lifelike appearance.

Buck Ruxton

orensic science can sometimes frustrate a murderer's most determined efforts to obliterate the identity of his or her victims. On the morning of September 29, 1935, a young woman on holiday in the Scottish countryside near the town of Moffat chanced to look down as she crossed a bridge over a stream. She was horrified to see a human arm protruding from a group of bundles on the bank. On searching the stream's banks immediately after, police found four bundles containing between them more than seventy pieces of human flesh, some wrapped in pillowcases, some in old clothes, and others in newspaper. There were two heads and one complete torso. As the fragments were examined, it became clear that extreme measures had been taken to disguise the identity of the corpses. The ends of fingers had been chopped off in one case and the ears, eyes, noses, lips, and skin had been removed from both faces.

ABOVE Parts of the Morecambe paper found wrapping body parts.

Further body parts were subsequently found at other sites in the area, including a left foot, wrapped in newspaper, at the side of the Carlisle to Glasgow highway, and an arm near a minor road a few miles away. All the body fragments were taken to the anatomy department of Edinburgh University, where they were painstakingly reassembled into two badly mutilated corpses. Every scrap of evidence found was carefully analyzed.

One of the newspapers used to wrap the remains was dated September 15 of that year. This helped investigators to establish some time frame for the dumping of the bodies, since between that date and the date when the body parts were discovered, the only time the stream had run high enough for the remains to be washed onto the bank had been before September 19.

Experts working on the corpses reported that one appeared to be that of a woman aged approximately twenty-one and about five feet one inch tall, and the other that of a man aged around sixty years, who had stood around five feet six inches tall. The terrible mutilations to the skull of the second victim had misled the experts, and as the reconstruction continued they revised their conclusions. They reported that the second body was in fact more likely to be that of a woman aged between thirty-five and forty-five. Police started searching their records for anyone who had been reported missing in the days leading up to September 19.

BACKGROUND Buck Ruxton with his wife and one of their children.

ABOVE Blouse which contained another bundle of remains.

ABOVE The lower legs of one of the victims.

The newspaper used to wrap the remains yielded further clues. One contained a report of the crowning of the local carnival queen at Morecambe, an English coastal resort more than one hundred miles to the south. Checks revealed that the paper was a local edition circulated only in Morecambe and the nearby city of Lancaster. At almost the same time the Chief Constable of Dumfries, in whose area the investigation was being pursued, happened to read in a Glasgow newspaper about a twenty-year-old housemaid called Mary Jane Rogerson who had been reported missing by her employer, Lancaster doctor Buck Ruxton, on September 14.

The Lancaster police found that Ruxton's common-law wife, thirty-four-year-old Isabella Van Ess, had also vanished at the same time. Questioning of Ruxton's neighbors, including the proprietor of the local newspaper shop, revealed that an edition of the paper with the carnival queen report had been delivered to Ruxton's house on September 15. One neighbor also recognized a set of child's clothes that had been used to wrap some of the body parts: she had originally given them to Mary Jane Rogerson to pass on to Ruxton's wife. When police subsequently searched Ruxton's house, in spite of the fact that it had been carefully cleaned they found traces of blood and human fat in the drains.

When comparing the remains of the second body with known details of the housemaid, pathologists found that the killer had been especially diligent in eliminating any special distinguishing features. Mary Jane suffered from a slight squint, and the eyes had been removed and destroyed. The skin over an appendix scar had been removed, as had a prominent birthmark and another scar at the base of one thumb. But the fingertips were still intact, and this allowed Mary Jane Rogerson's prints to be taken and matched with those in the Ruxton house.

Isabella's corpse was stripped of its identity in different ways. She had had a prominent nose and teeth, both of which had been removed. The hyoid bone in her throat was broken, which suggested that she had been strangled, but every part of her body that might have provided additional evidence had been cut away: the eyes, nose, ears, lips, and fingertips had been removed, which in itself pointed to the killer having expert medical knowledge.

Isabella Ruxton's remains were finally positively identified by superimposing a photograph of her over the skull of the victim. The match was conclusive. Ruxton was tried and convicted for the murder of the two women, to which he confessed before his execution in 1936.

ABOVE A photograph of Mrs Ruxton used to identify the skull.

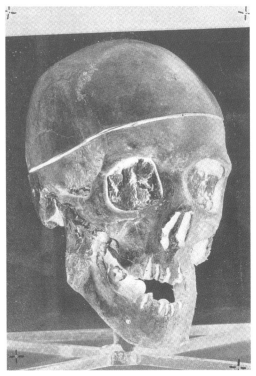

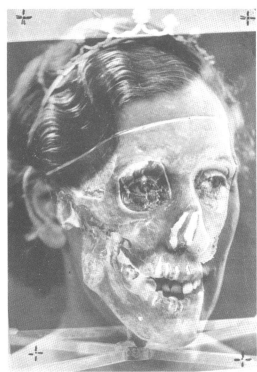

ABOVE A picture of Mrs Ruxton's skull, taken to match the position on the photograph.

ABOVE RIGHT The skull picture superimposed on the photograph of Mrs Ruxton.

ABOVE Fingerprints from Mary Rogerson's body matched with prints on a plate in the Ruxton's house.

John George Haigh

BOTTOM Police searching Haigh's Crawley "workshop."

BELOW Gallstones of Mrs Durand-Deacon found after her body was consumed in a bath of sulfuric acid.

John George Haigh was a professional confidence trickster, a smooth-talker who specialized in charming wealthy, middle-aged women out of their money, and then killing them and disposing of the bodies in a bath of acid. Convinced that he could not be caught and convicted without the physical evidence of the corpse, he was certain that he would evade all attempts to punish him for his crimes—but he was fatally mistaken in his belief.

Haigh's last victim was a rich widow named Olivia Durand-Deacon. It was his supreme confidence that led to his downfall. He admitted—off the record—that he had killed the woman, and even boasted that he had disposed of the body using acid at his workshop in Crawley, West Sussex, adding that only a layer of "sludge" remained. Sadly for Haigh, forensic pathologist Dr. Keith Simpson took up the challenge: he collected the "sludge"

and analyzed it in detail. As well as traces of human fat, Simpson found evidence of dentures and a gallstone. These items were enough to provide positive evidence that the victim was Mrs. Durand-Deacon, and that her body had been disposed of in Haigh's acid bath. Haigh was tried, convicted of murder, and hanged.

BACKGROUND John George Haigh arrives at Horsham Magistrates' Court.

RIGHT Detectives and police officers carrying one of the drums of acid into the court.

Wayne Williams

Between 1979 and 1981 a series of brutal stranglings of young men terrorized communities in the city of Atlanta. Almost the only forensic evidence linking the killings was a peculiar type of fiber found on the victims' clothing. This had an unusual, triple-lobed cross-section which appeared to correspond with fibers used in rugs or carpets.

Unfortunately, police efforts to track down the maker of this fiber were initially unsuccessful.

When reference to the fiber evidence appeared in newspapers in February, 1981, it changed the course of the investigation, because almost immediately the killer adapted his methods. From then onward his victims, wearing little or no clothing, were dumped in rivers so that the chance of finding any more fiber evidence was minimal. The killings continued, the murderer claiming more than twenty victims before police began to close in.

Early on the morning of May 22, 1981, a police patrol staking out the Chattahoochee River, where some of the corpses had been found, heard a splash. They rushed to the bridge where the James Jackson Parkway crossed the river and there they found twenty-three-year-old Wayne Williams, a music promoter, standing by his station wagon. Williams was questioned and then allowed to leave, but on May 24 the body of twenty-seven-year-old Nathaniel Cater was dragged from the river.

When police searched Williams' house and car ten days later, they identified unusual fibers matching those found with the first bodies but, in order to use them as evidence, they needed to prove that they were not commonly found. After further tests, they traced the fibers to a carpet manufacturer in Dalton, Georgia. Over a single twelve-month period the factory had made just 16,397 square yards of carpet using that fiber in the color—"English Olive"—found in Williams' home and car and on the clothes of the victims. It was calculated that the probability of finding that shade of that particular carpet in any house in Atlanta at the time was one in 7792.

A second significant fiber was found on the shorts of one of the murder victims and also in the carpeting in Williams' station wagon. The carpet had been made by General Motors, and checks revealed that just six hundred and twenty-eight out of more than

TOP Wayne Williams.

BACKGROUND The faces of Atlanta's murdered and missing children, at the time of the Wayne Williams case.

2.4 million cars registered at the time in the Atlanta area were fitted with this type of carpet, so the probability of finding this type and color of fiber in any of the others was one in 3828. This meant that the probability of another individual having the those same carpets in his or her house and car was almost one in thirty million. Evidence linking the murders was reinforced when similar fibers were found on another ten of the estimated twenty-eight murder victims. Williams was convicted and sentenced to serve two life terms in prison.

RIGHT Police and volunteers searching for clues.

BELOW Forensic industry consultant Dr Peter Mills uses the skull of one of the victims to establish the identity.

Weapons of the Criminal
Pure Poison

ABOVE "Poisonous" warning on a stoppered
chemical bottle.

Poisons were once the preferred choice of
the would-be murderer because of the
stealth with which they could be administered
and the difficulty involved subsequently in
linking murderer and victim. A wide range of
poisons still exists that can mislead medical
examiners because the physical symptoms they
produce can be confused with those of common
but fatal diseases.

The chemicals involved, however, are usually not widely available for purchase, so users tend to be professionals such as doctors or pharmacists who work in environments where contact with these substances is common or routine. Moreover, poisoning now accounts for only around one in every hundred murders in countries where highly skilled medical and forensic services exist, such as the U.S., Canada and in Europe.

But poisons can be responsible in cases other than murder where forensic evidence is needed to establish cause of death. Accidental poisoning, for example, usually results from mistakes being made with medical prescriptions or can occur when household chemicals such as weed-killers or strong cleaning preparations are stored in unlabeled bottles or simply left within reach of young children.

BELOW Detectives in Chicago investigating a case of poisoning.

Suicide poisoning usually involves substances such as painkillers or sleeping tablets that are commonly available in restricted doses but, if taken in excess, can be fatal. Strong or corrosive household or garden chemicals can be equally effective and may be used in cases where the victim, as the agent of his or her own death, has no necessity to cover his or her tracks.

Poisons in accidents and suicides

Strong mineral acids such as hydrochloric, sulfuric, and nitric acid, and alkalis such as caustic soda and caustic potash, are poisons too easily detected to be chosen for criminal use. They tend to be involved in accidental poisoning, unless the acids are so concentrated that their smell and fumes give the game away, and reveal the danger. Acids are still occasionally used by criminals for disposing of victims' bodies to destroy incriminating evidence.

Many suicides use common domestic medicines, such as ASA, in large doses. The stomach breaks the ASA down into acetic acid and salicylic acid, causing the victim to fall temporarily unconscious, before death. Chloral hydrate, which is used as a sedative and hypnotic, when taken in relatively large doses results in a coma followed by death in a matter of hours from heart and respiratory failure.

Other poisons involved in accidental deaths include disinfectants such as Lysol and phenol, which are corrosive, and oxalic acid, which is found in rhubarb leaves and was once a common bleaching agent. Oxalic acid deprives the blood of essential calcium. If taken orally, metacetaldehyde, which is used in slug-killing preparations and sold solid for camping stoves, produces cramps, hallucinations, tremor of the limbs, then coma and death from respiratory breakdown in a matter of days.

One of the most common accidental or suicide poisons is a gas, carbon monoxide, which is generated by automobile exhausts and sometimes by faulty gas appliances. Suicides often pipe the exhaust into a car through a length of vacuum-cleaner or garden hose, or run an automobile engine in a closed garage. When the carbon monoxide is inhaled it combines in place of oxygen with the hemoglobin in the red blood cells. Gradually the victim's blood becomes saturated with carboxy-hemoglobin instead of the normal oxy-hemoglobin, and he or she suffocates from the inside.

For the forensic examiner, the outward appearance of the victim usually provides sufficient initial evidence of the cause of death, since the presence of carboxy-hemoglobin in the blood turns the skin and the internal organs a bright cherry red. Carboxy-hemoglobin can be detected in the victim's blood for months after death, and this can provide a valuable pointer to forensic examiners checking victims found some time after death, or in cases where the

body was not found at the scene of the crime. If a body is found in a burned-out building, for example, where the fire may have been started deliberately to destroy evidence of a murder, investigators must try to establish whether the victim died in the fire or the body was dumped there before the fire started.

If a body has carbon monoxide in the blood, then the victim must have been alive when the fire started, otherwise the gases it produced would not have been inhaled. The subject is therefore likely to have been a genuine victim of the fire, though if other evidence shows that the fire was started deliberately, then the possibility exists that the victim was rendered unconscious before the blaze. If, on the other hand, the body shows no traces of carbon monoxide in the blood, then the victim did not inhale smoke and gases from the fire and must have been dead before it started, which in turn suggests that the fire was set in a deliberate attempt to conceal evidence of a murder.

ABOVE Domestic medicines, sometimes used by suicides.

LEFT Suicide attempt, using carbon monoxide from car exhaust.

Murderers' poisons

Most of the poisons listed above fail to meet the criminal's most important requirement: that the poison should be lethal but at the same time produce symptoms that suggest another, less suspicious, cause of death. At one time many poisons were extracted from plants and vegetables, so were relatively easy to obtain by those who knew what they were looking for. Poison hemlock, for example, can cause numbness which increases until the heart fails or breathing stops, and produces symptoms similar to those of suffocation. An examiner would look for signs of what caused the victim to suffocate, such as a confined space or an inadequately ventilated room, but there would be nothing to prove that a poison had been administered.

Aconitine is extracted from the flowers and roots of a plant called monkshood, and at one time was the most lethal poison known. It was used to relieve the pain of rheumatism by being applied to the skin as a poultice, where it produced a warming and anesthetic action. Unfortunately even absorption through the skin is dangerous and, once in the body, an extremely small dose of aconitine can be lethal, paralyzing all the body's organs in succession until the victim dies of heart failure or suffocation. The poison was well known to the Greeks, who believed it was contained in the saliva of the hound Cerebus who guarded the gates of the underworld. In Roman times its usefulness for poisoning inconvenient relatives or rivals earned it a mention in the *Satires* of the first-century Roman poet Juvenal.

Atropine can be extracted from plants such as deadly nightshade, and produces headaches, giddiness, hallucinations and finally a coma which ends in death from heart or respiratory failure. Where atropine has been administered, the pupils of subject's eyes dilate (for this reason, controlled doses are used in some eye treatments); heavy doses can make the eyes appear almost completely black.

ABOVE Herod the Great (74–4 BC) being reproached by his wife for the murder of her father and brother. In the foreground is Salome with a chalice of poison for the king sent by his wife.

At one time strychnine was another poisoners' favorite. This highly toxic vegetable alkaloid is obtained chiefly from the exotic *Strychnos nux-vomica* shrub found in the Indian subcontinent, where it was used in very small doses to build up immunity to bites from poisonous snakes. A dose of just one fiftieth of a gram of this intensely bitter-tasting extract can be fatal. It produces violent muscular contractions: the victim is rendered speechless by paralysis of the jaw muscles, the lips are drawn back into a terrible parody of a grin, and eventually death is caused by paralysis of the respiratory system. At one time, such deaths were usually assumed to have been due to tetanus or to severe epileptic fits, but once a reliable test for the presence of the poison had been developed, criminals were forced to turn to more subtle methods.

ABOVE Hair loss characteristic of thallium poisoning. Jethro Batt was a victim of English poisoner Graham Young.

Thallium is another powerful poison that offers would-be murderers a number of advantages. Not only do several different compounds containing the metal dissolve invisibly and tastelessly in water, but symptoms produced in the victim can be confusing. Once in the body, thallium substitutes itself for potassium in different body systems that nourish cells and nerve fibers; the patient becomes weaker and eventually dies from the cumulative internal damage. The outward symptoms, however, can be confused with those of influenza—except that thallium poisoning causes the victim's hair to fall out as the toxin begins its work.

The chemical element antimony, by contrast, administered in repeated small doses, produces symptoms resembling those of several stomach diseases. Sickness, pains in the stomach, loss of appetite, and diarrhea lead to extreme depression, painful cramps and convulsions, and finally heart failure.

Arsenic is another old favorite of criminals and crime-writers alike. Its taste can be disguised by food and symptoms produced by repeated small doses can be similar to those induced by severe food poisoning or even cholera and dysentery, which tended to be more common during the time when arsenic was popular with poisoners. Arsenic is an irritant poison and victims usually suffer from burning in the throat, nausea, sickness, stomach pains, and cramps. By the time the patient dies, traces of arsenic are present in all the body tissues.

One of the most famous victims of arsenic poisoning may well have been the Emperor Napoleon. Exiled to the island of Saint Helena in the South Atlantic following his final defeat at Waterloo, he fell into a routine of inactivity and depression, made worse by the poor relations existing between Napoleon and the Governor of the island, Sir Hudson Lowe. Napoleon first showed signs of illness at the end of 1817, just two years after he arrived on the island. The symptoms were seen as indicating an ulcer or even cancer of the stomach, which had killed his father when Napoleon was still a young man.

Two of his doctors had been dismissed as being too sympathetic to the prisoner, leaving only a fellow Corsican, Francesco Antommarchi, who seemed powerless to halt the disease. By the beginning of 1821, the illness became much worse. Napoleon was confined to bed from March, he dictated his will in April and he died on May 5th. When his body was

BELOW Baby food poisoned with arsenic by blackmailer Rodney Witchelo in England in the 1980s.

examined after his death, traces of arsenic were found in his hair and on his clothing. This was used to level the charge that the British had deliberately poisoned their prisoner, though traces of arsenic were also found in the wallpaper paste in the rooms he had occupied during his confinement on the island.

Cyanide works in the same way as carbon monoxide—by starving the blood of life-giving oxygen—but it works much more quickly, resulting in death within minutes. One characteristic sign of cyanide poisoning is a bitter almond smell which tends to linger in the mouth of victims and can be detected in the stomach contents.

Some of the deadliest natural poisons are found in fungi. Their efficacy as poison is partly due to their subtlety: by the time any symptoms are recognizable, the poison is already well established. The genus *Amanita* (which includes *Amanita phalloides* or the "death cap," the most dangerous fungus known) can cause intense suffering and often death even if taken in only the smallest quantities. The toxin works by destroying the body's cell nuclei. A side-effect is a speeding-up of the heartbeat, which in turn accelerates the spread of the poison through the system.

ABOVE Napoleon as a young man.

RIGHT Sample of Napoleon's hair containing arsenic traces.

LEFT Arsenic poisoning from the water supply due to war contamination in Bangladesh.

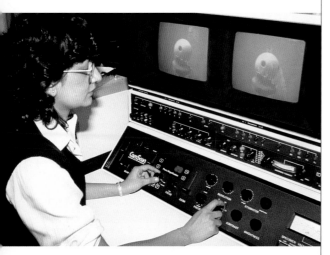

ABOVE A scanning electron microscope, used to examine the pellet that held ricin—the poison responsible for the death of Georgi Markov in 1978 (see pages 126–7).

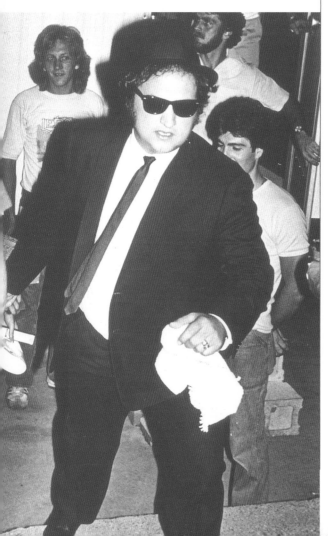

Ricin, derived from the seed of the castor-oil plant, is one of the more exotic poisons. It causes the victim's red blood cells to clump together and then attacks the other body cells, causing a high temperature followed by vomiting and eventually death from heart failure. Though its exceptionally deadly nature has led to rumors of its use as a potential biological weapon for military purposes, its only recorded use as a poison is that of the murder of Bulgarian dissident Georgi Markov.

Drugs and hallucinogens

More common today than the old poisoners' stand-bys of arsenic and antimony are different types of narcotics and hallucinogenic drugs that are taken because of their side effects. Here poisoning results from overdoses, from cumulative poisoning of the body system, from individual reactions to individual drugs and from contamination of the drug being used in an individual case.

In the nineteenth century the most popular drug was opium, often mixed with brandy to produce laudanum. The drug is obtained as a milky, sticky juice by cutting slits in the side of the unripe pod of the opium poppy, which is grown as a crop over wide areas of Asia. In relatively small doses, either taken as laudanum or smoked in a pipe, it produces drowsiness and a freedom from pain, together with a profound sense of well-being. As a poison it was too slow in its actions and too recognizable in its flavor to be of much use to the criminal, and its chief disadvantage to users was the danger of total addiction.

In the case of another popular drug of the time, hyoscine, which was obtained from deadly nightshade or henbane, the danger was much more direct, with even a small dose being lethal among susceptible victims. Nevertheless, it was

LEFT Actor John Belushi, best known for his appearance in "The Blues Brothers" died of a drug overdose.

popular as a prescription against travel sickness, and more recently to reduce inhibitions among prisoners being interrogated, to the point where they freely admit information they would otherwise strive to keep to themselves. In this form, it is usually described as the "truth drug" scopolamine, and it has also been used in the treatment of acute anxiety states. In larger doses, victims suffer from hallucinations, and a massive dose affects the heart muscles, causing death from cardiac failure.

Morphine is widely used for medicinal purposes as an analgesic that can relieve the severest pain by depressing the sufferer's central nervous system. It is derived from opium, which actually contains between 4 percent and 20 percent of morphine, and it also has to be administered with care, as it induces a high degree of physical dependence as the body's systems become accustomed to its effects.

Heroin, like morphine, is another derivative of opium and is popular among illicit drug users rather than used medicinally. It is produced by the reaction between morphine and either acetyl chloride or acetic anhydride, and because it dissolves readily in water, it can be injected directly into the circulation, for the maximum

ABOVE Two men smoking opium in China c. 1880.

BELOW Fields of opium growing in Afghanistan, one of the prime producers of this drug.

effect and the quickest results. Addicts often dissolve a small quantity of the drug in a teaspoon heated over a candle or a succession of matches to produce enough solution to administer through a syringe. Unfortunately the law of diminishing returns operates here too. The effect of the drug may initially last for several hours, but as the body becomes more dependent on it, larger doses are needed at more frequent intervals to produce a similar effect, and the pains of withdrawal from the drug become more intense.

Codeine is another drug derived from opium and is also used as an ingredient in common pain-killer preparations, and also as a cough suppressant in cough mixtures available from pharmacists. However, because it is considerably weaker in its effects than either morphine or heroin, it is rarely used by addicts.

Not all narcotic drugs are derived from opium, and a number of synthetic drugs that have similar effects on the body are commonly described as opiates. These include propoxyphene, originally marketed as a

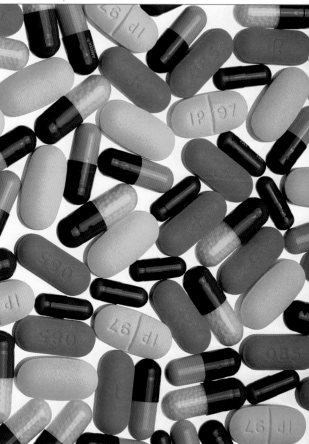

painkiller in the late 1950s, which has since been implicated in cases of addiction and overdoses, and methadone, which has been used in rehabilitation programs due to its unexpected effect on heroin users. If methadone is taken orally in regular doses, it appears to cancel out the euphoric effects of a dose of heroin or morphine, and involves little or no side effects. Consequently, it has been used in treatment regimes that have been successful in weaning addicts off heroin and in the longer term reducing or eliminating their dependence on illicit drugs of any kind.

Depressants

Other drugs that are classified as depressants also work to depress the action of the central nervous system. These include alcohol, the most widely used drug of all in the Western world, and also a wide variety of tranquilizers,

ABOVE RIGHT An assortment of medical pills, tablets, and capsules.

ABOVE Bags of opium from Afghanistan fuel the heroin trade.

barbiturates and the volatile chemicals contained in adhesive solvents, lighter fuels and hairsprays, which can be inhaled to produce the depressant effect. In general, these substances produce a feeling of relaxation, euphoria, exhilaration and ultimately drowsiness and sleep. In all cases, large doses can be harmful or even fatal.

Many of these drugs were developed originally for medicinal use. Phenobarbital acts slowly as it is absorbed through the digestive system, and generally only the faster barbiturates like secobarbital, pentobarbital and amobarbital are preferred by abusers. Even then, normal prescription doses do not usually produce dependence, so that abusers have to take the tablets in large quantities to produce the desired effect. In doing so, their systems become so dependent on the drugs that withdrawal causes extremely severe effects including convulsions and delirium, and may prove fatal if not carried out under close medical supervision. Tranquilizers too are safe in normal doses, though some users seem to become dependent on these drugs to cope with the stresses of modern life, and the stronger tranquilizers used to treat mental patients like chlorpromazine are more attractive to abusers.

Stimulants

Cocaine and amphetamines have the opposite effect, acting as stimulants to the central nervous system and producing feelings of confidence, boundless energy and loss of appetite. In most cases, these effects give way to sensations of dread, extreme fatigue and hunger, followed by a lasting depression. There is less tendency to addiction, but the body soon becomes acclimatized to the drug, and progressively larger doses are needed to produce the same effects. Crack cocaine is made by mixing cocaine with baking powder and water, and heating. The residue is then dried and broken down into lumps that can be smoked to release the drug in a way which can be absorbed more rapidly by the body, for a more powerful and immediate effect.

Hallucinogenic drugs

Apart from alcohol, marijuana is almost certainly the most widely available and widely used drug in both Europe and North America today. This hallucinogenic drug is normally obtained by crushing the leaves of the cannabis plant, which originally grew wild as a weed in many different parts of the world, and mixing them with different proportions of the stems, the seeds and the flowers. The sticky resin secreted by the plant is the foundation of hashish, a much more potent source of the drug. Another powerful form of marijuana is prepared by taking the unfertilized flowering tops of the female cannabis plants, after removing all male plants from the vicinity, to produce the substance called sinsemilla.

The active ingredient in all these variants of the drug is a substance called THC (for tetrahydrocannabinol), directly related to the strength of a particular formula of the drug and its effect on the individual user. The cannabis plant has an average THC content of approximately 1.5 percent, which rises in sinsemilla and orthodox hashish to around 3.5 percent. However, a much more potent preparation is produced by using a solvent to extract the resin, which contains the highest proportion of THC, as a thick oil, called "liquid hashish." This contains anything from 20 percent to as much as 65 percent THC, and as little as a single drop is enough to produce a very powerful effect on the user.

Marijuana appears to cause little or no physical dependency, though the blissful state

ABOVE Indian Hemp (*Cannabis sativa*), also known as pot, marijuana, or hashish.

of intoxication it produces can induce a state of strong psychological dependence among long-term users. On the other hand, researchers claim it does have certain medicinal benefits. For example, it has been found to reduce internal pressure on the eyeball in sufferers of glaucoma, and multiple sclerosis patients have apparently found it useful in coping with the effects of the disease. Other possible applications include its use as a muscle relaxant, or as a means of reducing the nausea produced by certain chemotherapy preparations in treating cancer.

A number of synthetic hallucinogens have also been developed with similar, and in many cases more powerful, effects. LSD is produced from a chemical called lysergic acid, which was originally extracted from ergot, a fungus which attacks grasses and cereal crops. It produces a mixture of startling hallucinations combined with mood swings and anxieties. Although there is little evidence of physical dependence, injuries and deaths have occurred when users succumb to the effects of the hallucinations it produces.

Another hallucinogenic drug called phencyclidine or PCP has become popular because it is fairly easy to make and produces effects similar to LSD. Abusers sometimes use a mixture of drugs, like a combination of LSD and PCP with amphetamines. These are taken as tablets, as a powder that is commonly called "Angel Dust" or as a liquid which can be sprayed on leaves and then smoked. Finally another hallucinogen, MPMA, more commonly known as Ecstasy or simply "E", was originally developed a drug for suppressing the appetite, but its side effects, including the capacity to produce feelings of relaxation and well-being, have made it popular among drug users. Unfortunately its other potential side effects are less enjoyable. They include increased blood pressure and pulse rate, nausea and muscle cramps, anxiety and confusion, and in several cases the drug has been fatal to users trying it for the first time.

Tests for poisons

Forensic scientists faced with a victim of poisoning have a daunting array of possible agents to search for at autopsy. The procedure often starts with samples of the victim's blood, urine, or specific tissues being dissolved in an acidified or alkaline solution. Acidified water is used when looking for evidence of acidic drugs such as ASA or barbiturates, which can be extracted from the solution using organic solvents such as chloroform.

A screening test can check quite rapidly for a wide range of drugs or poisons. Complicated

RIGHT Forensic drug testing. High pressure liquid chromatography is used to identify drugs in a forensic laboratory.

BELOW A gas chromatography machine connected to a mass spectrometer in a forensic laboratory. A sample injection robot transfers samples from small vials to the chromatography machine where they are evaporated and separated according to molecular weight. The spectrometer identifies the smallest traces of individual chemicals as they emerge from the chromatography tube.

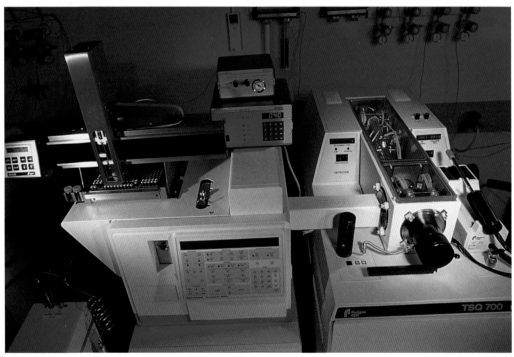

BELOW Forensic narcotic tests: a selection of vials used by police officers at the scene of a crime to test for illegal narcotics. Each vial is marked with the narcotic it can identify (from left; opiates and amphetamines; cannabis; LSD; cocaine). During a test the top of the vial is broken off and a sample of the drug inserted into the vial using a spatula. A positive result will be indicated by the clear crystals inside the vial changing to the color indicated on the vial.

Forensic analysts use thin-layer chromatography as a screening test to identify types of drugs. This works in a similar way except that it places the sample on a thin vertical film of silica gel or aluminum oxide. The sample is then split into its different constituents by a liquid solvent which rises up the surface of the film by capillary action, attracting some substances more strongly than others and carrying them further. When the process is finished, the plate carrying the vertical film is placed under ultraviolet light, which shows the different constituents of the mixture as dark or fluorescent spots. Alternatively a chemical agent can be used that reacts differently with each constituent, causing them to reveal themselves as different-colored spots.

Recently, forensic laboratories have been turning to immuno-assay techniques to test samples for very small amounts of drugs or poisons. This involves the development of antibodies that react with the substances being looked for. First, the drug in question is combined with a protein and the compound injected into the bloodstream of an animal. This stimulates the animal to produce antibodies, which are extracted from a blood sample, then added to the test sample. If the drug in question is present in the test sample, the antibodies from the animal's blood will be seen to react with it.

Confirmation tests usually involve a combination of gas chromatography and mass spectrometry. As each different component from the sample mixture emerges from the chromatography column, it enters into a mass spectrometer where it is bombarded by a stream of high-energy electrons. These electrons then cause the component to break up, producing a different but characteristic spectrum for each individual substance present.

mixtures can be broken down into their constituent parts using a technique called gas chromatography. A liquid sample is introduced into a heated injection port where it is vaporized and carried on a stream of gas through a liquid-filled column. The various constituents of the mixture travel at unequal speeds through the liquid column, and emerge at different times. By placing a detector at the end of the column, the individual constituents are revealed as peaks on a moving strip chart. Each of the peaks can be identified as a particular substance by comparing the strip chart with other reference charts, and the height of each peak shows the amount of each particular substance in the sample.

Aunt Thally

The death of an eighty-seven-year-old woman named Christina Mickelson in Sydney, Australia, in 1947 seemed a natural enough occurrence. When family friend Angeline Thomas died not long afterward this too seemed reasonable, given that the lady was also in her eighties. But the death of a much younger relative, sixty-year-old John Lundberg, a year later was more suspicious. Lundberg's hair had fallen out before his death, which made it all the more alarming when another member of the family, Mary Ann Mickelson, fell ill with similar symptoms, and finally she too died.

One factor common to all four deaths was the presence of Caroline Grills, the sixty-three-year-old stepdaughter-in-law of the first victim. Grills, who had married Mrs. Mickelson's stepson nearly forty years earlier, had nursed the old lady through her final illness. When Angeline Thomas fell ill, Grills had helped care for her too, preparing endless cups of tea to lift the invalid's spirits. She had also been there to minister to John Lundberg and Mary Ann Mickelson and, one after another, her patients' conditions had all deteriorated until eventually they died.

By 1948, the mystery sickness had begun to threaten the lives of John Lundberg's widow and daughter, both of whose conditions were worsening in spite of Caroline Grills' attentive care. Both women were losing their hair and complained of a heavy lassitude and difficulty in moving their limbs. Eventually a suspicious relative alerted the local police, who removed one of the cups of tea prepared for the suffering women and subjected it to forensic analysis. The fact that the victims' hair had fallen out during their illness suggested the presence of thallium as a poison. The laboratory checked by using the Reinsch test, which involves adding the suspect material to a solution of hydrochloric acid. A copper strip is dipped into the resulting mixture, and any metallic deposit forming on it indicates the presence of a heavy metal such as arsenic, antimony, or thallium. The specific identity of the contamination is then confirmed by further analysis.

Thallium was found to have been added to the tea. Discovery was made in time to save the lives of Mrs. Lundberg and her daughter, athough Mrs. Lundberg lost her sight as a result of the poison absorbed into her system.

Caroline Grills was tried and found guilty of the attempted murder of Mrs. Lundberg. She was sentenced to life imprisonment and, bizarrely, became popular among the other inmates who came to know her simply as "Aunt Thally."

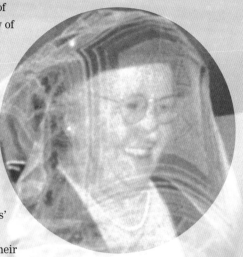

BACKGROUND A picture of Caroline Grills, who used thallium to poison her victims.

Dr. Hawley Harvey Crippen

ABOVE Dr Bernard Spilsbury in the pathology laboratory at St Bartholomew's Hospital, London.

BELOW Hilldrop Crescent in North London, taken in August 1910.

Dr. Hawley Harvey Crippen was an American-born dentist. He was married to a former music-hall singer whose stage name was Belle Elmore. After Mrs. Crippen disappeared early in 1910, neighbors' suspicions were aroused by Crippin's mistress, Ethel le Neve, who was seen wearing Mrs. Crippen's jewelry. Crippen and le Neve fled to Antwerp in Belgium whereupon, on July 13, police searched the Crippens' home at Hilldrop Crescent in north London, and found the mutilated body of a woman, but no proof of her identity.

British pathologist Dr. Bernard Spilsbury carried out an autopsy and was able to prove the existence of an appendectomy scar which helped to identify the body as definitely that of Mrs. Crippen. He also found traces of hyoscine, which showed that the woman had been deliberately poisoned. Because hyoscine produced symptoms similar to heart failure, and because it was available to medical practitioners for use in small doses as a treatment for anxiety and travel sickness, suspicion was cast on Dr. Crippen and police began a search for him and his mistress.

By this time, the couple were crossing the Atlantic on the steamship *Montrose*, posing as "Mr. Robinson and son." The captain became suspicious of their affectionate behavior and sent a wireless message to England. Chief Inspector Dew of Scotland Yard responded, boarding a steamer that reached

Canada before the *Montrose* was due to land. As Crippen's ship approached the Canadian coast, Dew went to meet it, disguised as a pilot. He subsequently arrested the couple and they were taken back to England for trial. Crippen, perhaps the first criminal to be caught as a result of a wireless message, was hanged later that year. Le Neve was tried as an accessory, but was later acquitted after her defense showed she had been unaware of the murder.

ABOVE Dr. Crippen walking down the gangway, his arm clasped by a detective, on their return to England.

ARRESTATION DU DOCTEUR CRIPPEN ET DE MISS LE NEVE SUR LE PONT DU «MONTROSE»

ABOVE The moment of the arrest on board the *Montrose* August 14, 1910, as depicted in the French magazine *Le Petit Journal.*

BELOW Dr. Crippen and Ethel Le Neve during their trial at Bow Street.

Arthur Warren Waite

POISONER AND THE ORDER HE SIGNED
FOR PROCURING SERVANT'S TESTIMONY.

Spaulding McClellan Co
Please give to bearer
R.C. Schindler One
Thousand ("1000.00)
dollars and
charge to my
account.

Arthur Warren Waite

DR.
ARTHUR
WARREN
WAITE

FROM PHOTOGRAPH
MADE LAST
DECEMBER

ORDER SIGNED by DR WAITE
for PROCURING
DORA HELLIER'S
TESTIMONY

Most poisons can be revealed by careful forensic analysis, but some murderers have tried to avoid suspicion by using genuine diseases to kill their victims. Dr. Arthur Warren Waite was a New York dentist who succeeded in poisoning his mother-in-law by lacing her food with a mixture of influenza and diphtheria germs. She died in January 1916. Dr. Waite then set to work on John Peck, his father-in-law, using in addition a nasal spray contaminated with tuberculosis germs. Though Peck proved more resistant to infection than his late wife, he died just two months after her. Among the tests conducted at Peck's autopsy was the standard test for arsenic poisoning, which had been developed by London chemist James Marsh eighty years earlier. Specimens of body tissue or stomach contents are placed on a zinc plate and sulfuric acid is poured onto the sample. Any arsenic is turned into a gaseous compound of arsenic and hydrogen, which passes along a heated tube to a cold section where arsenious oxide collects. In this case, the resulting white crystals of arsenious oxide showed that the impatient Dr. Waite had indeed added this more certain poison to his armory, and as a result he was convicted of his father-in-law's murder.

ABOVE A picture of Dr. Waite and the order he signed for procuring his servant's testimony.

OPPOSITE A newspaper report about the arrest of Dr. Waite, showing the victims. Mr. and Mrs. Peck, and below, their children, one of whom was the wife of Dr. Waite.

WAITE, IN DRUG STUPOR, UNDER ARREST, CHARGED WITH POISONING PECK.

POISONED MILLIONAIRE, DEAD WIFE, AND HEIRS

Mrs. JOHN E. PECK

JOHN E. PECK

MRS. ARTHUR W. WAITE

PERCY PECK

Detective Finds Dentist Unconscious in Riverside Apartment —In Lucid Moment Asks Doctor to Use Stomach Pump and Says He Took "Plenty" to Induce Sleep—Had Medical Book With Information About Poisons—Many Packages of Strong Chemicals in Pockets—Servant Tells Grand Jury She Saw Employer Pour "Medicine" in Aged Father-in-Law's Soup and Tea Two Nights Before Latter's Death.

District Attorney Swann at 10 o'clock yesterday morning ordered the arrest of Dr. Arthur Warren Waite, in whose apartment in the Coliosseum, No. 435 Riverside Drive, John E. Peck, a millionaire druggist of Grand Rapids, Mich., died on March 12.

The District Attorney's action followed hard upon the clue he found in the publication in The World of the suggestion of Miss Catherine Peck, a sister of the dead man, that he might have "gone to Dr. Waite's study, got the bottle of arsenic there, and taken a dose of it by mistake."

Physically, at least, Dr. Waite was not put under arrest, for Detective Cunniff of the District Attorney's staff found him deeply under the influence of drugs which he had taken, he said in intervals of coherence, at 11 o'clock Wednesday morning in an effort to induce sleep.

Waite continued violently ill at intervals throughout the day, but there was reason to believe that he would have recovered sufficiently by this morning to be placed actually under arrest and arraigned on a charge of homicide in connection with the death of Mr. Peck, whose son-in-law he was, and whose wife had died six weeks earlier, almost to the hour, in the Waite apartment.

Information on Poisons Marked in Books Found in Rooms

Mr. Swann found in the apartment yesterday, in the course of a two and one-half hours examination of it, several works on medical and chemical subjects. One of these was Woods on therapeutics and pharmacology. Between pages 811 and 812 was found a book mark, a yellowed strip of paper, that seemed to have been in place for a long time. On these pages the topic under discussion was "Arsenic: Effects on the System."

Between pages 158 and 159 was another mark, indicating a discussion of veratria (an organic alkali) and white hellebore. Between pages 662 and 663 there was still another mark, indicating a discussion of nauseating and depressive expectorants.

"These may be old references," said the District Attorney. "I don't say that they have any significance."

Mr. Swann, however, took the volume to his office with him.

Meantime the Grand Jury, sitting under Judge Nott of the Court of General Sessions, began an inquiry into the death of Mr. Peck. Two witnesses had been heard when it adjourned at 1.30 o'clock until 11 this morning—Dora Hillier, the West Indian servant employed by the Waites, and Dr. Jacob Cornell of Raritan, N. J., an intimate of Mr. Peck and, it is now believed, the author of the telegram signed "K. Adams," which prevented the cremation of the body of Mr. Peck and brought about the autopsies which revealed the presence of arsenic.

Servant Tells Strong Story

had seen Dr. Waite put "medicine" in soup and tea served to Mr. Peck one evening, about two days before he died. Dr. Cornell similarly told of having found Mr. Peck in apparently good health less than twelve hours before he died, and of finding himself a seemingly unwelcome guest when he visited the Waite apartment shortly afterward.

Witnesses called from Grand Rapids for appearance before the Grand Jury are on their way East, and may be heard to-morrow. Mr. and Mrs. Warren W. Waite, father and mother of the young dentist, started for this city last night. Assistant District Attorney F. X. Mancuso, who has been in Michigan with Dr. Otto H. Schultze, the District Attorney's pathologist, believes he has established facts of the utmost importance in the past three days. He telegraphed to his chief last night an enthusiastic account of his work, concluding:

"Check up bank accounts and hold up deposits."

Mr. Swann had already taken this action, impounding deposits Dr. Waite carried in a Fifth Avenue bank and the contents of a box in a safe deposit vault in East Fourteenth Street. The World established during the day that Dr. Waite had received from Miss Peck, his wife's aunt, considerably more than the $40,000 in cash of which she told Wednesday. Securities whose face value would bring the total close to $100,000 were also added to this.

Other Woman Still Unknown.

RECORDS OF BRITISH CRUISER AS FLOTSAM.

First Believed That Cumberland Had Been Sunk—No Dates Beyond 1908.

(Special to The World.)

NORFOLK, Va., March 22.—There was a sensation here to-day when members of the Coast Guard at Chicamicomcio, N. C., reported that they had picked up the log books of the British cruiser Cumberland, washed ashore on the beach.

The excitement considerably subsided when it was discovered that of the six books picked up, not one carried an entry later than 1908. They were, moreover, not the ship's log, but apparently some of the records of the engineer's force.

Many fishermen were ready to swear they had heard heavy firing at sea recently.

Communication with the British Embassy at Washington suggested the explanation that the books were discarded records.

FLETCHER ON WAY TO TALK TO LANSING.

PANAMA, March 22.—Henry P. Fletcher, the new American Ambassador to Mexico, passed through here to-day and sailed this afternoon on the steamer Corrillo for New York on his way to Washington from his former post at Santiago, Chili.

Mr. Fletcher said he was not prepared to discuss the problems confronting him in Mexico, because he was not possessed of information on the situation. He was going to Washington, he added, to receive instructions from Secretary of State Lansing and familiarize himself thoroughly with the conditions and with what was expected of him.

Knives and Blunt Instruments

ABOVE Some of the weapons used by "Yorkshire Ripper" Peter Sutcliffe.

With the decline in the general availability of poisons, and the increasing probability of their use being revealed by autopsy evidence, modern criminals tend to use other weapons to achieve their ends. In the U.S., where firearms and ammunition are relatively easy to obtain, a high proportion of woundings and murders involve gunshot wounds (*see* Chapter Eight). Nevertheless, use of a firearm often implies a degree of premeditation and can also provide evidence allowing forensic scientists to tie the weapon, and ultimately the user, to the murder. In less carefully planned attacks, cruder weapons are used, ranging from a stiletto, a switchblade, or kitchen knife, to the nearest heavy object able to inflict a sufficiently damaging wound—be it a wrench, a lamp, or a lump of wood. It is the job of the forensic scientist either to show that a particular weapon was the one used in a given case or, in cases where the weapon has not been found, to give a description of the weapon based on the victim's injuries to assist investigators in their search for evidence.

Evidence on the victim

In cases where a murder victim has been battered to death with a blunt instrument, the fatal blows are usually delivered to the head, and it is relatively unusual for one single blow to achieve the criminal's aim. A series of blows is usually sustained, each of which can cause ragged lacerations where scraps of tissue and blood vessels are driven into the surface of the underlying bones.

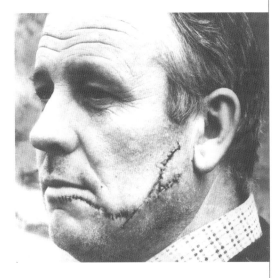

ABOVE Graham Backhouse slashed his own cheek after killing a neighbor, claiming he had been attacked and had shot back in self-defence.

The victim's head may show depression fractures where the bones of the skull were driven into the brain tissues, causing death by compression of the brain. In such cases, the shape of the fractured area may reveal something of the shape of the weapon used. The site of the fracture area, seen in the context of the victim's probable position when the blows were delivered, can also indicate the type of blow delivered, and even the relative height and strength of the attacker. There may be no discernible depression fractures, however, if the fatal injuries were caused by rupture of the blood vessels beneath the skull.

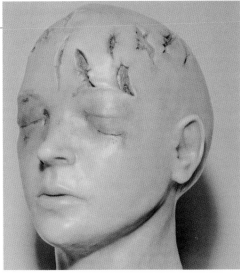

ABOVE A medical model of the head of Mrs. Marilyn Sheppard showing the horrific injuries she received. Her husband, Dr. Sam Sheppard, was found guilty of her murder in 1954, but was acquitted and released in 1966.

Sometimes the fatal injuries are only part of the evidence found on the victim's body. If the attack was prolonged, or a physical struggle preceded the murder, patterns of bruising can give an indication of what happened.

Bruises are caused by the breaking of small blood vessels beneath the skin. They might be caused by the attacker's fists, feet, or weapons, or by the victim falling against hard or sharp objects at the scene of the attack. Bruises can show forensic experts something of the order in which the attack progressed, and where and how the fatal blow was struck. Examination can also reveal whether the rupture of the blood vessels happened before or after death. In cases where the bruising was inflicted before death, a sample of the blood found beneath the skin at the site of the bruise usually shows a higher-than-normal white-cell count, because the body's normal reactions to an injury started to function immediately after the injury was sustained. If the bruise was inflicted after death, this process would not normally have progressed to the same extent.

Children who have been battered by their parents or caretakers are often too young or too frightened to give evidence regarding the nature of their injuries. Because bruises heal in a series of stages over several days or weeks, the injuries themselves can indicate that either a single incident or a series of repeated attacks was responsible.

For example, a fresh bruise usually appears purple or red in color, depending on the depth and size of the injury. Chemical changes that affect the blood that leaks into the tissues cause the bruise to change to brown, and then

to green, and finally to yellow before the signs slowly fade. Consequently, a victim showing fresh reddish-purple bruises, together with others that are brown, and others that are greenish-yellow, is likely to have been attacked on at least three separate occasions.

Knife Wounds

In countries where gun-control laws are tightly enforced, murders with knives are usually the most common type of killing. Even in the U.S., the number of knife murders is second only to the number of those involving guns. Though there is as yet no foolproof technique for positively linking an individual knife to an individual victim, as there is with guns and bullets (see Chapter Eight), knife murders do offer forensic experts some useful clues to help in their search for the perpetrator.

Knife wounds are almost always inflicted during close-range attacks. In the case of incised wounds, where the attacker makes a series of slashing moves, cuts to the victim's arms and hands often show where he or she has instinctively tried to intercept the blows in an attempt at self-defense. Struggles of this kind usually leave the attacker spattered or

LEFT AND ABOVE A Turkish debtor fatally stabs his creditor in broad daylight. The slaying was captured by a passing journalist.

Careful inspection of a stab wound can reveal useful details of the knife used. Though information on the width of the blade is often unreliable, because the knife may have been moved within the body after the initial stab, the weapon must have been at least as long as the depth of the resulting wound. A skilled anthropologist can often tell whether the wound was made by a double-edged blade or by a blade that has only a single sharp edge.

Not all stab wounds are caused by knives, of course. A victim could be stabbed with a chisel, a screwdriver, or a pair of scissors, for example. An elaborate technique is sometimes used to produce a cast of the wound, to give more accurate evidence of the shape and form of the

ABOVE In the case of one murdered woman, a pathologist found a knife blade tip in a neck wound, which fitted the broken blade of a penknife found in the pants pocket of her husband, the accused.

even drenched in the victim's blood: such bloodstains, if found, offer proof positive of the attacker's presence at the assault.

Forensic experts recognize another basic type of knife wound. Stab wounds are inflicted when the knife blade is pushed into the body, causing damage to the body's vital organs and producing internal bleeding. In these cases there may be relatively little external bleeding and, if the knife is removed, the wound can shrink so as to appear less obvious than an incised wound.

Stab wounds are usually fatal only when they are inflicted with a sufficiently long blade to the chest or abdomen. In attacks to the chest, blows are usually delivered upward so the knife tends to penetrate the chest wall between the ribs. A downward blow to the chest can result in the knife blade glancing off each of the ribs in turn, preventing it from entering deeply enough to inflict fatal damage to the victim.

weapon. This involves dissecting layer by layer the part of the victim's body that contains the wound, enabling a three-dimensional representation to be built up. In at least one case the victim's chest, and the fatal wound, were preserved in formalin after the autopsy. The murder weapon was subsequently found and presented as evidence; prosecutors were able to demonstrate in court that the shape of the weapon matched that of the wound.

Fatal incised wounds are usually those delivered to the body's most unprotected area—where the arteries supplying blood to the brain are exposed around the victim's neck. In reality, it is surprisingly difficult for an attacker to cut a victim's throat in the course of an equal struggle. If the throat has been cut, there is often evidence that the victim was held down, tied up or rendered unconscious before the fatal injury was sustained.

BELOW Bodies being recovered from a murder scene.

Homicide—or suicide?

Relatively few suicides use knives, though cases do occur, and forensic scientists have to recognize the signs that differentiate suicide and murder victims. In general, suicides who use knives target one of three sites on the body: they attempt to cut the throat, or to stab themselves in the chest or stomach.

In cases where a suicide stabs him- or herself through the heart or stomach, there are usually just one or two deliberate stabs. In most cases, clothing has been removed over the target area and the wound is located within the victim's easy reach to allow the blow to be delivered with sufficient force. In cases where there are multiple stab wounds over a wider area of the body, and where these are wholly or partly delivered through the clothing, then homicide is the more likely cause.

Where death has resulted from the severing of major blood vessels to the neck, the site of the cut and its appearance reveal a great deal

about how it was inflicted. A right-handed suicide usually inflicts a gash that starts high on the left side of the neck, sweeps across the throat and finishes lower down on the right side. A left-handed suicide commonly operates in the other direction, starting high up on the right side of the neck and sweeping across to finish low down on the left side.

Two further signs distinguish suicides from victims attacked by other parties. In a suicide where the throat is cut, there is often evidence of one or two shallower gashes caused by "trial attempts" made while the person built up sufficient determination to deliver the final, lethal cut. There is also a tendency for the suicide to raise the head at the moment of impact, intending to expose the neck arteries. In fact this can often defeat the object, because such action moves the blood vessels back to a position where they are at least partly shielded by the windpipe. Sometimes the attempt fails completely, or death results from suffocation when blood from the surrounding tissues enters the windpipe and prevents the victim from breathing.

Where the throat has been cut by an attacker, a fatal wound inflicted at one side of the neck often indicates whether the attacker was left- or right-handed or whether the blow was struck from in front of the victim or from behind. In addition, unless the victim was asleep or restrained at the time of the attack, there is usually evidence of defensive wounds to the hands, as well as to the arms, which is proof positive that the crime was homicidal rather than suicidal.

Even in cases where the criminal tries to disguise murder to look like suicide, telltale details can give the game away. In one case in England, a murderer placed a knife in his victim's hand, having deliberately inflicted cuts to his own body, and claimed he had shot his victim in self-defense. When checked by forensic experts the evidence revealed that the victim could not have continued to hold the knife after suffering the shock of a shotgun

ABOVE Mummified head of *Lindow Man*, dated between 20 and 130 AD, who met a violent end, being struck on the head and garroted, a method of strangling.

blast to the chest unless rigor mortis had set in immediately, and there was no evidence of this.

Furthermore, the nature of the wounds on the murderer's body was inconsistent with his story: they appeared to have been made while he was standing fairly still and there were no defensive wounds on his arms or hands to support his claim that he had tried to fend off the victim's attack. Another detail that cast suspicion on his story involved the state of the dead man's hand in which the knife was found. The palm was soaked in blood where the victim had clutched the massive wound to his chest. Had he actually been attacking with the knife when the shot was fired, the hand would not have been soaked in blood unless he had dropped the knife to clutch his wound.

Jeffrey MacDonald

ABOVE U.S. Army Captain Jeffrey MacDonald.

BELOW A military policeman stands guard as a crime lab technician works inside the MacDonald home.

Jeffrey MacDonald was a captain in the U.S. Army, living with his wife and two young daughters at Fort Bragg in North Carolina. Military police responding to an emergency telephone call in the small hours of the morning found the wife and daughters dead from numerous stab wounds. MacDonald was alive, and claimed he had been stabbed and knocked unconscious by three men and a woman: all "hippies," and apparently acting under the influence of drugs. He explained how he had warded off their frenzied blows by wrapping his blue pajama jacket around his hands, and how, after the attackers fled, he had first tried to revive his daughters with mouth-to-mouth resuscitation, then placed the jacket over his dead wife's body.

MacDonald gave detailed descriptions of all four attackers, but no evidence of their presence could be found. Officers were suspicious of MacDonald's story because the room had been in darkness at the time of the attack, and MacDonald had very poor eyesight. He needed glasses to read and to drive, so without them, his vision would have been blurred. When a forensic team searched the scene, they found blue fibers from his pajama jacket beneath his wife's body, in the children's bedrooms, and under the fingernail of one of the victims. But none was found in the living room where MacDonald claimed to have been fighting for his life, and where there was in fact very little disorder. The bloodstains in the different rooms were all identified, and

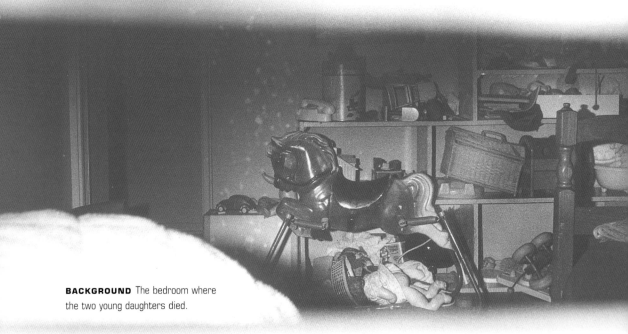

BACKGROUND The bedroom where the two young daughters died.

MacDonald's blood was found in the kitchen, in the bathroom, and on a pair of eyeglasses. No traces were found in the living room where he claimed to have been stabbed, or on either of the telephones he had used to call the police.

Nevertheless, many pieces of evidence had been lost by the time his trial was due, and charges were dropped. But when MacDonald subsequently appeared on a television chat show, his callous attitude and the flippant remarks he made regarding his family's tragic deaths revived suspicions as to his part in the drama, and his pajama jacket was sent to the FBI laboratory in Washington D.C. for analysis. Investigators found that all forty-eight holes said to have been made by the attackers' ice pick were smooth and round, rather as if the jacket had been held still while the holes had been made. There was also a large stain of Mrs. MacDonald's blood on both sides of a tear said to have been made during the attack. This suggested that the stain had been produced before the jacket was torn, although MacDonald claimed to have laid the jacket across his wife's body only after the attack was over and he had found her dead.

Finally in 1979 MacDonald was tried for the murders of his wife and children. During the course of the trial, forensic examiners demonstrated a simulated attack in the courtroom with an ice-pick and a pajama jacket. They showed that the pattern of cuts made in the pajama jacket was not consistent with the pattern of cuts that would have been made had the incident unfolded as MacDonald originally claimed. As a result, MacDonald was found guilty and ordered to serve three consecutive life sentences. A succession of appeals, started in October 1997, are still going on.

ABOVE MacDonald pictured on the day before he was accused of killing his pregnant wife and his children.

LEFT Artist's sketch shown at the preliminary hearing depicting a woman described by MacDonald as involved in the murders of his wife and children.

Strangulation and Suffocation

RIGHT Sketch of Colonel Edward Marcus Despart at New Surrey Gaol just before his hanging.

If an attacker has neither a gun nor a knife, and there is no object on hand that is hard and heavy enough to batter the victim with, a murderer may opt for strangulation or suffocation. Strangulation may be with a cord, a rope, or a length of wire, or it may be by the murderer's own hands. Suffocation may be due to a pillow or plastic bag over the face or by a weight (such as the murderer's body) being pressed on the chest of the victim making

breathing impossible. But forensic examination of the scene and body can still reveal exactly how the victim died, sometimes in spite of the criminal's best efforts to cover his or her tracks or to conceal the fact that a crime has taken place at all.

Accidental suffocation happens when the victim is starved of air because of where he or she happens to be, rather than because of the actions of an assailant. If a child happens to

find an abandoned refrigerator, for example, and accidentally becomes trapped inside, then unless he or she is rescued in time, the lack of oxygen will result in unconsciousness and eventually death. This would be classed as an accidental suffocation. On the other hand, if a kidnap victim is left concealed in a confined space and dies of suffocation, the case would be a criminal death, even if it was due to error rather than deliberate intention.

Victims can also be accidentally suffocated by what is described as crush asphyxia. If a

ABOVE The Hillsborough disaster at a soccer stadium in Sheffield, England, where stampeding crowds caused deaths from crush asphyxia.

victim is trapped in a crowd, or by a fall in a mine or quarry, or by falling concrete in an earthquake, the weight of other people or of the debris may bear so heavily on the chest that breathing is impossible. In such cases there are usually signs of hemorrhaging from the head and chest and around the eyeballs, which are often full of excess fluid.

Examining the clues

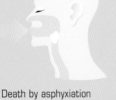

Death by asphyxiation results from air being prevented from reaching the lungs.

A victim of strangling often dies because the supply of blood and oxygen to the brain is cut off.

Excess pressure on the vagus nerve during strangulation can cause it to send a signal to the brain ordering the heart to stop beating.

Separation of the vertebrae can rupture blood and tear the spinal cord, causing instant death.

Smothering and "Burking"

When a victim dies because breathing is physically impossible, rather than owing to lack of oxygen, the cause of death is usually described as smothering. Victims can be smothered accidentally, as in cases where an unsupervised child puts a plastic bag over his or her head and cuts off the air supply. Sometimes—but not always—the influence of drink or drugs is involved in adult cases: people die from becoming entangled in clothing or bedding; from choking on food or vomit, or in cases of auto-erotic asphyxiation.

Nevertheless, some smothering cases occur as a result of a deliberate assault. Criminals sometimes choose the method in the hope that the absence of obvious injuries like bruising or knife wounds will lead investigators to

ABOVE The house at Tanner's Close in Edinburgh where Burke and Hare carried out their killings.

conclude that the victim suffered a seizure or heart attack. The notorious nineteenth-century "bodysnatchers" Burke and Hare made a living by murdering victims to sell their bodies to the anatomy departments of teaching hospitals in Edinburgh, Scotland. The murderers needed the bodies to be in good condition and have no external injuries. They therefore perfected a method of killing that involved their kneeling on the victim's chest and using their hands to close off the nose and mouth, a technique which ever since has been known to criminals and the police as "Burking."

LEFT Burke and Hare's common-law wives helped drug the victims with whisky before they were suffocated.

BELOW Burke and Hare soffocating one of their victims, to sell the corpse for medical dissection.

ABOVE Harry Dobkin killed his estranged wife Rachel (top) and hid her dismembered body in a bomb-damaged chapel in wartime London.

Manual strangulation

Where a victim has been strangled by the assailant's hands, there are two main causes of death. The pressure of the hands around the throat not only prevents the victim from breathing, but can also cut off the blood supply to the brain. As a result, a determined attack may render the victim unconscious—preventing any further resistance—before death occurs.

To a forensic scientist, the body of a victim of manual strangulation shows clear signs of what has happened. In order to cut off both respiration and blood circulation, the attacker has to apply enough force to cause bruising of the victim's neck and throat. The bruises are brought about by the pressure of the thumbs and fingertips and are usually approximately circular in shape and around half an inch in diameter. Curved marks may also be caused by

fingernails tearing into the victim's skin.

Other signs result from the victim's physical reaction to the strangulation. They may include the trapping of the tongue between the teeth, causing bite marks and bruising of the tissues. There may also be bruising of the surrounding area including the lining of the larynx, the voice box, and the floor of the mouth. As with any death from strangulation, it is likely that the hyoid bone, a curved bone at the base of the tongue, will have been broken, and if the attacker has used a great deal of force there may also be fractures of the cartilage of the windpipe and larynx. Another telltale sign of strangulation is the presence of pinpoint hemorrhages around the eyes.

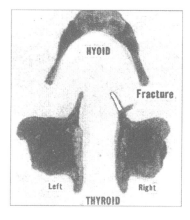

ABOVE Pathologist Keith Simpson found damage to the larynx that showed Rachel Dobkin had been strangled.

A fall—or a push?

The most obvious external evidence found on the body of a hanging victim is usually caused by the rope itself. The marks made on the victim differ according to the type of noose used. If the rope is tied as a running noose, the weight of the body tightens the rope to the extent that it presses an almost horizontal groove around the neck. With a fixed noose, on the other hand, there is enough slack for the rope from which the victim is hanging to distort the noose by pulling it upward at an angle, making a mark like an inverted letter V on the victim's neck. Because a fixed noose pulls to one side, the victim's head often tilts away from the vertical part of the rope, so the rope mark may not run right around the neck.

Whether the hanging was self-inflicted or the work of a murderer, the victim usually shows the effects of asphyxia. When the oxygen supply to the blood fails, the deoxygenated blood turns a characteristic blue color that can be seen in a blueness of the lips and tongue. The tongue often protrudes between the lips, the pupils of the eyes are usually dilated, and because the blood supply to the head is cut off by the rope, the face is literally deathly pale.

Since these effects can also be caused by straightforward strangulation, forensic examiners pay particularly close attention to the neck of the victim to search for any bruising or other injuries that would not have

OPPOSITE The beam where the murdered wife was supposed to have hanged herself in the 1925 case.

BELOW Michael Hutchence, leader of the musical group INXS, who allegedly committed suicide by hanging in 1997.

been caused by a noose. A search of the scene of the hanging may also reveal inconsistencies if there has been a deliberate attempt to confuse the picture. A genuine suicide, for example, found hanging clear of the ground, would have used a ladder or a chair to stand on while putting on the noose, and this would be found at the scene.

One murderer who tried to fake his wife's suicide in southern England in 1925 overlooked a most basic detail. He claimed to have found his wife hanging after she had committed suicide, and explained that he had cut down her body before calling the police. Forensic examiners checked the beam from which the rope was supposed to have hung and found it covered in dust with no sign of disturbance by a rope or anything else.

Strangulation by ligature

If a victim is strangled by a ligature, such as rope or cord, being pulled tight around the neck, forensic examiners will find marks on the neck revealing the cause of death. These

usually appear as a more or less horizontal groove, which is situated lower down the neck than it would be had the victim been hanged, since in that case the body falls into the ligature under gravity.

Some deductions about the type of ligature used can be made from the appearance of the marks. A deep and narrow mark indicates some form of wire, cord, or cable was used, while a broader, shallower scar is more likely to have been caused by a tie, a belt, pantihose or a scarf, for example. Generally speaking the softer the material, the less obvious the mark at first sight, but if enough force has been applied to cause the victim's death, then some kind of discernible mark is bound to be present.

If the ligature is found at the scene, it can become vital evidence in its own right. The material used may have a link with the victim or, more importantly, with the attacker. Even the way in which the ligature is used can provide clues. Some killers simply loop the ends around one another and pull, in the manner of the Thug ritual stranglers of ancient India; others use a knot of some kind. The ligature used by the infamous Boston

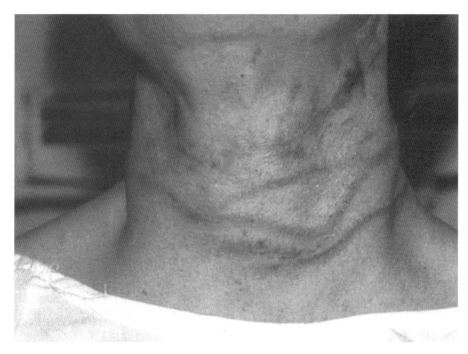

Strangler to kill his thirteen victims in the early 1960s was tied in a characteristic knot that identified each of the deaths as his handiwork.

The use of a ligature requires less pressure on the victim than is necessary in manual strangulation. As a result there is less obvious bruising around the neck, the cartilage of the larynx and windpipe may be intact, and there may be less muscular damage. Other hemorrhages may be revealed by blood in the brain tissues, for example, and there may also be damage to the neck muscles and thyroid cartilage.

Some victims found dead with a ligature around the neck are suicides. In such cases the

ABOVE A pathologist applies transparent adhesive tape to a ligature mark to lift any fibers onto paper for microscopic examination.

OPPOSITE The sensitive skin around the neck can reveal bruises from the strangler's fingers or abrasion from a strangling cord.

BELOW Murder equipment used by British serial killer Denis Nilson to torture and kill his victims.

ligature is usually deliberately tied with a double knot in order to maintain the pressure even as the victim loses consciousness. It may even be wound two or three times around the neck to make sure. However in suicide cases, the hyoid bone is usually found to be intact.

Hanging

The scene of a hanging usually betrays all too clearly what has happened, but still two main questions face forensic examiners. First, did the victim die from hanging, or was he or she already dead before the body was hanged? And second, if the victim died as a result of the hanging, was it murder or was it suicide?

Hanging is a special case of a ligature strangulation where the pressure around the neck is maintained by gravity acting on the victim's body. This causes the neck to be compressed, which closes off the vessels supplying blood to the brain and also the air passages, causing a loss of consciousness, and then death by asphyxia follows shortly after.

Other indications of the manner of death depend on how far the body has fallen, or the force with which the body fell, during the hanging. If the drop was only slight, there may be relatively little damage to the neck muscles, although there is often thyroid damage, and the hyoid bone is usually broken. If the body has dropped a matter of feet, then the neck muscles may be ruptured and the spine dislocated from the shock of the noose suddenly tightening around the neck under the full weight of the body.

Hanging victims can die without actually being clear of the floor. Suicides who lack a strong enough overhead fitting have succeeded in hanging themselves from furniture or doorknobs. Falling from a crouching position can exert the necessary pressure to the neck, even though most of the body weight is still supported by the floor. Dying by this method

BELOW The mummified body of Tollund Man dating from 240–20 BC. This well preserved body found in Jutland, Denmark belonged to a man aged between 30 and 40, hanged with a braided leather noose in either a murder or a religious sacrifice.

usually takes longer than it does by conventional hanging, and forensic examiners usually find signs of gradual asphyxia in the victim. These include a swollen face with a purple tinge and many pinpoint hemorrhages around the eyes, as well as in the voice box and windpipe.

In the eighteenth-century in England, when hanging was a common penalty for even trivial crimes, the convict was tied up, the noose placed around the neck, then he or she was hoisted off the ground by the rope. If the noose was not pulled sufficiently tight, the unfortunate criminal could take a long time to die, and it became common for friends, relatives, or the executioner—if suitably bribed—to hasten death by hanging on to the criminal's feet, thereby increasing the pressure on the neck. Later, efforts were made to ensure a quicker death by using a tighter noose and a longer drop. The rope then tightened with a jerk, dislocating the neck and severing the spinal cord, leading to almost instantaneous death of the victim.

ABOVE Re-enactment of a murder by hanging at Blackfriars Bridge, London.

LEFT A public hanging at Tyburn in London, in the early 17th century.

Michel Eyraud

TOP Michel Eyraud.

ABOVE Gabrielle Bompard.

In the high summer of 1889, the small riverside community of Millery near Lyon in southern France was disturbed by a terrible smell. A council workman was sent to investigate, and found a rotting corpse, tied up in a canvas sack, among bushes by the riverbank. The remains were taken to the Lyon city morgue, a barge on the River Rhône that smelled strongly of the investigations conducted on board. There the local forensic pathologist, Dr. Paul Bernard, began his examination.

Though the identity of the body was a mystery, Dr. Bernard found the injuries to the neck showed that the victim had died from strangulation, possibly with a ligature. Evidence from the skull led him to suggest that the victim's age had been about thirty-five.

Police investigations turned up a trunk that smelled as strongly as the body and had almost certainly been used to transport it. The trunk's labels showed that it had been sent from Paris to Lyon just over two weeks before the discovery of the remains. Checks of the missing persons files in Paris revealed that a notorious womanizer called Toussaint-Augsent Gouffé had been reported missing on the day that the trunk had been dispatched to Lyon. Assumptions that the corpse was that of the missing Gouffé were initially confounded when the man's brother-in-law reported that Gouffé had chestnut-colored hair: the hair and beard of the corpse were both jet black.

LEFT Engraving showing a reconstruction of the Gouffé murder.

When Dr. Bernard soaked a hair sample in distilled water, however, the black dissolved to reveal a bright chestnut color. The corpse was then delivered to the foremost criminal pathologist in France and a pioneer of scientific detection, Dr. Alexandre Lacassagne, professor of forensic medicine at the University of Lyon. Dr. Lacassagne was convinced that death had been caused by manual strangulation. Examination of the bones also showed a defect in the right knee which would have produced a definite limp. After studying the victim's teeth, he amended Bernard's estimate of the victim's age to about fifty. Since Gouffé had been forty-nine and had walked with a noticeable limp, the identity of the corpse seemed certain, especially when samples of hair from the corpse were matched with hairs from Gouffé's own hairbrush.

A huge publicity campaign, aided by a replica of the trunk used to transport Gouffé's remains to Lyon, produced a pair of suspects: Michel Eyraud and his mistress Gabrielle Bompard, who had been seen buying a similar trunk in Paris. It later emerged that the pair had lured Gouffé to Bompard's apartment, where they intended to kill him before raiding his offices. They tried to hang him by winding Bompard's dressing-gown cord around his neck and then passing it over an overhead pulley, but the knot failed to hold. Eyraud was forced to strangle Gouffé with his bare hands, after which the couple ransacked his office but failed to find most of his money.

After sending the trunk with Gouffé's remains to Lyon, the pair fled to North America. When Eyraud suggested repeating the crime they parted company, and Bompard returned to France. Eyraud was caught almost two years later in Cuba, and finally extradited to France where the couple were tried for murder. Bompard was given a twenty-year sentence, and Eyraud was sent to the guillotine.

ABOVE Engraving showing the arrest of Michel Eyraud in Havana, Cuba.

LEFT A replica of the trunk used to transport the remains of Gouffé's body, which was first identified by its smell.

Drowning and Burning

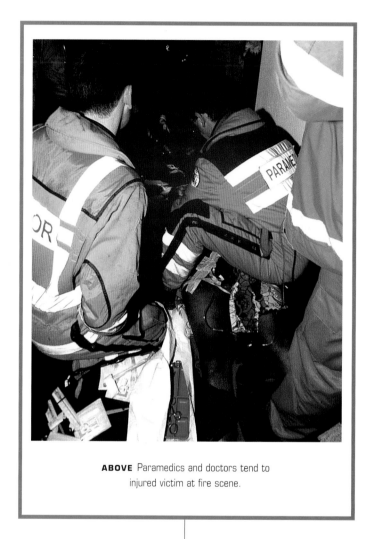

ABOVE Paramedics and doctors tend to injured victim at fire scene.

Drowning and burning are two further circumstances in which a victim may have suffered an accident or murderous attack, or have committed suicide. Deaths by drowning or burning are usually brought about by tragic accidents, though once again forensic experts check carefully that the apparent circumstances are indeed those in which the victim died, and have not simply been used to obliterate evidence of a more sinister death.

When a body is found dead in water in any circumstances—including lying face down in a puddle—forensic scientists must determine whether the victim died of drowning or hypothermia as a result of being in the water, or whether he or she was already dead before falling or being placed in the water.

From the medical point of view, drowning has similarities to asphyxia or suffocation, in that the victim dies because air cannot reach the lungs, blocked in drowning by water, and the body is starved of oxygen. Signs indicating this lack of oxygen are revealed in the systems of genuine drowning victims, but the clarity of the evidence depends largely on how fiercely the victim fought to escape drowning. In a few cases of accidental drowning, a person falls into water while heavily intoxicated, so the struggle to survive is not as intense or as prolonged as that of a sober victim who is swept away in a swimming or boating accident and is fully aware of what is happening.

Evidence of drowning

A person drowns when water enters the lungs. This produces a fine frothy mixture of water, air, and mucus that appears at the mouth and nostrils. The weight of water in the lungs causes the body to swell and increase in weight so that it tends to float lower in the water than a live person would.

The body of a victim who has fallen into a swollen river or been swept away in an accident may provide additional indications of the circumstances. If he or she clutched at the banks or at foliage in an attempt to reach safety, soil, stones, twigs or leaves may still be held in the hands in the vice-like grip caused by muscular spasms in the final phases of drowning.

Injuries on the body are more difficult to interpret. The signs that normally indicate whether the injuries that caused death occurred before or after the body entered the water may be blurred by the effects of immersion, which can cause chemical changes to the blood, for example. If the water is fast-moving, as in river rapids or where waves break on rocks, the body may sustain severe injuries after death by drowning: the clarity of the evidence depends largely on the length of time the body remained in the water.

The autopsy provides more detailed evidence. After death by drowning, the lungs appear waterlogged, swollen, and soft to the touch, so that pressure on the surface of the lungs leaves

BELOW A bound body recovered from the water may not be a murder victim. Suicides often tie themselves up, and put weights in their clothes to ensure their attempts to take their own lives succeed.

a mark that is comparatively slow to fade. The frothy mixture of water, air, and mucus that appears in the nose and mouth of the victim is also present in the windpipe and lungs, and in many cases water is found in the throat and stomach. The stomach may also contain organisms from the water in which the body was found. In addition, most genuine cases of drowning show hemorrhages in the middle ear that are not present if, for example, the victim had died from heart failure or upon falling into the water.

There are apparent drowning cases where the victim does not actually die from drowning, but from the shock of suddenly being plunged into cold water. This condition is called "reflex cardiac arrest," and the victim dies from a heart attack rather than from the oxygen starvation caused by the interruption of the body's air supply. In these cases, the normal signs of drowning will not be found on the body. Sometimes victims who were deeply intoxicated when they fell into the water may die from this condition. In other cases, they can drown in a puddle only inches deep because the mouth and nostrils were under water, and anoxia resulted before they realized what was happening.

Examining the clues

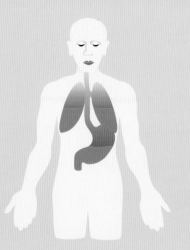

1 Wet Drowning—a mixture of air and water comes up from the lungs to fill the mouth and nostrils.

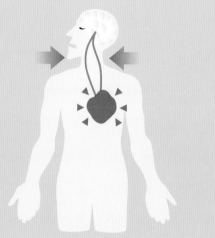

2 Vagal Inhibition—water enters the nose and causes a spasm of the larynx to press on the vagus nerve and stop the heart.

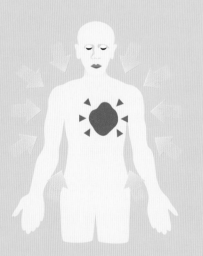

3 Shock—caused by sudden exposure to cold can result in an instant heart attack.

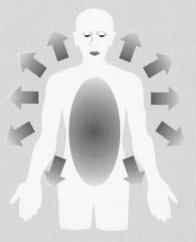

4 Hypothermia—caused by prolonged immersion in water, results in a drop in the body's core temperature, followed by unconsciousness and death.

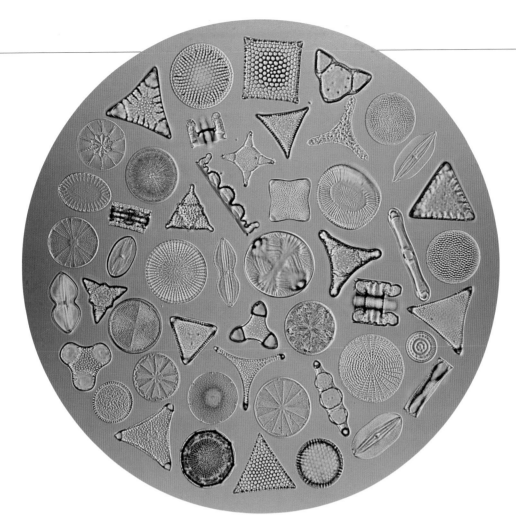

Time of drowning

The process of decay in water is different than that which occurs in bodies buried, or left exposed on land. First of all, in water the cooling process after death occurs twice as quickly, and in cases where a victim suffered death from hypothermia rather than by drowning, the core temperature of the body may already be appreciably lower than normal when the process of post-mortem cooling begins to set in.

Post-mortem lividity is less obvious with a corpse immersed in water: here the skin appears unnaturally white, with a "goose-flesh" effect from when the body's hair follicles became erect, a reflex intended to retain body heat as long as possible. Rigor mortis can take longer to develop and longer to disappear because the temperature of the water slows

ABOVE Diatoms, microscopic algae-like creatures found in the lungs, stomach, bloodstream, and bone marrow of drowning victims.

down the chemical processes that trigger these post-mortem changes. A body may be in water for up to four full days before all traces of rigor disappear.

After a week or more in the water, chemical changes within the body cause the abdomen to fill with gas. This increases the buoyancy of the body so that it floats on the surface of the water. As a result, many drowning victims not retrieved earlier tend to be found at this stage. The conversion of body fats into a hard residue, which normally takes place after around four to six months on land, may take much longer in water, particularly if the temperature is low.

Place of drowning

Blood tests can indicate whether a victim died by drowning in fresh or in saltwater, provided tests are carried out soon enough after death. Fresh water, found in rivers, ponds, and most lakes as well as canals and other inland waterways, is able to pass through the tiny blood vessels in the lungs and find its way into the heart and the rest of the circulatory system, where it has the effect of diluting the blood and reducing its chlorine content.

The salt in sea water, on the other hand, absorbs water from the blood, thereby increasing the proportion of chlorine present instead of diluting it. This clearly defined difference can help investigators faced with a body found where a river enters tidal water: the chemical changes that occurred when the victim drowned can indicate where and when the incident took place.

Another accurate pointer to the place of drowning involves analyzing body organs for the presence of tiny organisms called diatoms (see p. 103). These are present in all water sources that contain normal biosystems. A victim of drowning inhales these organisms along with the water that causes the drowning, and they are absorbed into the internal organs. When the autopsy is carried out, the presence of diatoms can be verified by dissolving sections of the internal organs in strong acids, which then reveal the silica shells of the diatoms if they are present. The shells can then be identified by close inspection under a microscope.

The presence of diatoms in a waterborne body gives two useful clues. First, it indicates that the victim was almost certainly alive when he or she entered the water. Second, there are many different species of these organisms and they are identifiable by the shape and size of their skeletons, so the species or combination of species found in the victim's body may help to show the approximate area where the original drowning took place.

Examining the clues

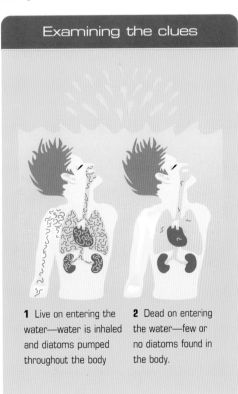

1 Live on entering the water—water is inhaled and diatoms pumped throughout the body

2 Dead on entering the water—few or no diatoms found in the body.

TOP A victim of Wayne Williams (see pages 60-1) lies face down in a boat after being pulled from the Chattahoochee river.

OPPOSITE Retrieving a body to find the cause and time of death.

Burning victims

As with drowning, cases of burning are more often than not the result of accidents rather than of homicide, though here too investigators must bear in mind that the body may have been deliberately burned in an attempt to disguise some other cause of death. This involves checking the body to determine which of the injuries were caused by burning, whether or not those injuries were inflicted before or after death, and which factors actually caused death.

There are six degrees of burn injuries, classified in ascending order of severity according to a scheme first set out by French surgeon Baron Guillaume Dupuytren almost two centuries ago. First-degree burns cause the skin to become inflamed and swollen and scales of the skin surface to be shed. Second-degree burns show blistering, third- and fourth-degree burns show partial or entire destruction of the victim's skin, and fifth-degree burns destroy the muscles. Sixth-degree burns, the most severe, also show bone destruction. Burn injuries are also classified in terms of the percentage of body area affected.

Many victims found in burned-out structures die from smoke suffocation or carbon monoxide poisoning, which happen

LEFT A fire at the entrance of the Happyland nightclub in New York's Bronx caused 87 deaths.

OPPOSITE ABOVE London's King's Cross disaster, in 1987, where smoke and fire poured through a crowded subway station.

quickly, rather than from the burns themselves. In such cases the autopsy shows signs of oxygen starvation. This may be caused by smoke inhalation, a possibility that can be confirmed by the presence of soot particles in the windpipe. Blood tests can also show the presence of carbon monoxide at a level high enough to cause death, while the presence of any carbon monoxide or soot within the victim's body confirms he or she was still alive when the fire started. If none of these signs are found, then the victim must have been dead before the blaze took hold.

Examination of the victim's burns can give an indication of the sequence of events. In general, burns suffered while the victim was still alive have a higher proportion of white cells in the blood count, because the body's natural defenses mobilized at the time in an effort to contain the damage. Fluid from the blisters at the site of the burns can also be tested for proteins: their presence indicates that the victim was alive when they formed.

Some severe burns—even those sustained after death—can cause the body tissues to rupture in a manner very similar to that caused by a battering from fists or blunt instruments. But careful analysis shows whether or not there has been underlying bleeding as a result of the wounds. If the splitting of the tissues was caused by heat, the blood will already have coagulated and there will be no signs of bleeding, as there would be in injuries caused by battering.

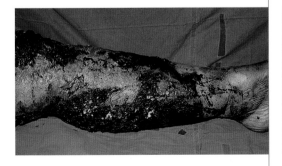

ABOVE Severe leg burns caused by the hot fat from a deep frier pan.

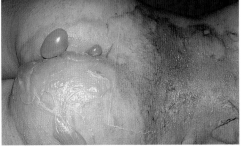

ABOVE Blistering and skin ruptures on the back of a fire accident victim.

Robert Maxwell

ABOVE Maxwell's yacht, the *Lady Ghislaine*.

BELOW Robert Maxwell shortly before his death in 1991.

In the fall of 1991, British publisher and newspaper tycoon Robert Maxwell was cruising in his luxury yacht, the *Lady Ghislaine*. One morning the crew was shocked to find he was no longer on board. He had last been seen on deck the evening before. A search was made and his dead body was eventually found in the sea off the Canary Islands in the northeast Atlantic Ocean. The subsequent enquiry came under the jurisdiction of the Spanish authorities, because the Canary Islands group is Spanish territory.

At the time, press speculation centered on Maxwell's known links with Israel and his rumored involvement with Mossad, the Israeli intelligence service, and there was a suggestion that his connections may have made him the target of a sophisticated professional assassination. Had that been the case, Maxwell would almost certainly have been dead before he entered the water, since otherwise the alarm might have been raised and Maxwell could have been rescued.

Spanish experts carried out an autopsy and found that diatoms were present in Maxwell's blood and body tissues, showing clearly that he had died after he entered the water. There was no evidence of other injuries to suggest that a murder attempt had taken place, but one curious feature of the body was the fact that the lungs were not full of water. This

LEFT Maxwell on board the *Lady Ghislaine* from which he disappeared.

could have been due to a condition known as "dry drowning," where the shock of falling into the water causes a spasm of the larynx. This triggers a body reflex which is similar to the reaction of the system to a sudden and severe increase in blood pressure: the heart stops, bringing about death in seconds. The only question the enquiry could not answer was whether Maxwell had entered the water accidentally or deliberately, since rumors of the shakiness of his business empire could have motivated him to make a suicide attempt.

BELOW Maxwell's body was found floating 12 hours after his disappearance and became the subject of a detailed and lengthy investigation.

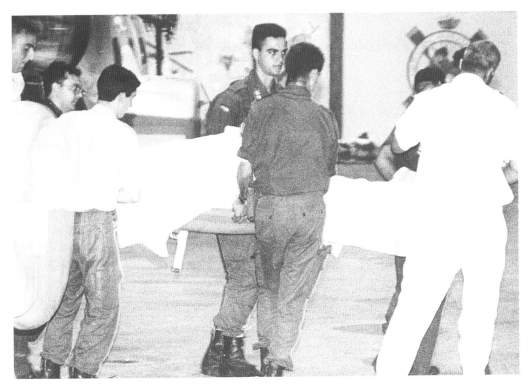

The Smoking Gun

ABOVE This 19th century engraving of French and Austrian soldiers at Edelsberg Bridge near Vienna in 1809 shows how the short range of smooth-bore muskets led to fighting at very close quarters.

Ever since smooth-bore pistols and muskets were replaced by mass-produced rifled weapons (in the late eighteenth century, around the time of the War of Independence), each spent bullet has had an individual tale to tell. Thanks to the process of rifling, cutting internal helical grooves similar to a screw thread in the barrel of a firearm, the fired bullet spins as it emerges from the barrel. This prevents the projectile from tumbling in flight and greatly increases its accuracy, making rifled weapons essential for hunters and soldiers alike.

RIGHT Bullets and spent cartridges can provide vital evidence.

From the viewpoint of forensic scientists, the main benefit of rifling is not that it makes a bullet fly more predictably to its target, but the fact that it imparts an individual identity to every single gun. When bullets are fired through the barrel, the rifling grooves create marks on the bullet's surface in a pattern unique to that weapon, and a similar pattern of marks appears on any bullet fired from that weapon, because the material of which bullets are made is softer than that of gun barrels.

When bullets were introduced that were encapsulated with the explosive charge in a single cased cartridge, more clues became available to investigators. As a charge explodes within the barrel it expands in both directions, driving the bullet forward and the cartridge case backward with considerable force against the breech of the weapon. The case, ejected as the shot is fired, carries imprint details of imperfections in the face of the breech and of parts of the gun mechanism such as the firing pin. These patterns once again vary from

weapon to weapon, but are virtually identical on any cartridge case used in a particular firearm.

ABOVE Weapons used in crime include revolvers and automatics, rifles and sawed-off shotguns.

BELOW High-speed photo of a .30 revolver bullet cutting through a playing card from edge to edge.

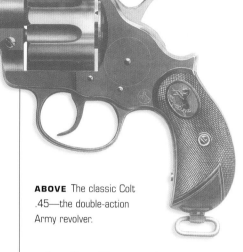

Classes of weapon

In mass-produced guns, particular makes and models of weapon are given the same standardized characteristics, including the barrel's internal diameter or caliber, the number of grooves in its rifling, and the direction in which the grooves spiral from breech to muzzle. This is very useful to forensic examiners and helps them to deduce the make and class of the weapon from any bullets found at the scene of a crime or in the body of a gunshot victim.

For example, Colt and Browning revolvers both have six grooves in the rifling, but those in the Colt turn anti-clockwise, whereas those in the Browning turn clockwise. Webley revolvers also have a clockwise spiral but have seven rifling grooves, while Smith and Wesson weapons have a clockwise spiral and only five grooves. Other variations between one make of weapon and another lie in the relative width of the rifling grooves and the "lands," the sections of barrel that are left between successive grooves.

ABOVE The classic Colt .45—the double-action Army revolver.

Firearm "fingerprints"

While the design differences between different classes, makes and models of weapon can help identify which kind was used at a specific

crime, the evidence needed for a positive identification of an individual weapon must be much more precise. The internal surfaces of an individual barrel carry fine lines or striations on both the grooves and the lands. These are

BELOW A French forensic laboratory analyzing the interior of a gun barrel.

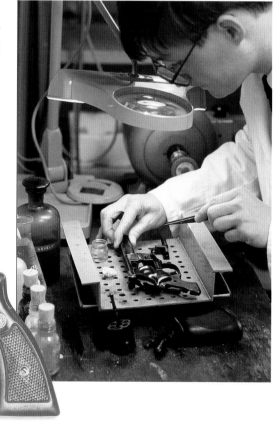

ABOVE The compact Smith & Wesson .38 revolver.

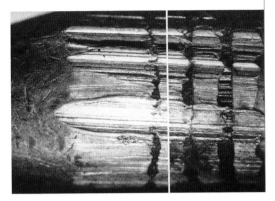

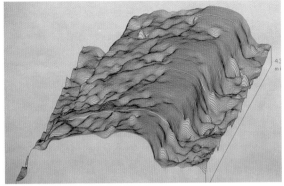

caused by surface defects on the cutting tool used to make the barrel, or by chips of steel scratched across the barrel's internal surfaces by the action of the cutter.

Unless the barrel is cut open for analysis, however, these striations normally remain unseen and cannot be recorded and measured. Nevertheless, the striations present in the barrel of each individual gun produce a characteristic set of marks on any bullet fired from that barrel. By firing a test bullet from a suspect weapon, then lining it up in a comparison microscope alongside a bullet from the crime scene, a positive match of these individual markings can be made with a greater degree of accuracy.

The New York Bureau of Forensic Ballistics was founded in 1923 by Charles Waite and Philip Gravelle. Waite was a deputy district attorney who had been appalled to see an innocent man almost executed six years previously because of worthless testimony regarding the identification of the murder weapon. Gravelle was the microscopist who invented the comparison microscope, a piece of equipment now indispensable to ballistics investigations (see Chapter One).

Waite died in 1926, but by then Calvin Goddard, a U.S. Army medical doctor and firearms expert, had joined the team. Goddard used Waite's collection of information on the standard calibers and rifling features of

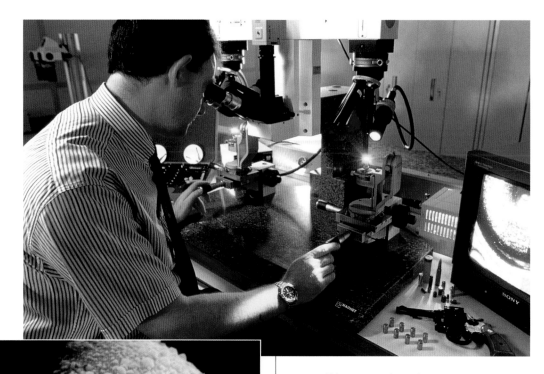

ABOVE Using a comparison microscope.

LEFT Scanning electron microscope image of particles of firing residue.

different makes and models of guns to great advantage. He also developed forensic ballistic techniques by working with the comparison microscope and a device called a helixometer, a hollow probe fitted with a light source and a magnifying lens that allows examination of the marks on the inside of a gun barrel.

The comparison microscope used for ballistics examinations has two cylindrical bullet-holders side by side beneath the examining lens system. Each of the holders can be rotated independently so that similar parts of the surface of the two bullets can be lined up to find a matching pattern. They can then be rotated simultaneously to compare other points of resemblance.

Experts cannot always establish a match complete in all respects. Sometimes particles of grit or rust within the barrel alter some of the markings impressed on bullets fired at different times. If a series of bullets has been fired between the firing of the suspect bullet and the test bullet, some internal wear of the barrel will have taken place in the intervening period. Similarly, if the bullet found at the crime scene is distorted, having passed through the victim's body or other obstructions, establishing a match is not straightforward. With expert knowledge and experience, however, it is usually possible.

Shotguns

The shotgun is an important exception as far as rifling is concerned. Instead of firing a single bullet, the explosion of the charge in the cartridge discharges a spray of small lead pellets which diverge as they fly through the air. Shotguns may be single- or double-barreled; in the latter the two barrels are arranged either side by side or one on top of the other. Each barrel usually needs to be reloaded once the cartridge has been fired. This is done by "breaking" the gun, folding the barrels downward to open the breeches and allow the discharged cartridges to be ejected and new ones to be fitted. The gun is then "cocked" by closing the breeches. Single-barreled shotguns are reloaded in exactly the same way.

Other types of shotgun, known as "pump-action" guns, carry several cartridges in an internal magazine, so the user can reload by pushing a slider backward and forward. Shotguns used for hunting have long barrels to minimize the spread of the pellets as far as possible, thus extending the weapon's lethal range. Shotguns are sometimes used by criminals at short range, however, a foot or more having been sawed off the barrels' length makes the guns easier to hide. At almost point-blank range, where the shotgun is most dangerous to a human target, the spread of the pellets is negligible.

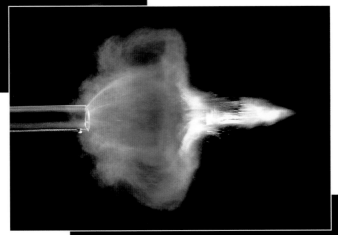

ABOVE High speed photograph of a charge of pellets leaving the muzzle of a 12-bore shotgun, taken 2.8 milliseconds after detonation.

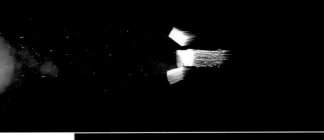

ABOVE RIGHT Four milliseconds after the cartridge detonates, a puff of smoke and gunpowder residues leave the barrel in the wake of the shot.

RIGHT The plastic wad separating from the shot after 5.7 milliseconds.

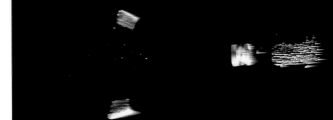

RIGHT After 7 milliseconds, particles of the wad that seals the front end of the cartridge falls away, and the charge of pellets begins to spread out.

Gunshot wounds

The appearance of a gunshot wound depends on the range at which the weapon was fired. Establishing the range is important in helping forensic investigators to determine exactly what happened. A case of apparent suicide would be immediately suspicious if the evidence showed that the gun had been fired from farther than arm's length from the victim's body. Equally, a claim of self-defense may be easier to prove if the evidence shows that the gun was shot at close range, when discharging the weapon might have been the user's last line of defense.

In cases where victim and assailant are at close quarters, and particularly where a struggle is taking place, the gun may be fired with the muzzle pressing against the victim's body. In such cases, the hot gases and soot particles produced by the discharge of the cartridge are driven into the skin and cause burning at the edges of the wound. If the wound was made through clothing, then the fibers around the hole in the cloth made by the bullet may be scorched or melted by the heat of the discharge, and the material may show a star-shaped tear pattern around the bullet hole.

If the gun is held more loosely against the body of the victim, there may be room for the

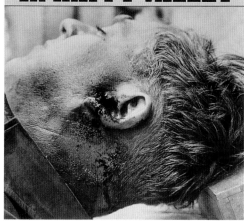

ABOVE Photo of the body of Josslyn Hay, 22nd Earl of Erroll, found dead from a gunshot wound to the head, in the "Happy Valley" scandal in Kenya in 1941.

LEFT Forensic examiner checking the clothing around a bullet hole for signs of the range at which the weapon was fired.

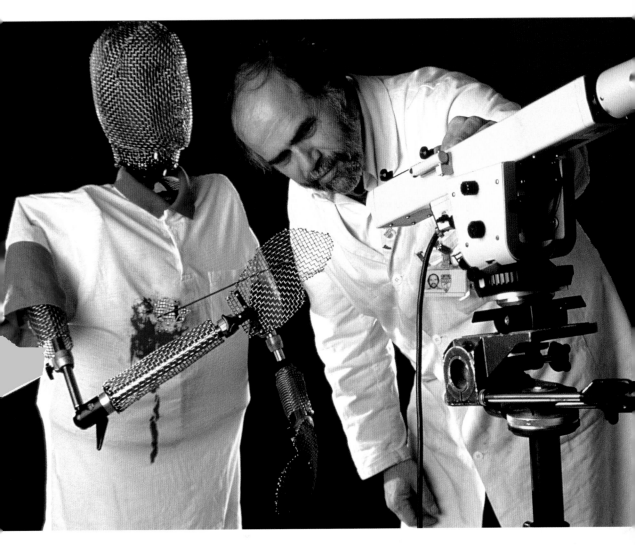

hot gases to escape through the gap between muzzle and victim. The gases, carrying particles of soot with them, then leave a wider ring of discolored skin around the entry wound. If the gun is pointing straight at the victim, the ring will be circular, but if it is pointed at an angle, the ring will be distorted into an oval mark, its longest axis lying along the angle at which the gun barrel was held.

If the weapon is fired from a slightly longer range, then particles of unburned and partly-burned powder are driven into the skin, causing a pattern called "tattooing." If the victim was alive when the wound was inflicted, the tattooing is usually orange or brown in color, but if the wound was inflicted when the victim was already dead, then the color is a

more subdued gray-yellow. If the wound is inflicted through the victim's clothing, the powder residues leave a clearly visible pattern, the spread of which is an indication of the range at which the shot was fired.

To make the most accurate estimation of the range, a ballistics examiner usually fires the suspect weapon from varying distances into cloth or fabric that is as similar to the victim's clothing as possible. The range that leaves the pattern most closely resembling that on the victim's clothing, given identical ammunition, is then the most likely range at which the shot was fired.

Entry and exit wounds

Examiners can expect to find patterns of soot around a bullet wound if it was made from a range of between twelve and eighteen inches. Scattered specks of unburned and partially-burned powder grains can be found if the shot was fired at a range of up to twenty-five inches, and scattered grains are occasionally found where the range was up to thirty-six inches. Beyond that distance, the only extraneous marking found around a bullet entry wound is a dark ring called "bullet wipe." The mark, made up of lead, carbon, oil and dirt, is brushed from the surface of the bullet as it enters the body.

In most cases the gunshot wound shows a circular or oval entry hole, drilled through the tissues by the shape of the bullet. By the time the bullet leaves the victim's body, it may have been distorted by impact with bone, or caused to tumble on its way through. Both these circumstances tend to produce exit wounds larger and more irregularly shaped than entry wounds, and there is no abrasion of the skin around the cavity.

Shotgun wounds, being caused by a spray of small particles, are entirely different. The degree of spread of the particles forms a measure of the range at which the gun was fired. At very short ranges, the shot has hardly any chance to spread and the whole charge tears a deep and concentrated wound through layers of the victim's body, leaving localized scorching and tattooing.

When the gun is fired more than three feet away from the victim's body, the pattern of holes caused by the pellets penetrating the skin begins to spread. At ranges of more than four feet the severity of the wound begins to reduce as the pattern of pellet-holes widens still further, leaving no sign of powder marking. However, the spread depends on the design of the weapon and the amount of "choke" or constriction of the barrel present. The choke is designed to extend the weapon's range by reducing the spread of the shot on leaving the muzzle. Once again the only reliable way for a forensic examiner to determine the range of the shot is to fire a series of test shots with the gun used in a particular incident to find the range at which the spread most closely resembles the signs found on the victim.

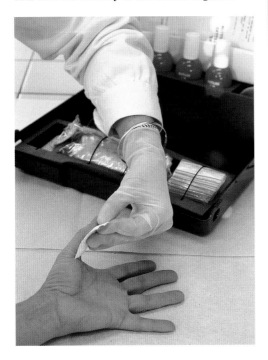

ABOVE Taking a swab from a suspect's hand to test for microscopic particles of gunpowder, and the presence of chemicals like cordite, widely used in cartridges as a propellant.

OPPOSITE PAGE The bodyguard of the speaker of the Egyptian Parliament, Rifaat al-Mahgoub, killed by a spray of automatic fire in a successful assassination attempt.

RIGHT Head X-ray of a murder victim shows groups of shotgun pellets across the face, and at the left-hand end of the jaw.

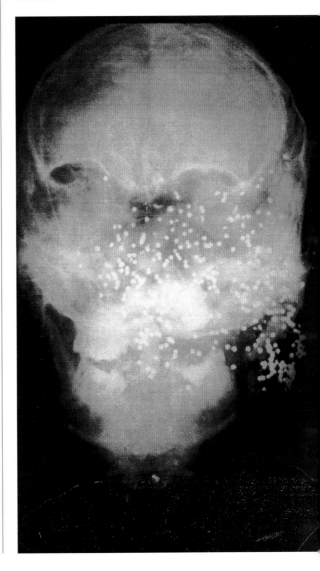

Other types
of weapon

Most firearms other than shotguns are categorized as either handguns or rifles. Handguns can be revolvers or pistols. Revolvers have a series of cartridges loaded into a cylindrical magazine which moves around at the discharge of each shot to bring the next round into the breech. They can be "single-action," where the user has to pull back the hammer to rotate the magazine and cock the firing mechanism, or "double-action," where this is achieved automatically by pressing hard on the trigger. Automatic pistols, on the other hand, usually have a series of rounds held in a vertical magazine inside the handle of the weapon. All the user has to do to fire the weapon is pull the trigger: the ejection of the spent cartridge, the loading of the next round into the breech and the cocking of the weapon are all carried out by the gun's own internal mechanism.

ABOVE Massed ranks of seized handguns in a court office.

LEFT A salesman demonstrates a Smith & Wesson .357 Magnum pistol in Florida, 1987.

Rifles can be classified as target, sporting or military, and their actions vary in a similar way to those of handguns. Many rifles carry a series of rounds in an internal magazine, but most use a bolt action to reload. When the bolt is pulled back, the spent cartridge is ejected; when it is pushed forward and turned, it pushes a new round into the breech and cocks the firing mechanism. Other rifles, particularly those designed for military use, eject the used round and load a new one by automatic action, so again all the user has to do is pull the trigger.

Not all weapons use explosively-propelled bullets. Poachers and hunters have traditionally used quieter air-operated weapons to shoot game. Commercially-made airguns and air pistols are hardly the most powerful weapons, though they can produce a serious wound at short range. Occasionally, however, investigators have had to deal with more powerful homemade weapons charged with compressed air and designed to fire larger, more deadly projectiles.

Another type of ballistic weapon, which has little in common with firearms, is the powerful crossbow used by archers in the Middle Ages. A handful of criminals in the United Kingdom and at least one in Canada have used crossbows, which are operated by tightening a short and exceedingly powerful bow with a pair of cranked handles. When the bow is fired, it releases a short steel bolt with lethal force and almost silent operation. Alternatively the classic English long bow, beloved of medieval outlaw Robin Hood, can fire an arrow with sufficient force to penetrate a suit of armor, and a skilled archer can fire a third arrow while the first and second are still in flight.

ABOVE The battle of Agincourt in 1415, where ranks of humbly-born English long bowmen slaughtered the flower of French chivalry with rapid volleys of arrows, deadly accurate and lethal through full armor.

LEFT Author and keen hunter Ernest Hemingway nets two pheasants. On July 2, 1961, depressed over his work, he committed suicide with a shotgun at his home in Ketchum, Idaho.

Bullets and cartridges

For more than one hundred and fifty years, the design of cartridges for both handguns and rifles has followed the same general pattern. A cylindrical cartridge case, usually made of brass, holds the main propellant charge used to fire the bullet. The front end of the cartridge is sealed by the bullet, and at the back a small cap contains a charge of primer. When the gun is fired, the firing pin strikes the cap and detonates the primer, which then sets off the main charge and fires the bullet straight down the barrel.

A ballistics expert can usually link the shape and design of the cartridge to a particular type and model of gun. Some cartridges have the primer cap in the center and others have the primer arranged around the rim of the cartridge case; there are also differences in the bullets used in the cartridges, and all this information can help the expert to identify the ammunition used in a given incident.

Most pistols and rifles used for sport or target-shoot purposes use lead bullets. These may be round-nosed, sharp-nosed, cylindrical or hollow-pointed so that they expand on

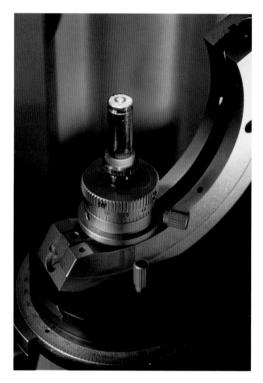

ABOVE Analyzing the marks left by the impact of the firing pin on the end of the cartridge case, for comparison.

RIGHT An instrument which can measure the pattern of surface roughness around a bullet, for identification.

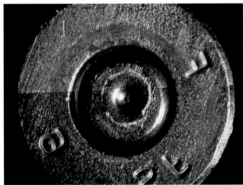

ABOVE Colt revolver and bullets.

ABOVE Different types of bullets and cartridges, classified and stored in a French ballistics laboratory.

LEFT Comparing the markings left on the bases of cartridges.

impact. They are essentially "soft" bullets and would be unsuitable for high-velocity weapons such as military rifles and automatic pistols. Such weapons use bullets with a lead or steel core that is wholly or partially enclosed in a jacket made of aluminum or alloys of copper with zinc or nickel. Specialized armor-piercing, tracer or incendiary bullets are also used in more sophisticated military weapons.

Shotgun cartridges are larger versions of rifle and pistol cartridges and comprise a charge, a case and a primer cap. Instead of a bullet, the front end of the cartridge is sealed by a wad, a disk of compressed cardboard, and a plastic body filled with small shotgun pellets. Crimped cardboard holds the pellets in place. Some shotgun cartridges, intended for shooting at large animals such as deer or bears, are fitted with solid, large-caliber bullets.

Sacco and Vanzetti

ABOVE Bullets recovered from the body of Allesandro Berardelli, together with cartridges found at the scene—the third bullet from the left, deformed by impact, inflicted the fatal wound.

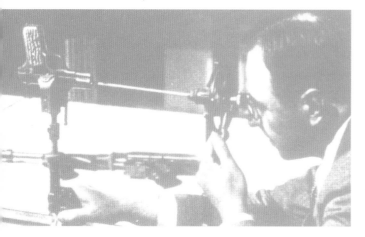

ABOVE Calvin Goddard inspecting a gun barrel with a helixometer.

On the afternoon of April 15, 1920, two security guards were delivering a shoe-company payroll of more than $15,000 in the small Massachusetts town of South Braintree. Two men suddenly appeared and opened fire, killing both security guards. They seized the cash and loaded it into a getaway car before driving off at high speed. Horrified eye-witnesses reported that the men were of "Italian" appearance, and one had a prominent drooping mustache. Police searching the scene discovered a range of spent cartridges that were later identified as having been manufactured by three different munitions companies: Peters, Remington and Winchester.

The getaway car was found abandoned in woodland, and a search revealed links to an earlier robbery that implicated an Italian criminal named Boda. When police raided his house they found he had fled, leaving behind the heavily mustached Bartolomeo Vanzetti, aged thirty-two, and Nicola Sacco, aged twenty-nine. Both men were carrying loaded pistols. Sacco's was of the same caliber as one of the guns used to murder the guards, and in his pockets were cartridges made by Peters, Remington and Winchester. Both men were arrested and charged with murder.

It emerged that the men belonged to an anarchist movement that openly advocated violence to settle society's injustices, and their trial sharply polarized opinion. The prosecution insisted the men were guilty, while defense attorneys insisted that they were being persecuted for their beliefs. As far as the ballistics evidence was concerned, each side produced experts whose testimonies contradicted the others'.

The outcome of the trial ultimately depended on whether or not the bullet that had killed one of the guards, Alessandro Berardelli, had been fired from Sacco's .32 pistol. The ballistics experts found that the bullet used was no longer in production, indeed it was so outdated that they could find no similar ammunition to use in firing test rounds—apart from the unused cartridges found in Sacco's pockets. After tests, the two bullets were compared and the match was close enough to secure a guilty verdict. The defendants were sentenced to death.

The verdict was overturned, however, after a self-styled expert named Alexander Hamilton appeared and denounced the ballistics evidence as false. Hamilton's evidence had succeeded in misleading a jury in a murder trial six years earlier, even though it had been scientifically worthless. At that trial Charles Waite, who went on to found the Bureau of Forensic Ballistics with his partner Philip Gravelle, had shown that Hamilton's assertion that a particular gun had been used as a murder weapon had almost convicted an innocent man. For the time being, however, Hamilton caused sufficient doubt to raise a motion for a retrial.

At the retrial, Hamilton brought two new Colt revolvers into court and dismantled them, together with Sacco's gun. When he was caught trying to fit one of the new barrels onto the alleged murder weapon, the retrial was cancelled. By June 1927, Calvin Goddard of the Bureau of Forensic Ballistics in New York was able to show that a test bullet fired from Sacco's revolver matched one of the murder bullets perfectly. He used a comparison microscope and a helixometer and produced evidence clear enough to convince even the defense experts, so Sacco and Vanzetti went to the electric chair on August 23, 1927.

Nevertheless, the legend grew that Sacco and Vanzetti had been put to death for a crime they had not committed, and in spite of the fact that a team of forensic experts re-confirmed in 1961 that Sacco's gun was the murder weapon, the governor of Massachusetts in 1977 issued a special proclamation establishing the men's innocence, half a century after their execution. Yet another investigation in 1983 reaffirmed the truth of the ballistics evidence. Nevertheless, to this day the case remains highly controversial.

RIGHT Vanzetti and Sacco (center and right) being led to court in handcuffs.

BACKGROUND One of the demonstrations organized in support of Sacco and Vanzetti.

Georgi Markov

ABOVE Bulgarian dissident Georgi Markov was the second to be attacked by agents of the Bulgarian government.

Some twenty years before the collapse of the communist regimes of Eastern Europe during the 1990s, Georgi Markov was a Bulgarian dissident working for the BBC World Service in London, broadcasting to his former homeland. On the afternoon of September 7, 1978, he was waiting for a bus on Waterloo Bridge when he felt a sharp stabbing pain in his right thigh. He turned to see a man carrying a furled umbrella; the man mumbled an apology in a thick accent and hurried off to hail a cab.

Once home, Markov inspected the wound. It was a small red puncture mark at the back of his leg. By the following morning he was vomiting and running a high temperature, and was taken to hospital where the wound, now inflamed, was X-rayed. Nothing suspicious showed up on the films, but his temperature and blood-pressure were now dropping and his pulse racing. His white-cell count soared to three times the normal level and doctors suspected blood poisoning. He was treated with antibiotics but became delirious and subject to violent fits. He eventually died four days after the mysterious wound had been inflicted.

An autopsy was carried out and the section of tissue that contained the puncture wound was sent to the Porton Down chemical warfare research laboratories. There experts found, buried beneath the skin, a spherical pellet approximately the size of a pinhead with two tiny holes drilled in it. No trace could be found of any poison that might have caused Markov's illness and death, and the pellet was sent to the Metropolitan Police forensic laboratory where it was examined under a scanning electron microscope.

The pellet proved to be made of an alloy of platinum and iridium that was exceedingly hard and immune to corrosion—and virtually invisible on an X-ray plate. The holes in the pellet were large enough to hold a minute trace of poison, but their contents had dissipated. It was thought that the tiny pellet had been fired by some form of gas-operated gun hidden in the furled umbrella in a bid to assassinate Georgi Markov.

Identifying the poison became a process of elimination. Considering the minute size of the dose and its catastrophic effects, it was decided that the pellet must have been charged

BACKGROUND The specialized pellet gun concealed in the furled umbrella and used to murder Markov.

with ricin (see Chapter Four), a potential chemical warfare agent five hundred times more lethal than cyanide. The theory was tested by injecting a pig with a quantity of ricin similar to that which could have been contained in the pellet. The animal died within twenty-four hours, and its organs showed damage similar to that found at Markov's autopsy.

Though the Bulgarians denied any responsibility for the murder, another expatriate Bulgarian named Vladimir Kostov had suffered a similar attack in Paris a year earlier, but had recovered because the pellet had been fired into his back, well away from the main blood vessels. When a surgeon examined him, an identical pellet was found buried beneath his skin.

Following a change of regime in Bulgaria in 1991, the new government admitted that assassination attempts had been made on a number of former citizens living in the West, including Markov and Kostov.

TOP Scanning electron microscope used to examine the fatal pellet.

ABOVE Photomicrograph of the fatal pellet recovered from Markov's body.

RIGHT London's Waterloo Bridge, where the fatal blow was delivered.

The USS *Iowa*

he U.S. Navy is the only service in the world to maintain battleships as part of its active fleet since the end of World War Two. The Iowa class have a main armament of nine sixteen-inch guns mounted in three triple turrets. Each gun can fire a shell weighing some 2700 pounds with a range of up to twenty-four miles. To provide the colossal energy needed to achieve this, the guns are loaded with between five and seven bags of nitro-cellulose explosive, each bag weighing 93.4 pounds, in addition to the heavy shells.

During a firing drill on the battleship USS *Iowa* on April 19, 1989, five bags of the explosive being loaded into the center gun of number two turret exploded without warning, killing forty-seven seamen, including the entire crew of the armored turret. A Navy investigation found that the explosion had been caused by sabotage on the part of the petty officer in charge of the gun turret, in an attempt to commit suicide and claim the life of a former friend working at the bottom level of the turret. Both men died in the explosion, but their families strongly criticized the Navy's findings.

The Senate Armed Services Committee decided to commission explosives experts at Sandia National Laboratories to carry out a full technical investigation. When they checked the drill used to load the gun, they found that once the shell was placed in the barrel, the bags of explosives were pushed slowly up the barrel by a power-operated rammer until they were close to, but not in contact with, the shell. On the day of the exercise, the left gun was loaded in forty-four seconds and the right gun in sixty-one seconds. A recording of intercom messages showed that the sailor controlling the rammer of the center gun had reported a problem: eighty-three seconds later, the charges exploded.

The naval investigators claimed that analysis of debris in the gun-barrel showed traces of steel wool, brake fluid and calcium hypochlorite. They insisted that this had been

RIGHT Gun turrets of the USS *Iowa*—number two turret is in the background with its guns trained out to the side.

deliberately placed in the barrel as an incendiary device and had set off the charges when the pressure of the rammer was applied. The Sandia experts analyzed the traces and found they were made up of steel fibers, calcium and chlorine. But these elements were also found in the other gun turrets of the USS *Iowa*, as well as in those of her sister ships USS *Wisconsin* and USS *New Jersey*. Traces of these elements were found in lubricants and cleaning fluids used in the gun turrets, and in some cases were also found in sea water.

If the Navy's theory that there had been a deliberate attempt at sabotage and suicide was mistaken, what had really caused the explosion? Examiners found that the rammer on the center gun was pushing the explosive bags two feet farther up the barrel than it should have done, and other evidence suggested that the sailor controlling the rammer had been inexperienced and had operated the rammer much too quickly. Both these factors may have led to the explosives being slammed against the bulk of the shell with some force, but tests showed that such action did not detonate them. However it was found that extra sticks of explosive had been arranged in a loose layer at the top of each bag to make up the weight, and this would have imposed the additional stress necessary to cause the explosion.

When tests were carried out by dropping a steel weight representing the rammer onto bags of explosive containing a loose top layer, the bags exploded. As a result the Navy was able to change the loading procedure and ensure that a similar accident could not happen. Had the explosion been ascribed to sabotage, more sailors might have died in similar circumstances.

BELOW Crew members fighting the fire after number two turret exploded.

RIGHT Bodies of the gun turret crew at Dover AFB, Delaware.

Fire and Explosives

ABOVE Remains of a house totally wrecked by a gas explosion.

The terrible power of fire and explosives to obliterate evidence is harnessed by criminals both to achieve their aims directly and to disguise crimes committed by other means. Buildings and property are deliberately destroyed for insurance fraud; letter bombs and remote-control devices eliminate specific targets; and evidence of violence and theft are burned in the hope that all possible links with the perpetrator will be destroyed. Nevertheless, as the techniques available to forensic examiners become increasingly sophisticated, this potential avenue of escape for the criminal becomes ever more remote.

Human bodies prove extraordinarily resistant to complete destruction by fire and explosives: the tiniest scraps of evidence can now provide viable leads for investigators. When homemade bombs have been constructed from chemicals, or even when commercial explosives have been used, sufficient residues remain at the scene to help identify, and in some cases locate, the perpetrators.

Sometimes these residues are well hidden, having soaked into what remains of the furnishings where the explosion took place. But investigators can produce a solution of the residues by removing all potentially absorbent

ABOVE Smoke patterns on the outside of a burned-out house.

RIGHT Fire in an apartment block.

BELOW Evidence from a fire, bagged and ready for examination.

materials from the crime scene and treating them in acetone. Any residues can then be tested by chromatography to give an accurate blueprint of the explosive materials present. A similar technique can be used at scenes of suspicious fires, to discover whether any highly flammable materials were used to help start or maintain the blaze.

Fires, like explosions, need a source of energy to trigger them. Materials burn only when enough heat is applied to raise them to their ignition temperature. The ignition temperature of kerosene, for example, is approximately 445° F, that of benzene is 1045° F.

In other more complex materials, such as wood or coal, sufficient heat must be applied to cause the chemical breakdown of the material and the release of gases, which then ignite and start the material burning.

Fires do not normally start spontaneously: even a gas leak needs a stray spark to set it off. But some materials generate their own sources of heat and can spontaneously combust. Coal is one example: temperatures at the center of a large stack can reach levels high enough to ignite it. Similarly, hay stacked in badly ventilated storehouses can reach high temperatures because of the heat produced by bacterial activity, and can eventually burst into flames without warning. But most fires, whether accidental or deliberate, leave some clue as to the heat source that started it, whether it was a lit match or a bolt of lightning.

Explosions are even less likely to occur unless a specific combination of ingredients has been brought together to cause a rapid chemical reaction. Close inspection of the aftermath almost always reveals traces of those ingredients.

Fires burn at different temperatures depending on their fuel. As a result, they burn with differing colors of flame and smoke. Wood and cloth fires, for example, burn with reddish-yellow flames and gray-brown smoke. Gasoline and kerosene fires burn with yellow-white flames and black smoke, and cooking oil burns with yellow flames and brown smoke.

Accident—or arson?

In any case of death apparently resulting from fire, a crucial part of the forensic examination is directed at determining the cause of the fire. If a victim's body has been burned in an effort to conceal a murder, for example, there is usually evidence to show that the fire was started deliberately. Alternatively the fire may have been started to enable a fraudulent insurance claim to be made, to destroy evidence of fraud, even to eliminate a business rival, or it may simply have been started to gratify the psychological appetite of a pyromaniac.

In most cases, setting a fire involves the use of some kind of accelerant to help the flames take hold. Fires tend to spread upward as well as outward, so the search for the start-point is usually focused on the lowest point of the burned-out area. There may be traces of gasoline or other flammable hydrocarbons, either lingering in the air or present in fabrics or surfaces on the edge of the area. These can be identified by laboratory analysis, either by being heated in water to liberate a

ABOVE Smoke patterning on the ceiling of a room in a burned-out building.

characteristic and identifiable scent, or by gas chromatography, which reveals the chemical composition of the hydrocarbons in question. This latter technique is so accurate that it can be used to differentiate between different makes and grades of gasoline. Each grade has a different chromatography "fingerprint" depending on the proportions of the different chemicals present. In some cases the chemical make-up can be measured so accurately that

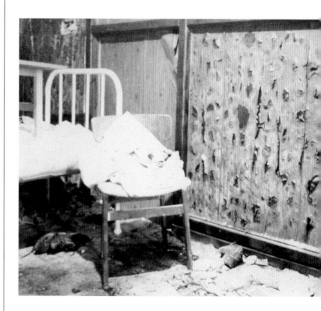

ABOVE The pattern of smoke on the wall of a room can help to show where a fire started and how it spread.

the gasoline can be traced to an individual gas station, or even to the fuel tank of a particular vehicle.

Piles of ash at the base of a fire may indicate where an arsonist piled material before lighting it. Any signs that the blaze had more than one point of origin strongly suggest that the blaze was deliberately started; evidence of breaking and entering can also point to arson. Where appropriate, investigators can check security or sprinkler systems to see whether they have been deliberately disabled. Where fraud or insurance swindles are suspected, investigators search carefully for the remains of goods or burned documents on the premises.

Where a fire is genuinely accidental, the cause is usually all too clear. The starting point may be found to be a fault in the building's electrical wiring, a gas leak, or a lighted cigarette carelessly disposed of. In other cases, evidence of a lightning strike or the presence of volatile materials stored near natural heat sources may show the cause.

ABOVE AND RIGHT A horrific fire at King's Cross station on the London subway system in 1987, which killed 31 people, was thought to have been started by a carelessly dropped cigarette setting light to an old wooden escalator.

In this reconstruction, the flames, which can just be seen in the top picture, have spread to cover the whole right-hand side of the escalator.

Within minutes, the wooden framework of the escalator is fully ablaze, preventing the trapped passengers using it as an escape route to the surface.

Explosive evidence

Explosions are caused by a combination of materials which, when detonated, set off a fast-burning reaction that produces gas. The gas causes the pressure inside the bomb's container to rise rapidly until the casing bursts and the pieces are blasted outward at high speed. Damage is inflicted and casualties caused not only by these fast-moving pieces but also by the blast effect of the expanding gases that are suddenly released from confinement and travel at speeds of up to 7,000 miles per hour.

Explosives are normally classified as one of two types, depending on how quickly the chemical reaction takes place. In "low" explosives, the reaction produces light, heat, and a subsonic pressure-wave flying outward in all directions from the detonation. In "high" explosives, the speed of the reaction is far greater, producing an almost instant build-up of heat and gases and a supersonic pressure-wave of destruction.

In most criminal cases involving explosives—excluding those organized by large, well-funded terrorist groups—the incendiary devices used are likely to be homemade. Most homemade explosives are low explosives, made from ingredients that are relatively easy to obtain. One traditional mixture, a black powder once used in muskets and pistols, is made from combining charcoal, sulfur and potassium or sodium nitrate. Others contain the essential combination of a fuel and an oxidant using ingredients as familiar as sugar and weed killer.

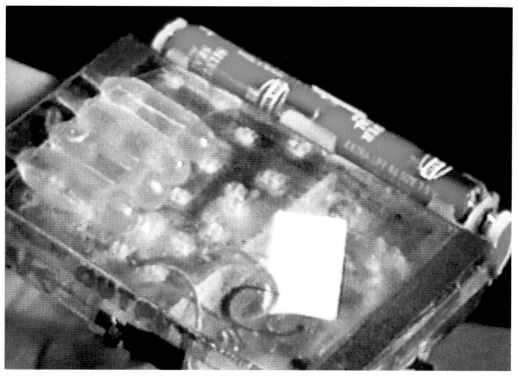

High explosives are more complex in their action. The most powerful of all, such as dynamite, TNT or RDX, are quite inert in themselves, and can be handled and even set on fire without exploding. For these, a primer is needed, a small charge of an explosive that is even more sensitive to heat or shock. Primer charges are usually detonated by blasting caps, which are triggered by lighting a safety fuse or applying an electric current. If the remains of one of these caps is found at the scene, it is usually safe to assume that the explosion was deliberately executed. The blasting caps of high explosives leave fragments that can be identified by sifting and then closely examining the debris found at the center of the explosion.

Searching for evidence

Even the most powerful and efficient explosives are not completely consumed in a deliberate detonation. Some residues inevitably remain at the scene, and forensic examiners now have a range of powerful tests at their disposal to reveal the presence and type of these traces.

In most cases, an explosion leaves a crater at the center of the blast, and debris is taken from this area for further tests. Fragments of softer materials such as wood, rubber or insulation may have absorbed traces of the explosives. Harder materials, such as metals, may have traces deposited on their surfaces.

OPPOSITE ABOVE The casing of a radio used to hide the bomb placed next to it.

OPPOSITE LEFT Part of the bomb used to destroy the PanAm Boeing Flight 103 747 over Lockerbie in 1988.

RIGHT Searching through the wreckage left when an El Al Boeing 747 freighter crashed into a block of flats near Amsterdam's Schiphol airport on October 4, 1992, a disaster that was eventually found to be caused by metal fatigue in the aircraft's mountings.

All these materials can be tested using chromatography equipment, and a portable machine that can be used at the scene itself is now commonly used. A vacuum pump collects vapors from suspect surfaces and passes them through its own high-speed gas chromatography equipment to identify their constituents. The device can detect commercial and military explosives, including the more sophisticated types of plastic explosives.

The detonator that sets off a low explosive is also usually homemade: an electrical detonator is sometimes linked to a battery

ABOVE Explosives investigation trucks at the scene of the Waco siege and shoot-out in Texas at the end of the 51-day standoff in April 1993.

ABOVE Part of the bomb used to blow the PanAm Boeing 747 airliner out of the sky over Lockerbie in 1988 (see p. 134).

through a device set to trigger the circuit. This might be an alarm clock, which allows the bomb to be set to go off at a particular time, or a mercury tilt switch, so that if the device is moved the circuit is completed and the bomb goes off. Many car bombs are wired to the vehicle's ignition, so the act of trying to start the engine sets off the explosion.

In some cases, analysis of the victims' bodies yields essential evidence. When a British European Airways Comet airliner was brought down in the eastern Mediterranean in

BELOW The victim of a Mafia assassination in Italy, lying next to his burning vehicle.

1967, the aircraft wreckage settled at the bottom of the sea and there was little of the plane left to show what had caused the disaster. Passengers' bodies floated to the surface, however, and autopsies were carried out. Forensic pathologists discovered that fragments of the bomb-casing had been driven deeply into the skin of one of the passengers. The site and severity of the wounds (together with the passenger manifest) enabled accident investigators to eventually determine the location of the bomb on the aircraft and the break-up sequence of the airliner, even though the airplane itself lay unrecovered on the sea bed.

Sabotage

Not all the evidence found at the scene of a fire or an explosion relates to the blaze, the detonation, the victims or the wreckage. The criminal may have broken into the area before setting the fire or planting the bomb, and left other pieces of evidence in the process. A tool such as a chisel or a screwdriver, when used to force open a door or window, leaves marks on the wood or metal that record the most minuscule shape and surface defects of the implement.

In cases such as vehicle sabotage, the criminal may have used saws and wire cutters, each of which leaves its signature impressions on the material being cut. Even knife scratches can give valuable evidence, especially if the suspect item is recovered and can be used to produce a test mark for comparison purposes. The pattern of marks resulting from the manufacture of the tool, together with any nicks and scratches acquired in its ordinary use, can be enormously helpful in ascertaining its origin and history.

TOP Wreckage and bodies in the aftermath of another Italian terrorist killing with a car bomb.

ABOVE This car was blown over by a bomb in a Mafia assassination in Palermo, Sicily.

Steven Benson

ABOVE Steven Benson at his trial in 1986.

Steven Benson came from a wealthy Florida family and expected to inherit a large sum of money on the death of his older relatives. On the morning of July 9, 1985, he arrived at his grandmother's home in Naples, Florida, to pick up some equipment to mark out a site for a new home. He loaded the family car, a 1978 Chevrolet Suburban, with stakes and plans, then he drove to a local store for coffee and rolls to bring back for the family breakfast.

Just before 9:00 AM, he and his mother, sister and adopted brother Scott went out to the car, ready to drive to the site. Finding that he had forgotten his tape measure, Steven threw the car keys to Scott and went back into the house. Scott climbed into the driving seat, turned the ignition key, and the car exploded in two separate but devastating blasts. Other than Steven, the only survivor was his sister Carol Lynn.

When forensic investigators arrived, they noted that Steven seemed remarkably calm considering that he had narrowly escaped being blown to pieces and had lost two members of his immediate family. As they searched the wreckage of the car, investigators' suspicions intensified. They found the remains of a bomb that had been made from a length of galvanized metal pipe, threaded at both ends and sealed with end-caps. One of the end-caps carried the letter G for its maker, Grinnell, and the other bore a U for Union Brand. Close to the site of the explosion,

BELOW Aerial view of the crime scene, with the wreckage in front of the Benson house in Naples, Florida.

fragments of four 1.5-volt batteries were found together with a manual switch and a piece of circuit board that was not part of the Suburban's electrical system.

Teams of investigators visited local hardware stores, junkyards and construction sites to check the sources of the pipes and end-caps. One store had sold two Union Brand end-caps four days before the explosion, and the description of the purchaser, who had been tall and heavily built matched that of Steven Benson. The sales tickets for the components were then chemically treated and revealed Steven Benson's palm print, proving that he had bought the bomb-making equipment.

On August 21, 1985, six weeks and a day after the fateful explosion, Benson was arrested. Almost a year later he was found guilty of the murders of his mother and brother. It emerged that Steven Benson had been stealing from his mother for some time. Having found him out, she was about to amend her will so that Steven would not inherit the ten million dollars he had been expecting. To prevent that from happening, he had been prepared to literally blow his family apart.

BELOW The twisted wreckage of the Chevrolet where Steven Benson's mother and brother died and (inset above) close-up of part of the wreckage.

Pan Am Flight 103

ABOVE Impact craters and debris from the crashed airliner in Lockerbie.

BELOW The nose and flight deck of the 747, found in a field more than two miles from the town.

At 6:25 PM (GMT) on December 21, 1988, A Pan American Boeing 747 originating in Frankfurt took off from London and headed for New York. Many of the two hundred and forty-three passengers on board were looking forward to spending the Christmas holiday with their families in the U.S. By 6:56 PM the airliner had reached its cruising altitude of 31,000 feet and was flying over southwestern Scotland following its Great Circle route toward the Atlantic. Seven minutes later, air-traffic controllers noticed with alarm that the airplane's echo had faded from the radar displays: it was replaced by several smaller, vanishing traces.

The disintegrating airliner fell out of the sky and hit the small Scottish town of Lockerbie, almost six miles below, with all the fury of an earthquake. One engine blew a crater fifteen feet deep in the northeastern part of the town, and the wing exploded in a fireball a quarter of a mile wide. Twenty-one local houses were destroyed in an impact registering 1.6 on the Richter scale; many more were badly damaged. Tragically, all two hundred and fifty-nine people aboard the aircraft died, as did eleven more on the ground.

The fact that the airplane victims were found to have suffered lung damage from violent decompression suggested that some catastrophic failure had made the aircraft disintegrate in the air. In order to establish the sequence of events leading to the disaster, investigators needed to collect as much of the wreckage as possible even though the debris was widely scattered.

Fragments had drifted in two trails of wreckage covering an area of almost a thousand square miles of northern England and part of Scotland. Nevertheless more than four million pieces were traced.

Eventually over ninety percent of the airplane's structure was recovered and used to reconstruct the plane in a huge hangar at a former army ammunition store.

At first the evidence seemed confusing. There had been no radio message giving a distress call. The flight data recorder showed that the control settings had been correct for normal

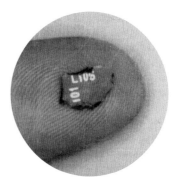

flight, and there was no sign of fatigue or corrosion in the engine or bodywork that could account for the airliner's disintegration.

Investigators examining the fragments found signs of explosive damage in luggage containers from the forward baggage hold: it seemed that a bomb had been detonated next to a container floor. Microscopic particles were found in the container walls and the aircraft skin panels, and a tiny piece of printed circuit board, part of a Toshiba radio cassette player, was found trapped in the container paneling. There were traces of Semtex (a plastic explosive), and residual fibers showed that the cassette player had been hidden inside a brown suitcase.

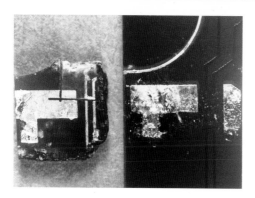

The aircraft's disintegration appeared to have started when the bomb blew a small hole in the fuselage. The fuselage edges were then pulled back by the slipstream, the nose section tore away and the plane entered a steepening dive, breaking apart as it fell. In little more than ninety seconds, just 2.2 pounds of Semtex had blown apart a three-hundred-ton airliner, leading to the deaths of two hundred and seventy people.

Investigators started to focus on a detailed three-dimensional reconstruction of the part of the fuselage that held the bomb. Explosives experts assembled a series of identical devices, packed clothes in suitcases similar to those that were on the plane, and detonated them in identical luggage containers in an effort to establish the exact location of the device. The results showed that the case containing the bomb was loaded above the bottom layer of baggage in the container, which indicated that it was loaded onto the 747 at Frankfurt where transfer passengers boarded.

Forensic specialists found garment fibers in the fragments of the case. These were traced to clothes bought in Malta and flown to Frankfurt on the day of the crash. Investigations on Malta traced the purchase of the clothes to a Libyan who did not actually board the flight to London, though the baggage containing the clothes was accepted.

As a direct result of these findings, airlines have re-examined their policy on baggage loading, aiming to ensure that such a tragedy never happens again. Security checks on luggage have been intensified, and unaccompanied baggage can now be located before take-off. If passengers have checked in but fail to board a flight, their bags are removed from the hold.

Research is currently being undertaken to see how airplanes can become more resistant to the forces of internal explosions. To guard against the possibility that terrorists will respond by making more powerful bombs, increasingly sensitive explosives detectors are being developed. These can reveal the presence of minute quantities of the chemicals used in incendiary devices by using variants of neutron activation analysis (see Chapter Twelve).

World Trade Center

On February 23, 1993, a yellow van was parked in the underground garage of the northernmost tower of New York's World Trade Center. It contained a massive bomb that, when detonated, killed six people and injured more than a thousand. Five hundred million dollars worth of damage was also caused.

Specialists from the FBI's Materials and Documents Unit conducted detailed searches of the crime scene and managed to isolate trace evidence of urea nitrate. From the extent of the damage it was clear that at least twelve hundred pounds of the explosive was used.

Agents hunting for the bombers got an early break when an immigrant named Mohammad Salameh called at the rental office to claim back his $400 deposit on the rented Ryder van used in the bombing, which he said was stolen from him by Ramizi Ahmed Yousef, one of the principal conspirators, the day before. The police found Salameh's fingerprints on bomb-making chemicals once their investigation led them to a Jersey City apartment and a nearby storage shed used by Yousef as a bomb factory.

The fingerprints of Yousef and his chief conspirator, Eyad Izmoil, were found on chemicals and bomb-making manuals at the site, although the two men had left the U.S. on a flight from Kennedy Airport immediately after the bombing. A $2 million reward was posted, and two years later Yousef was arrested in Pakistan, after earlier sightings in Manila and Bangkok, and extradited to the U.S. to stand trial. Izmiol was later arrested in Jordan, and in November 1997 the two men were put on trial together with their follow plotters.

Six men with links to Arab countries were eventually tried and convicted of conspiracy to carry out the bombing. Their motive was to punish the U.S. for its continued support of Israel. It transpired that the carnage they caused had actually fallen far short of their intentions. Their aim was to blow up one tower, causing it to topple onto the other. Had they succeeded, the resulting death toll could have run into hundreds of thousands. All six conspirators were sentenced to life imprisonment.

ABOVE LEFT Investigators examine the rubble in the basement of the World Trade Center.

BACKGROUND The conspirators hoped that one of the Center's twin towers would collapse, bringing down the other, with a much greater loss of life.

The Oklahoma Bombing

ABOVE Bags of ammonium nitrate, commonly available as fertilizer in garden stores, and used in the Oklahoma bombing.

BELOW Devastation at the Alfred P. Murrah Federal Building in Oklahoma City after the bombing.

On April 19, 1995 the story of the Trade Center bomb was eclipsed by a much larger explosion—in the Alfred P. Murrah Federal Building in Oklahoma City, Oklahoma. One hundred and sixty-eight people died, many of whom were children attending a day-care center in the building.

Again, the forensic examiners' first priority was to collect and sift through tons of rubble in an effort to trace clues to the identity of the bombers. Almost 13,000 pieces of potential evidence were taken from the site of the explosion—including particles of metal removed from the bodies of the victims—and examined in detail. In fact one of the pieces of debris found in the earliest stages of the search gave investigators their most promising lead. A mangled piece of metal found close to the center of the blast was identified as part of a distorted truck axle. Close examination revealed a partial vehicle identification number that, when fed into the National Crime Insurance Bureau database, revealed that the axle belonged to a 1993 Ford truck. The truck belonged to Ryder Rentals of Miami, and investigators found that the vehicle had been hired out from a Ryder office in Junction City, Kansas.

Computer-enhanced artist's impressions were produced from descriptions given of the two people who hired the vehicle. Copies of the pictures were issued to more than a thousand agents from the FBI and the Bureau of Alcohol, Tobacco and Firearms, who began questioning staff at hotels, diners and gas stations between Junction City and Oklahoma City to see whether anyone remembered seeing or serving the suspects.

The manager of the Dreamland Hotel in Junction City thought one of the sketches resembled a man who stayed at his hotel and who drove a Ryder truck. The guest gave his name as Timothy McVeigh. The same sketch, which was also broadcast on television, prompted a one-time colleague of McVeigh's to call the FBI. He reported that he had been surprised by the vehemence with which McVeigh had reacted to news of the Waco shoot-out, in which FBI agents stormed the fortress of the Branch Davidian extreme religious sect.

Another lucky coincidence boosted the investigation at this point: initial attempts to locate McVeigh revealed that he was actually in custody already, having been arrested for an unrelated offense. The day after the bombing, Oklahoma State Trooper Charles D. Hangar spotted a yellow Mercury Marquis without a license plate on Interstate Highway 35. He asked the driver to pull over, and then found he was attempting to conceal a semiautomatic pistol. Details of the driver, who gave his name as Timothy McVeigh, were duly entered on the record.

Since McVeigh's name had been suggested by at least two sources in the FBI's inquiries into the bombing, it was keyed into the National Crime Information Center database. An immediate match was flagged, and inquiries revealed that the suspect was being held at Noble County Jail.

McVeigh's driver's license, which he had been carrying when he was arrested, gave a Michigan address. Local enquiries revealed that two brothers, Terry and James Nichols, had also been living there. Terry Nichols was eventually identified as suspect number two.

Forensic examiners believed that the explosives used in the bombing had been contained in fifty-gallon plastic barrels. Remains of barrels found at the bomb-site showed markings very similar to those found on empty barrels at Nichols' home. Furthermore, traces of the chemicals used in the explosives were found on the suspects' clothes.

Some of the assumptions made by forensic examiners concerning the type and amount of explosives used were later criticized, and some argued that the chemical traces found on the suspects' clothing might have come from a totally unrelated source. But the evidence linking the men to the truck that had contained the explosives proved unshakeable. Nichols was sentenced to life imprisonment and McVeigh, identified as the prime mover in the bombing, was sentenced to death.

McVeigh's attorneys appealed against his conviction on the grounds that the public climate at the time of the bombings prejudiced his right to a fair trial. The appeal was denied in March 1999. Nichols' appeal was quashed on October 12, 1999.

ABOVE Rescue teams sifting the wreckage of the building, searching for survivors.

BELOW Timothy McVeigh being taken by FBI agents from the Bonle County Courthouse in Perry, Oklahoma, where he had been arrested for a traffic offense and carrying a concealed firearm.

Unmasking the Criminal Frauds and Forgeries

ABOVE Testing a US currency bill under fluorescent light to reveal evidence of forgery.

The examination and testing of documents is an increasingly important area of forensic science. All kinds of clues to the identity of a criminal can be revealed by fragments of writing ranging from personal letters to ransom demands, or by printed documents from pawnbroker's receipts to airline or train tickets.

In other cases forged or altered letters, bank drafts, checks and similar financial documents can be profitable for a criminal if they can be passed off as genuine. Forensic specialists, however, can use a wide range of techniques to reveal even the most convincingly forged documents as fakes.

Other documents such as diaries and works of apparent historical significance are also tested to help prove their authenticity, usually by analysis of the writing and scientific testing of the paper and ink. Watermarks and

RIGHT Cleaning a medieval manuscript to ensure any tests carried out on it are accurate.

signatures can be checked to identify forgeries, and minute characteristics unique to individual typewriters or printers can be identified in pieces of text as a starting point for locating the machine that was used. Some techniques even allow deliberate corrections made at the time a document was created to be rendered transparent so that the underlying text is revealed.

Handwritten text

Most people are taught to write by copying a particular handwriting style. However, as individuals become more accustomed to writing and have to write more quickly, letters and words begin to acquire idiosyncrasies associated with that person's individual experience and coordination. Individual variations from the standard writing styles are the elements handwriting experts are most interested in, especially any differences that may be characteristic of, and so help identify, the writer.

Handwriting experts study in detail how particular letters have been formed in any given sample. For example, the letter "i" may be not be dotted, may be written without an upstroke, or may have one or more small "eyelets" where the movement of the pen changed direction in forming the letter. Not only do these characteristics show up throughout a particular sample of hand-written text, but in many cases they are

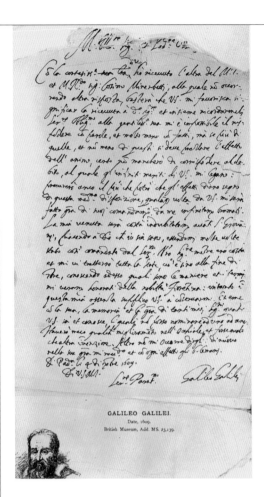

GALILEO GALILEI.
Date, 1609.
British Museum, Add. MS. 23,139.

TOP Genuine handwriting of the Italian astronomer and physicist Galileo.

BELOW LEFT Researchers working on a computerized system for handwriting recognition.

present even when the writer is trying to conceal his or her identity, or attempting to imitate someone else's handwriting.

Another area of analysis involves the proportion or relative height of different letters. Even in an individual's ordinary handwriting, of course, variations do occur, but certain established ratios are usually consistent. For example, the ratio between the part of the letter "g" above the line to the overall height of the letter tends to remain the same in an individual writer, regardless of the writing style adopted.

The overall slant of the writing from the vertical is another fairly consistent factor. This

147

can range from thirty-five degrees to the right to as much as fifty degrees to the left in different styles, but it should be more or less consistent for a given person's hand. Experts measure the inclination using a transparent protractor, concentrating on the longest letters such as "f," "h," or "g."

Spacing of individual letters, words and lines is another respect in which writers' styles differ. In particular, a signature or a complete line of text tends to follow a consistent path for an individual. The baseline is either straight and level or angled or curved upward or downward or both. The presence or absence of connectors, the strokes that join letters in handwritten text, is another common individual variation.

Signatures

Perhaps no written words have as much forensic importance as signatures, and suspect examples are invariably checked against the genuine signature. Although each example of an individual's signature looks very similar, there are always subtle differences between them. If a suspect example, placed over a genuine example on a light box, looks completely identical, investigators automatically suspect forgery.

In order to establish whether or not a signature is genuine, forensic examiners gather as many copies of the genuine signature as possible. Ideally the collection includes casual scrawls as well as more formally written

ABOVE Magnifying glass placed on a sheet of genuine Salvador Dali signatures, which can be used to authenticate unknown examples of the painter's work.

visors in your agency become fully informed of the import of this Order. I am convinced that good personnel manage- ment can make a substantial contribution to the efficiency of the government.

igations that are properly responsibilities of the States Government. Any arrangement proposed for the ion of this currency should include provisions designed as possible to avoid any windfall to speculators.

of the President following appropriate discussions with yourself, Dr. Bush and the Director of Central Intelligence.

LEFT President Harry S. Truman invariably placed his signature on typed documents close to the last lines of the text, as shown in the top and center examples. When checked by drawing a circle using the vertical stroke of the letter "T" in the signature as a radius, the forgery at the bottom is clearly too far from the text.

signatures, signatures written with different kinds of pens and, since handwriting can change with the passing of time, as many samples as possible dating from around the period when the suspect signature was supposed to have been written.

Although signatures made by one individual all differ slightly, there are certain features in each example that remain consistent; the placing of the signature relative to the typed or printed text in a letter, for example. Other similarities are associated with the actual shape of the signature rather than the formation of individual letters. By putting a sheet of tracing paper over a signature and marking the tops (or the bottoms) of each of the letters and then joining them up, a zigzag line is produced. Different genuine examples of the same signature all show a very similar line but a forgery, even one that seems convincing at first glance, often shows quite a different pattern from the original.

Other comparisons can be made by marking any gaps in the signature which, once again, produce a characteristic pattern. The baseline of the writing is another important element. Some forgers, concentrating on the formation of the letters, fail to notice the way in which the signature as a whole climbs or descends from left to right. The distinctive signature of Abraham Lincoln, for example, was characterized by a stepped baseline in which the initial "A" and the final "ln" lay on different levels from the rest of the name—an idiosyncrasy missed by several would-be forgers of his day.

Microscopic examination can show further discrepancies between a genuine signature, usually written quickly and confidently, and a forgery, where the writer took care to make the shape as convincing as possible. A microscope reveals any breaks in the lines, tremors, patching (where badly-shaped letters were corrected), or any pencil tracing and eraser marks made when the signature was transferred from a genuine example.

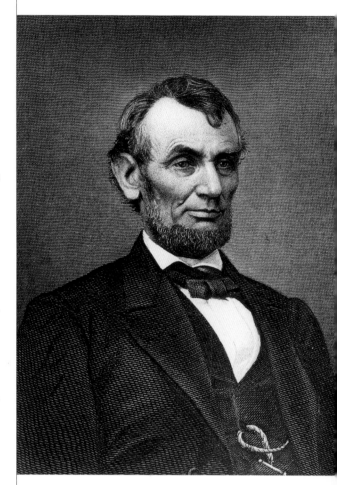

ABOVE Abraham Lincoln and his genuine signature, showing the characteristic three steps of the baseline, a feature often missed by forgers.

Disguised writing

Not all criminals try to imitate the writing of others. Some try to disguise their own writing to avoid revealing their identity. There are several common ways of doing this: some would-be forgers change the direction in which the letters slant, others change the size of the letters, print in block capitals, or even write with the other hand. Writing quickly or slowly, deliberately misspelling words or trying to copy another handwriting style are other tricks of the trade.

Many of the most obvious changes are ignored by experts when comparing disguised

ABOVE Impression of handwriting on a receipt book, found at the scene of the murder of Vivian Messiter in Southampton, England in January 1929, when viewed in oblique light revealed the handwriting and signature of W. F. Thomas an alias of his murderer, William Henry Podmore.

writing with a sample produced by a suspect. Smaller, more subtle signs of individuality, such as the forming of individual letters, are more difficult for the writer to eliminate. Other clues are the way in which the writer starts or ends a particular letter each time it appears.

One way of confirming the identity of a writer is by locating the origin of the

ABOVE W. F. Thomas (left), alias William Henry Podmore, hanged in April 1930 for the murder of Vivian Messiter (right).

document in question. A search of a suspect's home or office may uncover partially destroyed drafts, or examination of the remaining pages of a notepad or the desk blotter may show pressure marks of the pen where a document was written. Modern forensic science can bring powerful techniques to bear on both these possibilities. Fragments of torn-up and burned documents can be reassembled and read by photographing them under infrared light, or alternatively under light that is reflected at different angles off the burned surface of the paper to produce the greatest possible contrast between the writing and the scorched background.

When an imprint is left on paper that was underneath the document at the time of writing, as in the case of successive pages of a notepad, for example, electrostatic detection can provide a lot of useful information. Each page of the notepad is placed in turn over an electronically charged wire mesh and tightened against it using a shrink-wrap technique. A form of photocopier toner is then applied which clings to the parts of the document that were pressed down by the action of the pen on the top sheet. These came into closest contact with the charged mesh, so picking up an electrostatic charge. This technique is so sensitive that images can be retrieved from several pages torn off the pad in succession. It is even possible to reconstruct the order in which the pages lay in the original pad, and therefore the order in which different sections of text were written.

Typewriting and printing

The introduction of typewriters and computer printers forced forensic examiners to meet new challenges in identifying the origins of machine-written documents. Manual typewriter text analysis is based on the fact that different pressures on the keys and differing wear on individual letter keys eventually build up a series of discrepancies that are distinguishable in text typed on any particular machine. Some letters become displaced upward or downward from the line of text, others skew from the vertical as type bars become twisted. Some letters become broken or indistinct with use, all of which helps in identifying a suspect machine.

Developments in typing and printing technology have tended to reduce the value of this kind of analysis. The introduction of electric typewriters, in which even pressure is applied to all key strokes, reduced variations in the weight with which different letters were typed, though faults in the mechanism can replace the action of the typist's fingers in creating new inconsistencies. The availability of golf-ball typewriters, which allow a whole font to be changed by substituting another ball in a matter of seconds, also complicates the experts' task. But perhaps the advent of

ABOVE AND ABOVE LEFT Typebars of a typewriter with raised and reversed letters and symbols, can become worn and displaced with use, producing characteristic misalignments like the raised figures of the date in the sample of text.

computer-controlled printers has provided the greatest obstacle to those seeking the individual quirks and variations that identify a particular machine.

In the first word-processors, output was often delivered on a daisy-wheel printer, where the type was set on bars that formed the spokes of a wheel. These were susceptible to wear and tear in a similar way to typewriters, and because the mechanisms of both golf-ball and daisy-wheel machines can become slightly misaligned with use, documents printed on a particular machine could still be identified with some accuracy.

Since then, the increasing popularity of ink-jet, bubble-jet and laser printers has tended to eliminate these useful inconsistencies. Other ways of linking the author to the document have had to be found, such as tracing the original word-processor files on the hard disk of the computer, for example. Although the writer may have taken care to delete the files in question, they can often still be retrieved by computer experts who know how and where to search for them.

Inks and papers

Elaborate forgeries of printed documents can be extremely convincing to casual inspection, but are often revealed as counterfeit when tests are carried out on the paper or the ink used. Modern inks fall into four basic types. Most black inks contain dye material and iron salts in a suspension of gallic or tannic acid. India ink, or carbon-black ink, is made from a suspension of carbon particles in gum Arabic, and a whole range of colored inks is made using synthetic dyes with different polymers and acids. Ball-point pens use inks made with synthetic dyes or insoluble pigments in a range of solvents and additives.

ABOVE The English poet Lord Byron with a genuine sample of his handwriting.

LEFT Testing inks using chromatography to reveal their exact composition.

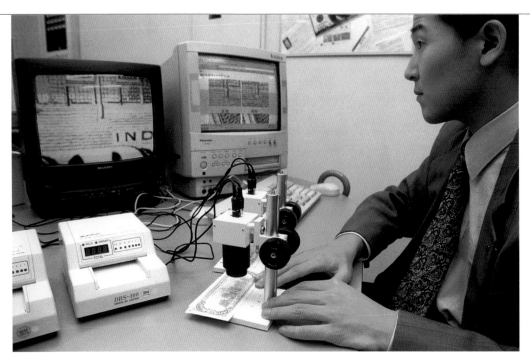

ABOVE A Japanese machine for identifying forged currency, using infrared and magnetic sensors.

BELOW RIGHT Bank notes illuminated by ultraviolet light.

Within these basic types there are thousands of variations. Each can be isolated by using methods such as spectrometry or thin-layer chromatography. The U.S. Bureau of Alcohol, Tobacco and Firearms has a database of more than 3000 different ink chromatograph traces that can help to identify a particular ink composition.

Paper too can be classified by the different materials used in its manufacture. Some papers have particular watermarks, others are made from synthetic fibers or have optical brightening agents like fluorocarbons added to make them whiter and less transparent for high-quality color printing. Papers also differ in the surface treatment used to prepare them for printing: some are hot-rolled, others treated with size, synthetic resins or starch.

Specialists are often able to ascertain the date when a particular paper or type of ink was originally introduced, and this can reveal an otherwise convincing historical document as a forgery. A document once thought to be an original manuscript by the English poet Byron was found to have a watermark showing the paper was manufactured in 1834, ten years after his death.

Some forgers attempt to increase the value of postage stamps to collectors by faking the cancellation stamps, and many attempt the most difficult forgeries of all by producing counterfeit currency. Here, of course, the papers and the printed designs used by mints are chosen specifically to make the forger's task as difficult as possible. Even where the reproduction of the printed design is perfect to the naked eye, techniques such as

microspectrophotometry can reveal the absorption spectrum of the ink used in individual printed lines, making it a simple matter to distinguish between genuine and forged notes.

So numerous and varied are the obstacles facing the would-be currency forger that in one classic case, the criminals thought of an original twist to simplify their task. In 1924, using inside knowledge, they forged "official" letters to a British printing firm that produced Portugal's currency notes. These letters ordered a special printing of five-hundred-

ABOVE A tungsten-halogen lamp with a set of filters reveals the luminescence of the ink, and a transmitted light source shows masked or obliterated text on a document.

BELOW The original check (top) is altered by the forger to pay a much larger amount (bottom) by a few additional pen strokes.

escudo notes for the Portuguese colony of Angola. The notes, according to the letter, were to be normal Portuguese currency, to be overprinted "Angola" by the Portuguese themselves. The notes were printed, collected by the criminals using forged letters of authorization, and then used to buy shares and foreign currency.

The ingenious twist to this case was that the notes were perfect, and the crime came to light only when a check was made on the number of five-hundred-escudo notes in circulation. The check was ordered after a batch of genuine notes had been printed with the same serial numbers as those ordered by the criminals. Even then the main culprit managed to delay his trial by five years by producing more forged letters, this time implicating the governor and directors of the Bank of Portugal in the deception and portraying himself as an innocent scapegoat.

Changing checks and drafts

Many criminals avoid the need for complex and difficult forgeries by altering existing documents such as checks and bank drafts, either by changing the name of the payee or by increasing the amount involved. Such changes often involve erasing one or more characters on the existing document by scratching away the surface layer of the paper, and then typing or writing over the alteration. Microscopic analysis usually reveals the signs of such an alteration when the document is lit from one side to highlight changes in the surface layers.

In other cases, criminals erase existing characters by using a chemical agent. This works by reacting with the ink to produce a colorless product, but the part of the paper to which the chemical is added reveals its secret when examined under infrared or ultraviolet lighting. Even if a skillful forger does not remove any of the existing text or figures and simply adds to them, examiners can use a

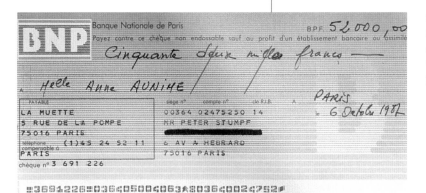

technique called infrared luminescence to reveal these later alterations.

By shining blue-green light onto the document, then photographing it using infrared-sensitive film, investigators can highlight differences in the luminescent properties of the inks. Illuminating the document with infrared light before the infrared photography also shows discrepancies in the capacity of different inks to absorb infrared light. In either case, the alterations appear different from the original writing, making it clear that the document has been tampered with.

In the Clifford Irving case (see Chapter Fifteen) the criminal did not even have to alter the check, which had been made out to the subject of a so-called authorized biography. The check was given to Irving for transmission to the reclusive billionaire Howard Hughes, but Irving's wife opened a bank account in the name of Helga R. Hughes. The check, which was made out to H. R. Hughes, was paid into the account, therefore, without any alterations being necessary.

RIGHT The forgery is revealed using infrared luminscence.

The Hitler Diaries

ABOVE Gerd Heidemann with some of the volumes he claimed were the diaries of Adolf Hitler.

In 1981, twenty-seven volumes of handwritten text believed to be the diaries of Adolf Hitler were bought by the German publishing firm, Grüner and Jahr, together with a previously undiscovered third volume of Hitler's *Mein Kampf*, for a sum equivalent to two million dollars. The story was that the volumes had been smuggled out of Berlin in the last days of World War Two, but the airplane carrying them had crashed in what was later Communist East Germany. The papers had fallen into the hands of a collector of Nazi documents whose brother had been an East German general. The collector had brought the documents to Gerd Heidemann, a journalist on the staff of the German news magazine *Stern*, which was also published by Grüner and Jahr.

Naturally the documents were checked for authenticity against known samples of Hitler's handwriting. Two experts were brought in to carry out the checks, Max Frei-Sultzer, former head of the Zürich police forensic science department, and Ordway Hilton, a specialist in document verification from Landrum in South Carolina. Both men, together with another German police documents expert, confirmed that the texts had been written by the same person, which was actually true. The diaries had been forged by a small-time criminal named Konrad Kujau, who

BACKGROUND The Remington typewriter on which Hitler had written *Mein Kampf*.

RIGHT Hitler's dedication and signature on a first edition of the book.

had also succeeded in forging the sample used to check the
diaries' authorship!

The truth was revealed by West German police and
government forensic tests. Instead of checking the handwriting,
they concentrated on the paper and ink used in the diaries. After
testing the paper under ultraviolet light, they found it contained
a whitening agent that had first been introduced in 1954. The
threads attaching the official-looking seals to the volumes
contained viscose and polyester,
materials that had been
developed since the war, and
none of the four different types
of ink used had been available
when the diaries were supposed
to have been written. Finally,
the evaporation of chloride from
the ink was tested to establish
how long the ink had been on
the paper—the results showed
that the documents had been
written less than a year before
the tests were carried out.

The Diary of Jack the Ripper

An unemployed scrap-dealer from Liverpool, England, named Michael Barrett, claimed in 1991 to have been given a Victorian scrapbook that appeared to contain the diaries of Jack the Ripper, the notorious nineteenth-century serial killer. Barrett claimed that he had been given the scrapbook by a friend, Tony Devereux, who had since died. Rumors linked Devereux with workers who had carried out rewiring at a house formerly owned by the alleged author of the diaries, Liverpool businessman James Maybrick, who had died of arsenic and strychnine poisoning in 1889.

A series of tests has since been carried out on the diary, even though Barrett himself later claimed to have forged it, but then retracted his confession. One senior London psychiatrist found the variation in handwriting and the phrases used could be consistent with a potential serial killer. Again the tests were designed to analyze two distinct elements: the handwriting and the materials. Comparisons were made between the handwriting in the diary and that used in Maybrick's will, to show whether or not they could have been written by the same person; the paper and ink were analyzed to see whether their make-up was consistent with that used during Maybrick's lifetime.

ABOVE James Maybrick—Murder victim, or serial murderer?

BELOW One of the letters which was sent to the police at the time of the Ripper Murders, and which was supposed to have been written by the killer himself.

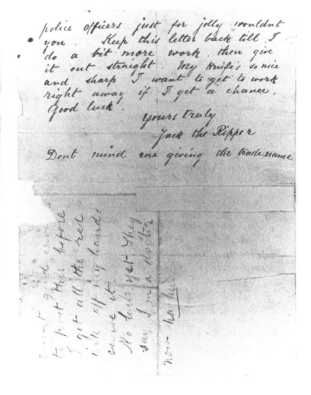

Scientific opinion remains divided. Handwriting analysis by the former forensic document expert for the Chicago Police Department concluded that the handwriting differed from the signature on Maybrick's marriage license and that on his will. But there are those who believe the diary reveals details that would be unknown to a forger, and some contend that the will was the faked document. Such a possibility was indeed aired at the time of Maybrick's death, since the will disinherited his own children. Believers also argue that Maybrick's formal signature is too small a sample to use for objective comparison.

On the paper and ink used in the diary, opinion is similarly split. Tests carried out by Dr. Nicholas Eastaugh, a document specialist who worked for the auction house Christie's as well as London museums and art galleries, indicated that the ink could have been right for the period. Analysis of the paper showed no trace of any modern additives. But Michael Barrett in his confession claimed to have bought an antique Victorian scrapbook and a bottle of "Victorian ink" to carry out his forgery, which he composed with the help of detailed library research. To confuse the picture still further, one American document specialist referred to an ink solubility test carried out in the U.K. which "appeared to show the ink was barely dry on the pages." For the moment it is not clear whether the Ripper diaries are authentic or not.

BELOW The envelope sent to the Central News agency contained a letter from the Ripper (background picture).

Fingerprints and Footprints

ABOVE Individual identifier—a false-color computer graphics image of a human fingerprint.

The fact that every living person has a unique pattern of ridges and depressions on the tips of their fingers is one of the founding principles of forensic science. It offers not only the possibility of positively identifying an individual victim or criminal, but also of proving the presence of a suspect at the scene of a crime.

The principle was recognized three thousand years ago in ancient China, where it was common for legal contracts to be endorsed by the fingerprints of the parties involved. The custom was also adopted by the Japanese. In the nineteenth century, an Englishman named William Herschel working in the Indian Civil Service introduced a similar practice; contracts were "signed" by the print of the signatory's right hand, which had been inked by being pressed on the ink pad normally used for rubber stamps.

The technique of using fingerprints as a way of identifying individuals was developed by another British expatriate, Dr. Henry Faulds, a Scot working in a Tokyo hospital. He was involved in a case where a thief had left a fingerprint on a whitewashed wall. When a suspect was identified, Fauld noticed that the patterns of ridges and whorls on the suspect's

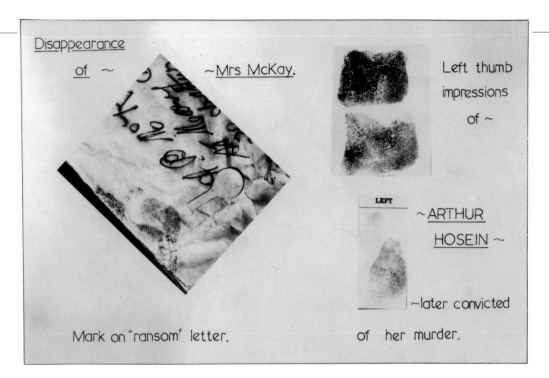

Disappearance of ~ ~Mrs McKay.

Left thumb impressions of ~

LEFT

~ARTHUR HOSEIN ~

~later convicted

Mark on 'ransom' letter.   of her murder.

fingers were quite different from those left in the whitewash. When an alternative suspect was apprehended, his prints were taken and the patterns compared—this time they matched perfectly.

Faulds published his conclusions in a scientific paper in 1880, and even volunteered to fund a fingerprint bureau at Scotland Yard, London's police headquarters, hoping that a practical method for identifying criminals could be developed. At the time, the "vital measurement" teachings of Bertillon (see Chapter One) still seemed to point the way forward, and Fauld's offer was declined. What Scotland Yard needed was an accurate and reliable method of classifying prints, as well as practical illustration that fingerprint evidence could prove an individual's identity with greater certainty than Bertillon's methods could.

Thanks to the work of Sir Francis Galton in England, Edward Henry in India and Juan Vucetich in Argentina, it became possible to classify and describe prints in such a way that matches could be reliably confirmed or rejected. The superiority of fingerprint evidence over Bertillon's "vital measurement" records was confirmed, in the United States at

TOP Fingerprints of Arthur Hosein, convicted of the kidnap and murder of Mrs Muriel McKay in England in 1968, matched with prints on the ransom note.

MIDDLE Fingerprint comparator with a glass magnifying lens and a cool-white fluorescent light source.

BOTTOM Recording fingerprints on a standard form.

least, by the case of a prisoner named Will West who arrived at Fort Leavenworth Prison, Kansas, to serve his sentence. The prison records showed there was already another prisoner in the penitentiary named William West, totally unconnected with the first Will West. The two men looked alike and their records, according to the Bertillon system, were identical. The only way they could be reliably distinguished was by their fingerprints.

Classifying fingerprints

Prints are classified by the pattern of ridges on the surface of the skin. At different points on the fingertip, these ridges come to an end, or divide, or cross; and the resulting complex

ridge patterns are different in every single individual. The general ways in which the ridges are arranged follow a series of recognizable patterns which allow prints to be systematically classified so that a search for a match can begin with general characteristics, then proceed to more detailed points of resemblance.

Two-thirds of the human population, for example, have ridge patterns that form loops. These are classified as "radial" (from the

ABOVE Another type of fingerprint comparator, which presents two prints side-by-side for detailed matching under high magnification.

LEFT AND BELOW Fingerprint classifications including different types of loops and arches.

Ulnar loop

Central pocket loop

Plain whorl

Double loop

Plain arch

Tented arch

Double loop

Accidental

Tented arch

Radial loop

radius bone of the forearm) if the loops open toward the little-finger side of the hand; "ulnar" (from the ulna bone) if they open toward the thumb. The center of the loop is called the core, and the triangular pattern where the outermost looped ridge lines meet the horizontal ridge-line pattern running across the base of the fingertip is called the "delta."

Almost one-third of the population has ridge patterns in whorls, which can be further split into plain whorls, double loops, central-pocket loops and accidental loops. Approximately one person in twenty has ridge patterns arranged in arches, which are described as plain arches if they follow a smooth, wavelike pattern, or tented arches if they end in a sharper point at the center.

Henry's system, and the later development of this system used by the FBI, splits the possible variants into 1,024 coded groups to simplify searches. Each of an individual's ten prints is assigned a numerical value. First of all, the prints are arranged as a double row in the following sequence:

Right index finger   Right ring finger   Left thumb   Left middle finger   Left little finger

Right thumb   Right middle finger   Right little finger   Left index finger   Left ring finger.

Each print is then given a value depending on the pattern of the print and the finger in question. If either of the fingers at the beginning of each row (the right index finger or the right thumb) has a whorl pattern, it scores a value of sixteen. If either finger of the second pair (the right ring finger or the right middle finger) has a whorl, it scores eight. The third, fourth and last pairs score four, two and one respectively if either of them has a whorl; any finger that has no whorl pattern is given a zero score.

The scores on each row are then added up and one further point added to each unless all the fingers on that row have whorls. The result is presented as a fraction, such as 14/8 or 16/9,

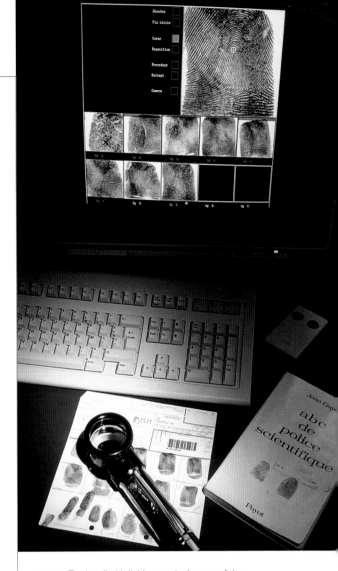

ABOVE The handheld digitizer at the bottom of the picture is used to transfer old paper copies of criminals' fingerprints from existing records into data which can be fed into computer databanks.

which provides an overall class figure, and this acts as a starting point in any search for a matching print.

This type of pattern recognition is an ideal application for computers, which can scan and store a given fingerprint as a digital pattern, taking account of the type and location on the print of each individual feature. These automated fingerprint identification systems (A.F.I.S.) can search a file of hundreds of thousands of digital print records for a match in less than a second, and offer a series of close matches for final scrutiny by a fingerprint expert. The computer also makes it feasible to

163

find a match for a single print found at a crime scene, even though the original FBI formula was based on a knowledge of all ten prints.

Computer-based storage systems also allow prints to be compared on high-resolution monitors and can enhance poor-quality or smudged prints to produce a sharp image. In addition, data can be exchanged with other A.F.I.S. systems and prints can be sent across the world to be compared or matched with locally obtained prints.

Revealing and recording prints

The fingerprints searched for at crime scenes fall into three main categories: visible, plastic or latent. Visible prints are the easiest to spot, being those made by fingers that have been in contact with a marker such as wet paint, ink, or blood. Plastic prints are made by the fingers pressing on a material like soap, wax, or putty which retains the image of the finger-tip ridges. Latent prints, however, the most common type, are also the hardest to see and need to be exposed before examination.

Latent fingerprints are made when the natural oils and perspiration present between the fingertip ridges are transferred to a surface by touch. The method used to reveal such minute traces

depends on the type of surface being tested. Hard and non-absorbent surfaces like glass, painted wood, tiles or metal are usually dusted with fingerprint powder which sticks to the traces of oil and perspiration left by the fingertip. The powder is made in different colors so that investigators can select the one that provides the sharpest contrast with the surface being dusted. Fine carbon powder is used to reveal latent prints on light-colored surfaces, while aluminum powder reveals prints on dark surfaces. Fluorescent powder can also be used, and this is photographed under ultraviolet light so that the fluorescing latent print will stand out even against the most brightly colored or patterned surface.

Soft or porous surfaces such as cloth or paper can yield fingerprint evidence through the use of chemical methods. The oldest method is iodine fuming. The article is examined by being placed inside an enclosed cabinet with iodine crystals and then heated. The iodine vapor given off by the crystals combines with the traces of the print in a chemical reaction that leaves a visible pattern.

ABOVE Magnetic powders and applicators help to reveal latent prints.

Other chemical methods use a ninhydrin spray that forms a purple-blue color when combined with the traces of amino acids in human perspiration; or silver nitrate, which reacts with the salt in perspiration to form silver chloride, which in turn is revealed under ultraviolet light.

A newer technique is known as superglue fuming because it relies on cyanoacrylate ester, the active ingredient in this type of very strong, quick-acting adhesive. The fumes can be applied by heating the object in a closed cabinet, as with iodine fuming, or by filling the whole of a closed space, such as the interior of an automobile, with fumes to reveal every latent print. Hand-held wands have also been developed that heat a small cartridge containing a mixture of the active ingredient

and a fluorescent dye. These wands can be used to test a suspect area that includes both porous and non-porous surfaces.

One of the latest techniques for revealing latent prints involves illuminating them with laser light, which causes chemicals in human perspiration to fluoresce in darkness. Different chemicals are used to intensify this effect. Alternative types of lasers or other high-intensity light sources such as quartz or xenon arc lamps can be set up relatively easily in most locations. In all these cases, the prints have to be placed on permanent record by being photographed or "lifted" using adhesive tape or plastic sheet to attract the fingerprint powder and preserve the all-important patterns.

ABOVE A fiberglass latent print brush and latent print-lifting tape.

Fingerprinting the dead

Fingerprinting has now become a standard part of autopsy procedure, effected after all other possible trace evidence has been removed from the fingertips and fingernails. If some time has elapsed since the death of a victim, "reconstructive" procedures have to be undertaken to ensure a clear set of prints.

Taking fingerprints from dead bodies is usually carried out when rigor mortis has passed off and after the body has been kept in cold storage. Bodies that are badly decomposed sometimes have to have the hands, or occasionally individual fingers, removed to aid the taking of the prints. Mummified bodies may need to have the fingertips softened by being soaked in a mixture of glycol, lactic acid and distilled water, sometimes for several weeks, before prints can be taken.

The most difficult subjects are those in which the skin has been softened by damp or immersion in water. In some cases glycerine or liquid wax has to be injected into the fingertip from below the joint. If the damage to the tissues is more extensive, the skin can be stripped away from the hand to be mounted on a surgical glove for prints to be taken. In one case in 1933 in Australia, the unidentified body

of a murder victim was found in the Murrumbidgee River with one hand missing and the other badly mutilated. The discovery of the outer skin of the missing right hand further along the river bank enabled this technique to be used to retrieve the prints. As a result the victim was identified as a down-and-out named Percy Smith, and eventually a fellow vagrant named Edward Morey was convicted of his murder.

Other identifiers

The patterns of the ridged skin on the palms of the hands and the soles of the feet are also unique to each individual, but prints of these are not usually kept for record purposes. Nonetheless, if a barefoot print or a palm print

BELOW Taking the fingerprints of a corpse.

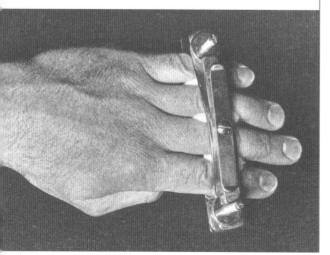

ABOVE A postmortem record strip holder for fingerprinting the dead.

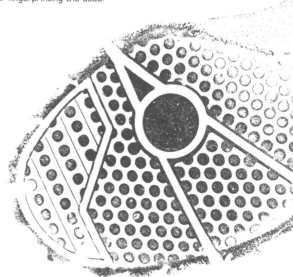

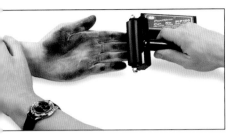  

is retrieved at the scene of a crime, potential suspects can be eliminated if their prints do not match. In some countries, the barefoot prints of new babies are used to provide positive proof of individual identity in maternity hospitals, since babies' fingerprints are too small for their features to be easily identified.

Other individual features are used to help identify faces from security-camera recordings. The basic proportions of the face can be computer-processed to enable them to be

TOP ROW Inking a subject's palm (left), rolling the palm on to the record card (center), and the finished palm (right) showing clear ridge details.

compared with photographs of a suspect taken from different angles and perspectives. The shape of the ears is one highly individual characteristic, since this varies from one person to the next and remains virtually the same for the whole of a subject's lifetime.

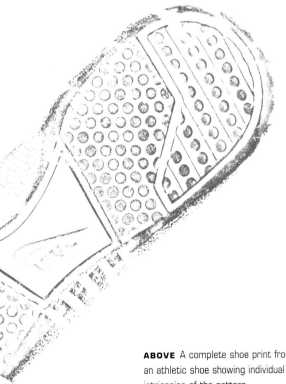

ABOVE A complete shoe print from an athletic shoe showing individual intricacies of the pattern.

RIGHT Comparing a heel print photograph taken at a crime scene with the shoe of a suspect.

Thomas Jennings

The Hiller family lived on Chicago's West 104th Street. In the early hours of September 19, 1910, Mrs. Hiller woke her husband Clarence and told him the gas lamp outside their daughter's bedroom was not burning properly. He got up to check and met a stranger on the landing. Hiller challenged the intruder, the two men fought and both fell down the stairs. The intruder then fired two shots and fled, leaving Clarence Hiller dying on the floor.

Neighbors arrived to help and the police were called, though a suspect had already been arrested less than a mile from the murder scene. Four off-duty officers had seen a man running as if evading pursuers, constantly turning to look behind him. When they stopped and searched him, they found he was carrying a loaded revolver. His name was Thomas Jennings and there were bloodstains on his clothing which he claimed had been made when he fell from a streetcar.

When officers searched the scene of the murder, they found three unused cartridges close to Mr. Hiller's body and some traces of sand and gravel at the foot of the daughter's bed, but these proved less significant than the fingerprints found in the kitchen. The day before his murder, Clarence Hiller had painted some railings next to the window through which the killer had gained access. The paint was still wet and had preserved a perfect set of four fingerprints from the intruder's left hand.

The Chicago police force was one of the first in the United States to recognize the value of fingerprinting. When Jennings' prints were compared with those at the Hiller house, they proved a perfect match. The case against Jennings was reinforced by a match between the bullets found in Clarence Hiller's body and test bullets fired from Jennings' gun, and he was found guilty of murder. His attorneys appealed on the grounds that fingerprint evidence was not admissible, but the verdict was confirmed on appeal. Jennings, the first felon in the United States to have been convicted on fingerprint evidence, was sentenced to death on December 21, 1911, and on a later date hanged.

BACKGROUND Thomas Jennings, whose fingerprints in wet paint at the crime scene resulted in his conviction for murder.

The Shark Arm Case

O n April 25, 1935, a tiger shark at Sydney's Coogee Beach aquarium appeared to suffer a violent fit, thrashing backward and forward in the water. The cause of the shark's discomfort finally became clear when it managed to regurgitate the obstruction—a human arm.

Forensic experts found that the arm was muscular and well developed as a result of regular exercise. An unusual tattoo of two boxers fighting was still visible. An early priority was to take fingerprints, even though the skin of the hand was in a very fragile condition. By removing the skin in small flakes and reassembling the fingertips piece by piece, the police managed to obtain the prints they needed to identify the owner of the arm. The tattoo alone had not proved enough of a distinguishing characteristic, even among missing persons, to provide the lead the police needed.

The arm was eventually traced to one James Smith, a former boxer with criminal connections who had vanished from his home on April 8 that year, telling his wife he had rented a cottage for a fishing holiday with a friend called Patrick Brady. Brady, who had links to drug trafficking, was arrested but denied all responsibility for Smith's death, casting suspicion instead on the local boatbuilder, Reginald Holmes.

Close examination of the arm showed that it had been hacked from Smith's body by a sharp knife, not bitten off by the shark's teeth, and that this had happened some time after Smith's death. At the rented cottage, police checked the owner's inventory and found that a trunk, a length of rope, a mattress and three mats were missing. They assumed Smith had been killed in the cottage and his body cut up on the spot. They also assumed that most of the body parts had been crammed into the trunk but they discovered that the remainder, including his arm, had been roped to the outside of the trunk before it was dumped at sea.

In spite of all these promising leads, the murderer was never found. Holmes claimed Brady had carried out the murder, but Holmes himself was murdered before he could testify at the inquest. Brady was still the prime suspect in the Smith killing, but he had still been in custody at the time of Holmes' death. Although both the motive and perpetrator remain unknown, the extraordinary sequence of events leading to the identification of the victim earned this case a unique place in the history of forensic science.

ABOVE The arm of James Smith, disgorged by a captured Tiger Shark in a Sydney aquarium, and showing the tattoo of a boxer.

ABOVE The murderer of James Smith (right) has never been found.

Peter Griffiths

BELOW Peter Griffiths.

June Anne Devaney was a three-year-old patient in the children's ward of Queen's Park Hospital in Blackburn, England, in 1948. She was recovering from a bout of pneumonia. During the early hours of May 15 the child was abducted; less than two hours after the alarm was raised, the search revealed her fearfully battered body lying dead in the hospital grounds. She had been raped and there were teeth marks on her skin, but there was no other evidence to help identify her killer.

The police concentrated on the ward from which she had been taken. They checked every footprint on the polished floor and discovered a set of prints of stockinged feet that could not have belonged to any of the nurses. The tracks led first to a trolley at the end of the ward, from which a bottle of sterile water had been taken, then to the child's bed. The bottle had been left under the bed. The police then checked every print on the bottle and, having painstakingly eliminated those belonging to the hospital staff, were left with one single set: those of the killer.

The place where the child's body had been left suggested to police that the culprit was someone with local knowledge. They undertook the daunting task of fingerprinting every male over the age of sixteen in the whole city area—more than 46,000 men. Almost eight weeks later, having completed that search and checked all local records, they had still not found a match.

At that time, some aspects of wartime rationing were still in force in Britain and all adults had to be issued with ration books. The electoral registers, which had been used for the fingerprint campaign, were cross-checked against registers of ration-book holders. Police were surprised to find that these second registers contained details of more that two hundred men who had not appeared on the first lists. Checking was resumed and, on August 11, police found that the prints of subject number 46,253, a twenty-two-year-old Blackburn flour mill worker called Peter Griffiths, provided a perfect match.

BACKGROUND A record from the mass fingerprinting campaign.

LEFT Entrance to the hospital ward from which June Anne Devaney was abducted.

RIGHT Fingerprints on a glass bottle made visible by dusting with fingerprint powder.

BOTTOM A policewoman at the headquarters of Blackburn CID hands over fingerprint record forms to a plainclothes police officer working on the case.

Peter Griffiths was identified by the world's first mass fingerprinting campaign. Other evidence linking him to June Devaney's terrible murder was discovered by matching fibers from the child's nightgown with some found on his clothes and by fitting his stockinged feet to the prints found on the hospital floor. His niece had been a patient in the hospital at the same time as his victim. Though initially he denied any involvement, he finally confessed, was found guilty at trial and hanged in November 1948.

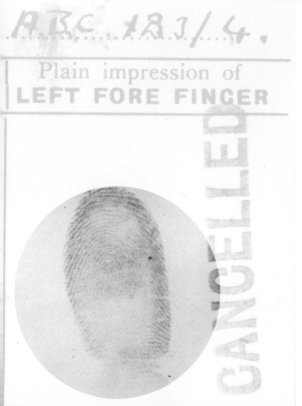

Ted Bundy

ABOVE, LEFT TO RIGHT Three of Bundy's alleged victims: Laura Aime, Debbie Kent, and Melissa Smith who all disappeared in 1974 in Utah.

BELOW Ted Bundy appears in court, restrained by handcuffs and a leg brace.

Serial killer Theodore (Ted) Bundy killed more than forty young women in a spree spanning almost a decade. The killings began in 1969 in California and spread through Oregon and Washington and into Utah and Colorado. The murder victims all shared certain physical characteristics, and when the different police forces compared notes on suspects they found Bundy's name was another recurring theme—but none had proof of anything more sinister than his presence in the vicinity of the crimes.

Bundy made his first mistake in Salt Lake City in November 1974 when he tried to abduct 18-year-old Carol DaRonch by claiming to be a plainclothes police officer. She climbed into his car, but when he produced a pair of handcuffs and tried to attack her with a crowbar, she managed to struggle free and escape. She reported the incident, but it was not until August the following year that a Salt Lake City police officer noticed a Volkswagen driver behaving suspiciously, and stopped him. A crowbar and handcuffs were found in the car, prompting an association with the attempted abduction of Carol DaRonch. She identified Bundy, and he was sentenced to fifteen years' imprisonment for the attack.

Unfortunately, while being taken to Colorado to be charged with another murder in June 1977, Bundy escaped. He was recaptured after eight days, but within six months he had escaped again. In January 1978, he attacked four women in the Chi Omega sorority house at Florida State University in Tallahassee. Two of the women were killed and two were left seriously injured. An hour and a half later, he attacked another

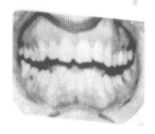

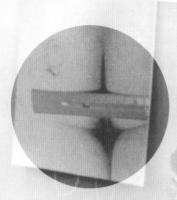

woman on the same campus. She survived and was able to provide a description.

Bundy was eventually recaptured in Pensacola and put on trial for the Florida murders. The crucial evidence was a bite mark on one of the victims that had been photographed and measured as part of the autopsy. Bundy's teeth were photographed and he was also forced to cooperate in the making of a cast of his bite. Because of peculiarities in the arrangement of his teeth in the jaw, which matched the injuries exactly, the jury accepted that he was the murderer. Once he had been convicted of the murders of the Florida State University students and sentenced to death, he intimated that he could have been responsible for a total of between forty and fifty murders. He was finally executed in 1989.

ABOVE Photographs of Bundy's teeth, which were linked to the bite-mark left on the buttock of one of the victims, Lisa Levy.

BACKGROUND Dr. Lowell Levine, chief consultant in forensic dentistry to the New York City Medical examiner, explaining the individual features of Bundy's teeth to the assembled court.

BELOW Dentist Dr. Richard Souviron shows the jury the bitemark evidence.

Trace Elements

ABOVE Highlighted spots of trace evidence on the road where murder victim James Byrd was dragged in Texas in 1998.

One of the basic assumptions of forensic science is that a person present at the scene of a crime exchanges trace evidence with the location in a number of different ways. Traces may be found at the scene that can be linked to a suspect, and traces found on the suspect may link him or her to the place where the crime was committed—or indeed to the crime itself. Hairs, fibers, particles of dust or soil, plant debris, paint flakes and other microscopic evidence can trap even scrupulously careful criminals and prove their involvement in the most meticulously planned crimes.

ABOVE Examining evidence through an optical microscope.

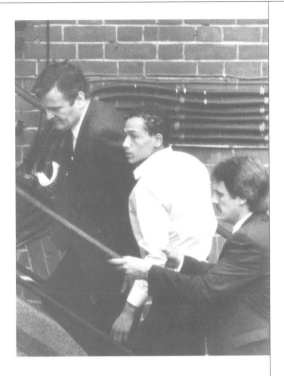

Paint Samples

Traces of paint evidence offer similar possibilities. In some cases the shape and color of a flake of paint can be matched with the surface from which it was taken. In others, the chemical constituents and other precise properties of the sample must be determined to prove whether or not they match the suspected source.

Paint samples are particularly important in cases involving vehicles, and forensic laboratories maintain large databases on the precise compositions and ranges of colors used by the larger manufacturers. The surface finish of any vehicle is usually built up as a series of layers, from the initial primer to the final coats of clear gloss. Colors can be compared under the microscope, and the polymer binder that holds each layer together can be broken down and analyzed by pyrolysis gas chromatography, where the paint chips are heated to release their constituents in gaseous form. This effectively creates a single "fingerprint" for each layer and helps to establish points of comparison with other samples.

TOP FOUR Cross sections of different samples of red paint and underlying layers from different red automobiles.

BOTTOM FOUR Cross sections of red household paint.

TOP LEFT Kenneth Erskine, who was traced to a crime scene through samples of his hair.

175

Hairs

Hairs found at the scene may belong to the criminal, to the victim or to animals associated with either individual. Whatever their origin, hairs provide useful evidence because they retain their structure for a long time: the tough outer covering of the cuticle partly accounts for this resistance to decay. It is made from overlapping cells that show different patterns in different species of animal.

Inside the cuticle is the cortex, a regular array of cells running along the length of the hair. This carries the particles of pigment which give the hair its characteristic color. The way in which these particles are shaped and distributed, and their precise color, can help identify the hairs of particular individuals.

At the center of the cortex there is usually, but not always, another inner layer of cells called the medulla. The medulla is rarely continuous. In both human and animal hair, it may be interrupted or fragmented, and it varies in shape and appearance.

Unfortunately for investigators, there are often significant variations in the structure of different hairs from a single individual, especially if they are from different parts of the body. For this reason the widest possible range of comparison samples is taken for analysis. In general, hairs from the head are of circular cross-section, as are those from eyebrows and eyelashes, though these generally have more tapering tips. Hairs from the beard are generally triangular in cross section, while those from the armpits are oval.

Racial differences can sometimes be discerned by examination of the hair alone. People of Mongoloid origin, for example, tend to have hairs with a continuous medulla, while the particles of pigment in Afro-Caribbean hair are denser and less evenly distributed than those in Caucasian hair.

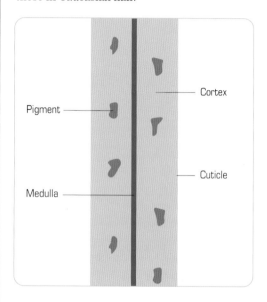

ABOVE Diagram showing the different internal components of a human hair.

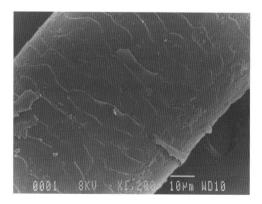

ABOVE Photomicrograph of a human hair, magnified 1200 times.

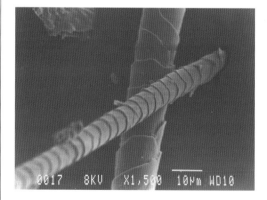

ABOVE Photomicrograph of a cat hair to the same scale as the human hair (left) is clearly thinner, with a different pattern of overlapping scales.

Using microscope technology, it is possible to tell whether a hair has been artificially bleached or colored. Depending on where the colored or bleached zone ends relative to the root of the hair, estimates can be made of when the last coloring or bleaching was actually applied.

Hairs can sometimes reveal the presence of poison in the body of the person they came from. In cases of drug abuse or poisoning by arsenic, the part of the hair in which these traces are found gives an indication of when doses were administered.

Further information can be gathered through neutron activation analysis, a process that was introduced in the late 1950s. A sample of potential evidence, such as a hair, is bombarded with neutrons in the core of a nuclear reactor. The neutrons collide with the atoms of the different trace elements making up the sample and render them radioactive. By measuring the resulting gamma radiation, the most minute traces of every constituent of the sample can be measured. Neutron activation analysis can identify traces of billionths of grams of fourteen different elements in a single hair. Calculations have shown that the likelihood of two different individuals having the same concentrations of just nine of these constituents is around one in a million. More recently, this powerful but fairly cumbersome

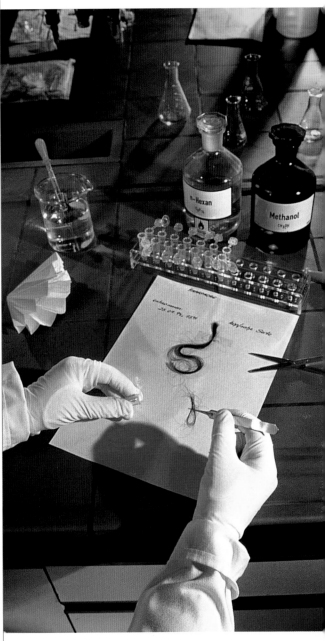

ABOVE Preparing a hair sample for microscopic analysis.

technique has been superseded by the use of hair as a source for producing samples of a subject's DNA (see Chapter Fourteen).

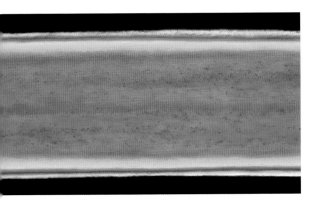

ABOVE Photograph of a human hair taken under polarized light, revealing the medulla as a darker central filament.

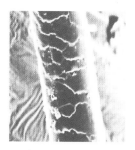
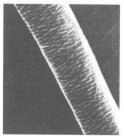
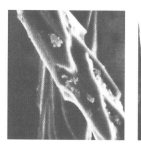

Fibers

All fibers used in clothing and furnishing fabrics are natural, man-made, or a combination of the two. Natural fibers include wool and silk, vegetable fibers like cotton, hemp, sisal, flax (used in making linen) and jute; a wide range of animal hairs such as cashmere, camel hair, mohair and alpaca; and furs like mink or sable. Each one has a characteristic appearance that enables it to be

ABOVE, FROM LEFT TO RIGHT Dog, deer, rabbit and horse hair.

BELOW False-color scanning electron micrograph of cotton fibers and (bottom) sheep hairs, one broken to show its internal honeycomb structure.

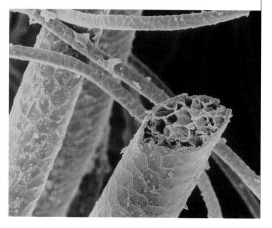

distinguished from human and other animal hairs when examined under a microscope.

As with most fiber evidence, the usefulness of any particular sample depends on its rarity. Cotton, for example, is so widely used in clothing that the presence of undyed cotton fibers is normally of little use, though different dyed colors can narrow the field to a significant extent. Animal hairs found at a crime scene may belong to pets rather than furs, and these too need to be checked carefully with any traces found on a suspect's clothing.

Man-made fibers, however, offer much more to the forensic examiner. Since the development of rayon and nylon before World War Two, a wide range of different materials has been produced including acetates, acrylics, and polyesters, each of which has different properties and identifiable characteristics. They are all formed from polymers, molecules built up from long chains containing millions of individual atoms that account for the elasticity and durability of many of these fabrics.

It is sometimes possible to identify fragments of fabric without sophisticated technology. For example, forensic examiners can sometimes match a length of fabric from the clothing of a hit-and-run victim with a fragment found on the vehicle responsible

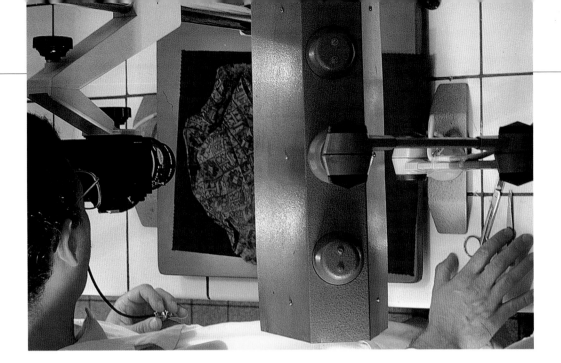

without needing to ascertain precise details of the material's composition.

More often, however, forensic examiners find relatively few fibers, so their value as evidence depends on their exact constitution. This can be checked through a microscope by pinpointing the fiber's precise diameter, its exact color, and any other distinguishing features such as striations running along the fibers from the production process, or particles of agents such as titanium dioxide, which is added during manufacture to modify the fabric's texture and surface shine.

The colors of fibers, even when only small fragments have been retrieved, can be compared very accurately by a technique called microspectrophotometry. This involves shining a beam of visible or infrared light on a sample of the fiber under a microscope to display the absorption spectrum of the fiber on a computer screen.

Chromatography can be used to separate the individual chemicals used to make the dye by dissolving the dye in a suitable solution. The fiber itself can be identified by additional tests such as birefringence. This is carried out by shining a beam of light onto a synthetic fiber: the light emerges refracted and polarized. The light emerging parallel to the axis of the fiber has one refractive index; that emerging perpendicular to the axis has another. By measuring the two refractive indices accurately, the fiber type can be identified.

BELOW, LEFT TO RIGHT Synthetic fibers, showing discernible differences in structure: acetate, nylon, and vivrelle.

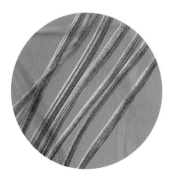  

Glass and Dust Analysis

Samples of glass from vehicle windows or headlights, or from windows or glassware at the crime scene, can provide important evidence. Large fragments of glass can sometimes be fitted into the lamp or window pane from which they were broken for a positive match, or the glass can actually preserve a record of the order in which events happened. When a window pane is penetrated by a series of gunshots, for example, the first shot makes a hole surrounded by a set of radial fractures that in turn are linked by concentric fractures. These fracture patterns can tell forensic examiners which side of the glass received the initial blow from the stress marks along their cross section. Because developing fractures stop at the point of any existing fracture lines, the radial fractures from a second bullet hole end where they meet the radial fractures from the first. Fractures produced by a third bullet hole terminate where they meet fractures radiating from the first two, and so on.

Different types of glass have different densities and refractive indices. Density is measured by placing the glass fragments in a mixture of two chemicals of different known densities: bromoform and bromobenzene. The proportions of the two ingredients are adjusted until the glass particles remain suspended in the liquid, at which point their densities are equal.

The refractive index of glass is determined by immersing samples in a liquid that changes its refractive index according to its temperature. Controlled heat is applied until the contrast between the liquid and the glass particles disappears, at which point the refractive indices of the glass and the liquid are the same.

Although a particular combination of density and refractive index is not usually unique, the FBI laboratory maintains data on the frequency with which any individual combination is likely to be found. If two samples with the same properties come from a relatively rare type of glass, their significance in terms of evidence is increased.

Particles of dust picked up at the crime scene or on a suspect's clothing can also reveal important evidence. Soil from gardens, open land, tracks or woodland can be valuable because of the plant spores, pollen particles, insects and micro-organisms contained in it, all of which can be revealed by microscopic analysis and can help to indicate its likely source. Other dust particles of concrete, flour, coal or brick, for example, can suggest connections with a person's place of work or occupation.

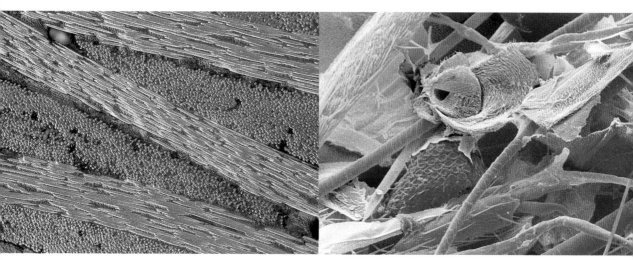

ABOVE Bullet holes in a glass window producing radial and concentric fractures, where the intersections reveal the order in which the shots struck the glass.

FAR LEFT Photomicrograph of glass fibers in a polypropylene matrix.

CENTER LEFT Color-scanning electron microscope image of household dust, made up of particles of soil and sand, skin scales, household fibers, and pet hair.

LEFT False-color scanning electron micrograph of glass fibers.

Stephen Bradley

On July 7, 1960, eight-year-old Graeme Thorne was snatched by a kidnapper while on his way home from school in Sydney, Australia. His parents, Bazil and Frieda Thorne, had won the state lottery five weeks previously, and their newfound wealth had clearly made them a target. Sure enough, the kidnapper made two telephone calls demanding a $52,500 ransom for the boy's safe return; then all communications ceased.

Witnesses claimed to have seen a blue 1955 Ford Customline in the vicinity on the day of the kidnapping. The boy's schoolbag was found, then his cap, coat and books. Finally, on August 16, his body was discovered ten miles from his home, wrapped in a rug. The boy had been suffocated and then clubbed to death. The evidence was taken to the Sydney forensic laboratory to be studied in detail.

Scientists found a curious pink granular substance on parts of the boy's clothing, together with animal and human hairs. There were also traces of mold on his shoes and socks. Analysis revealed that the animal hairs were almost certainly from a Pekinese dog and that the pink grains came from a mortar used in house-building. The development of the mold indicated that the boy had probably been dead for five to six weeks, and so had been killed almost immediately after the kidnapping. Investigators also set out to identify all the plant material found on the rug and the body. Their finds included seeds of a rare variety of cypress that did not grow in the area where the body was discovered. A public appeal asked for details of houses that had both pink mortar between the bricks and this type of cypress in the garden. One such house was located in the suburb of Clontarf, where the tenants gave promising details of the previous occupant. He had been a Hungarian and had assumed the name of Stephen Bradley. His spoken English had been heavily accented—much like that of the man who had made the ransom demands—and he had left the house on the day of the kidnapping. A search of the premises yielded a picture of

ABOVE Confident kidnapper Stephen Bradley, trapped by trace evidence.

OPPOSITE A handcuffed Bradley arrives at Sydney Coroner's Court.

Bradley, picnicking with his family on the very rug that had been used to wrap the boy's body. A tassel that had become detached from the rug was also found in the house.

Bradley was also known to have had a Pekinese dog, and to have sold a blue Ford Customline on the day of his disappearance. Police located the car at a local dealer's and found traces of pink mortar in the trunk. The dog, whose hairs matched those found on the boy's clothes, was traced to a veterinary hospital. Bradley himself was found, bound for England on the liner *Himalaya*. The ship was intercepted at Colombo in Sri Lanka, and Bradley was arrested. At trial he was convicted of the boy's murder and sentenced to life imprisonment.

Malcolm Fairley

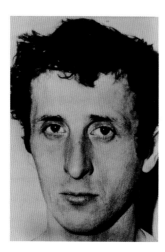

ABOVE Multiple rapist Malcolm Fairley, alias "The Fox."

RIGHT Detective Chief Inspector John Branscombe shows the crudely made hood worn by "The Fox" during his attacks, against a background of other pieces of evidence, including gloves, shotgun cartridges, and a sawed-off shotgun.

A series of burglaries and attacks on householders in southern England in 1984 became increasingly serious when the attacks began to escalate into violent assaults. The burglar threatened his victims with a shotgun he had stolen from one of his earlier robberies, and eventually took to raping his female victims and assaulting their male companions.

The man wore a hooded mask, but witnesses were able to report that he spoke with a northern-England accent and was clearly left-handed. Though a huge police hunt was mounted for the man, dubbed "The Fox" by newspaper reporters, he managed to evade capture for months.

On the night of August 17, however, when driving north to Yorkshire to visit his mother, "The Fox" made a careless mistake. He stopped on the outskirts of a village called Brampton and decided to strike again, even though he had left his hood at home. He concealed his car in a field and cut a new mask from a pair of green overalls. He then walked to the village, broke into a house, tied up the male occupant and raped his wife. He then coolly removed traces of physical evidence, even cutting away a square of bed sheet, and left.

When police searched the area they found tracks that showed where the car had been parked. They also found a flake of yellow paint where the car had scraped against a tree while being reversed into the hiding place, a leather glove, the piece of bed sheet and the burglar's crudely-made mask. Nearby, under a covering of leaves, they found the shotgun. Convinced that the suspect would return to retrieve the gun, police mounted a stake-

RIGHT Armed police officers at Linslade Wood, near Leighton Buzzard, searching for the rapist known as "The Fox."

BELOW The search for "The Fox" extends to a house in the Bedfordshire village of Edlesborough.

out operation, staging a fake road accident to account for their presence in this quiet country area; but the suspect did not return.

The paint sample was analyzed and the color identified as "Harvest Gold." That color had been used on only one model, an Austin Allegro made between May 1973 and August 1975. Police also searched the national computer for details of burglars from the north of England who were known to have moved south, and the computer produced data on more than 3000 potential suspects.

The laborious police search continued until September 11, when two officers went to check an address in north London. The resident was one Malcolm Fairley, and officers found him outside washing his car—an Austin Allegro, painted in Harvest Gold. They questioned him about his recent movements, noting the pronounced northern accent that characterized his evasive answers. On the back seat of the car was the suspect's watch, which the police asked him to put on. He complied, and in doing so showed he was left-handed. The car itself bore evidence of damage at a height consistent with position of the paint flake found on the tree near Brampton. Fairley's flat was subsequently searched and two more sets of overalls identical to those used to make the mask were discovered. The suspect confessed and on February 26, 1985, Macolm Fairley was given six life sentences for a series of violent attacks and rapes.

BACKGROUND Malcolm Fairley's apartment in Kentish Town, North London.

John Vollman

On a spring afternoon in May 1958, sixteen-year-old Gaetane Bouchard failed to return from a shopping trip in Edmundston, New Brunswick, Canada. Her anxious father telephoned her friends to ask if they knew where she might be. Several mentioned a boyfriend, a twenty-year-old printer and part-time musician named John Vollman who lived across the U.S. border in Madawaska, Maine. When asked about Gaetane, Vollman claimed he had not seen her since he had become engaged to another woman.

Bouchard notified the police and resumed his search. He checked an abandoned gravel pit that was popular with young couples in parked cars—and there he found his daughter's body. She had been stabbed to death. At the scene police found tire tracks, and two flakes of green paint that had probably been dislodged from a vehicle by stones thrown up by its wheels as it accelerated away.

Witnesses were found who reported that, earlier that day, Gaetane had been seen buying chocolate. She had also been seen talking to the driver of a 1952 green Pontiac with Maine license plates, and been seen inside the car, which was thought to be the vehicle that had left tracks at the murder scene.

Detectives checked Vollman's car and were able to match the larger paint flake with a corresponding chipped patch below the passenger door. Inside the glove compartment there was also a half-eaten bar of chocolate bearing traces of lipstick. The most important evidence, however, was a hair found clutched in the dead girl's hand.

Samples of Gaetane's hair, Vollman's hair and the hair found at the scene were tested by neutron activation analysis (see page 177). One result gave the ratio of sulfur radiation to phosphorus radiation in each sample: Gaetane's hair registered 2.02, Vollman's registered 1.07 and the sample found clasped in her hand registered 1.02.

Though Vollman's attorneys attempted to have the evidence rejected as inadmissible, it prompted Vollman to change his plea of innocence to one of guilty of manslaughter. Nevertheless he was convicted of murder and sentenced to death (the sentence was later commuted to life imprisonment) and he became the first criminal to be convicted by the powerful new technique of neutron activation analysis.

ABOVE Scanning electron micrograph of the surface of a shaft of human hair shows how irregular each individual strand can be.

Blood

ABOVE Murder victim Ghislaine Marchal apparently wrote the words "Omar killed me" in her own blood on the door of the room where she died, and the message provided vital evidence in the conviction of her accused attacker, Omar Raddad.

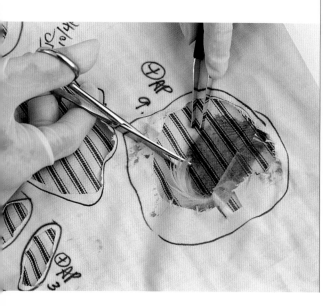

An adult has some ten pints of blood circulating around the body, driven under pressure from the heart's pumping action. This presents a potential attacker with something of a problem. Any cutting or piercing of major blood vessels can produce a deluge and result in significant traces of blood being left at a crime scene. Such traces can indicate how an attack was made and help identify all manner of objects associated with it. Even the attacker's own blood, shed in a violent struggle, can tie him or her to the scene as securely as a photograph or an eyewitness identification.

LEFT Checking bloodstains on a pillow recovered from a crime scene.

For these reasons, criminals often go to great lengths to remove bloodstains from a crime scene. They may satisfy themselves that all traces have been eliminated, but once the crime has been discovered the police search usually extends to areas beyond the perpetrators' control. Forensic experts check beneath washbasins and inside drawers, between floorboards or in drains and waste-pipes leading from baths or sinks that may have been used for washing or for cleaning the murder weapon.

Bloodstain evidence

At one time, blood found at the crime scene was significant to forensic scientists simply by its presence. Because blood tends to dry quickly on exposure to air and to remain clearly visible unless cleaned away, bloodstains and splashes can often tell their own story. Drops of blood that fall onto a horizontal surface, for example, give examiners some idea of how far they fell before hitting the surface,

and so suggest the position at the time of the individual who shed the blood.

If the blood falls only a short distance, the marks are circular or, if the surface is at an

ABOVE Bloody footprints provide evidence at a crime scene.

BELOW At the crime scene collecting blood samples for analysis.

angle to the horizontal, elliptical in shape. If the drops fall a few feet before hitting the surface, the edges of the circular mark are crenellated, the degree of crenellation increasing proportionately with the length of the fall. If drops fall from a height of six feet or so, there are usually side spurts radiating from the site of the main drop.

Drops of blood shed from a moving source have a different appearance. They may have fallen from an already blood-soaked weapon being swung to deliver a blow, or from a wounded victim trying to escape. In such cases any drops hitting floors or walls often take on the appearance of a stretched exclamation mark: the end of the stain showing the smaller blob indicates the direction of the subject's movement.

Stains made by blood spurting under pressure from a major blood vessel show where a serious or even fatal blow was delivered. The height reached by the spurting blood, if it splashed on a wall or partition, for example, can show whether the victim was standing, sitting, kneeling or lying down when the blow was struck; the quantity of blood spilled, when compared with injuries to the victim's body, can be correlated with particular wounds. Pools of blood can also indicate where the victim died, even if the body was later moved.

Tests for blood

In many cases, blood spilled at a crime scene is all too obvious. But even if criminals have tried to clean away the evidence, examiners must ensure that they locate every remaining trace. There are several chemicals that can differentiate between blood and other substances with a similar appearance, and others that can be used to highlight bloodstains. In using these chemicals at the scene, great care must be taken to avoid contamination, since some of the tests are sensitive to chemicals other than blood. The first test simply uses a powerful light. The

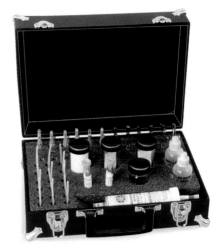

ABOVE Portable blood test kit for field and laboratory use.

BELOW Forensic scientist places a sample of bloodstained clothing into a sample tube for analysis.

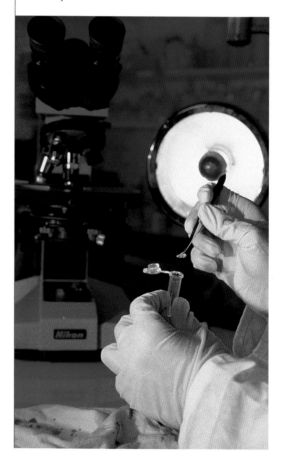

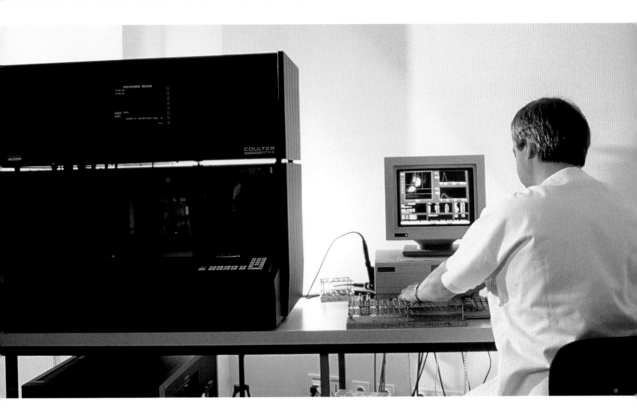

ABOVE A forensic technician displays the results of a blood analysis test on a computer screen.

light's beam, held at an angle over every surface at the scene, can often reveal traces of blood that would otherwise remain unnoticed.

A more powerful test relies on a chemical called luminol, which reacts with blood to produce a faint luminescence. Examiners darken the room being tested and spray all suspect areas with the chemical. All spots and stains of blood then emit a faint blue glow, the intensity of which varies according to the amount of blood present. The test works even on old bloodstains, which react by glowing more vividly than recent marks. Luminol can reveal bloodstains even if they are diluted by a factor of 10,000, but it does have one unfortunate drawback. The chemical can destroy many of the properties of bloodstains that examiners need to preserve for further analysis, so it is normally used only to check for bloodstains that would otherwise remain invisible to the naked eye.

If examiners wish to confirm that suspicious-looking marks are in fact bloodstains, chemical indicators such as phenolphthalein can be used. When mixed with hydrogen peroxide and a blood sample, these chemicals react with the hemoglobin in the red cells to produce a deep pink color. Unfortunately, they also react in a similar way to constituents of potatoes and horseradish, so examiners must guard against any potential contamination from such sources.

To identify blood as human blood, a sample is placed in a test tube above a layer of specially prepared rabbit serum that has been sensitized to human blood. This is prepared by injecting a rabbit with human blood, allowing the appropriate antibodies to form in the animal's bloodstream, then extracting a sample. If the sample found at the crime scene is human blood, a cloudy ring will appear at the junction of the suspect sample and the rabbit serum.

Blood groups

Blood is a mixture of red and white blood cells suspended in a watery liquid called plasma. Plasma accounts for more than half the blood's content. The job of the red blood cells is to absorb oxygen from the lungs and carry it to the body tissues. The red cells carry chemicals called antigens that can react to the presence of blood of a different group by causing the cells to clump together, or agglutinate. This adverse reaction caused the death of many patients given blood in early transfusions toward the end of the nineteenth century.

In 1901, Austrian biologist Dr. Karl Landsteiner identified two different blood groups, A and B, that had different antigens on their red cells. He found that blood of either type could be mixed with blood of the same type from a different person without any adverse reaction, but if the two types were mixed with each other, agglutination occurred. Landsteiner subsequently identified a third group that he classified as type C, and this had affinities with both type A and type B. A fourth

group was also found that could be mixed with groups A or B without agglutination, and this was classified as group AB.

In time further human blood classifications were defined and the Rhesus factor recognized. The Rhesus is an antigen occurring in the red cells of most people: where it is present, the blood is described as Rhesus positive (Rh+); where it is not, the blood is described as Rhesus negative (Rh-). Different enzymes and proteins were also isolated, and these can now be identified even in dried bloodstains, adding further detail to investigators' findings.

Every detail extracted from a blood sample helps to narrow the field of possible sources. For example, some forty-two percent of the U.S. population has type A blood, about nine percent has type B, forty-six percent type O and three percent type AB. An enzyme called phosphoglucomutase 2-1 (PGM2-1) is also found in thirty-six percent of the population, regardless of blood group. So if PGM2-1 is found in a sample of type A blood, for example, the field of potential sources is narrowed to 0.36 x 0.42 or fifteen percent of the population. Traces or absences of other proteins and enzymes can be used to identify an individual blood sample more particularly, with the result in some cases that the field of possible sources is narrowed to hundredths of one percent of the population. Such accuracy is of course highly useful in both eliminating or implicating suspects.

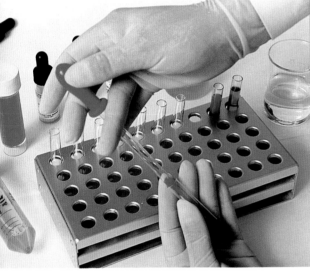

TOP LEFT A gloved hand transferring blood into a sample bottle.

LEFT AND ABOVE Blood from a shoe is reconstituted in a saline solution before being dropped into a test tube (above) containing different antibodies to determine the blood group.

RIGHT A program called FAScan displays the results of blood analysis.

Secretors

Irrespective of blood group, around eighty percent of the population qualify as "secretors" because the antigens, antibodies, proteins and enzymes that characterize their blood are also found in other body fluids like tears, sweat, saliva, vaginal fluids and semen. The remaining twenty percent or so of the population carry this information only in the blood; but in secretors, samples of skin and muscle tissue, and even saliva left by a smoker on the butt of a cigarette can contain a great deal of evidence. Forensic examination is then simplified by the fact that just a sample of saliva, which can be quickly and easily obtained once a suspect is identified, can be tested and the results checked against crime-scene evidence.

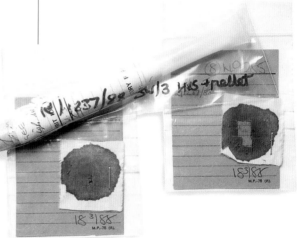

ABOVE Two pieces of bloodstained cloth and a vaginal swab from a rape investigation.

BELOW A forensic serology laboratory, specializing in testing and analysis of body fluids.

RIGHT Photomicrograph of human spermatozoa.

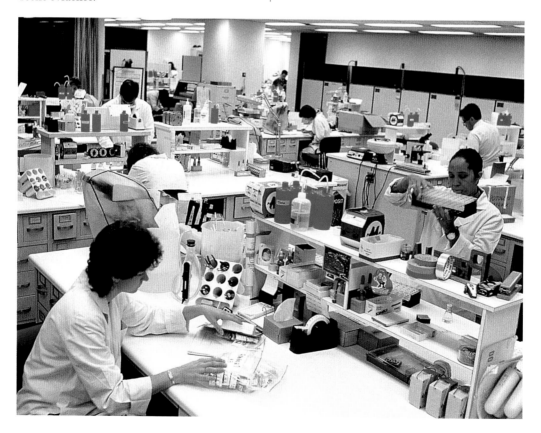

Seminal fluid

In cases of rape and other sexual crimes, the seminal fluid left by the attacker on the victim's body or on clothing or furniture presents another powerful source of evidence. Since the sperm in the fluid remain alive for only a relatively short period, the condition of the sample can give a reasonably accurate indication of the time of the attack. In the case of secretors, such a sample contains information on blood group and the presence or absence of other enzymes and proteins that can help to concentrate the search for a potential subject.

Samples of seminal fluid are isolated using tests similar to those used to reveal the presence of bloodstains. These tests are particularly useful where attempts have been made by the criminal to remove or wash away incriminating traces.

The usual test is for the presence of an enzyme called acid phosphatase, which is normally secreted into the seminal fluid by the prostate gland. Filter paper is rubbed over the suspected area and any acid phosphatase present is partly transferred to the paper. A few drops of a mixture of sodium alphanaphthylphosphate and a chemical called Fast Blue B solution are then dropped on the paper, and if the enzyme is present a deep purple color quickly appears. Again, the test is sensitive to other substances such as fungi and some types of fruit and vegetable juice, but these fluids do not usually produce a reaction as quickly as seminal fluid does.

Another more specific test developed in the 1970s looks for a protein called p30 or Prostate Specific Antigen (PSA). This is found only in seminal fluid and the test is similar in principle to that used to identify bloodstains as human. A sample of p30 is injected into a rabbit to induce the animal to produce antibodies to the protein. Then a sample of blood serum containing this antibody (anti-p30) is taken from the rabbit and used to test the

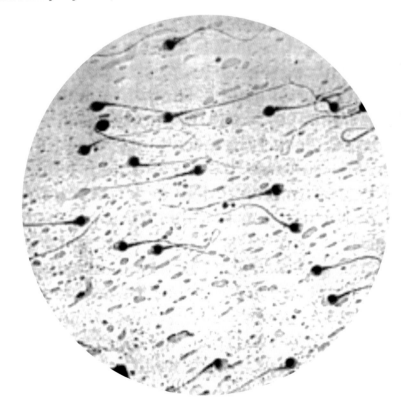

ABOVE FROM LEFT TO RIGHT Suspect semen extract and sample of anti-p30 added to their respective wells of an electrophoretic plate; antigen and antibody move towards one another under electric charge; formation of a visible straight line between the two wells reveals the suspect fluid contains semen.

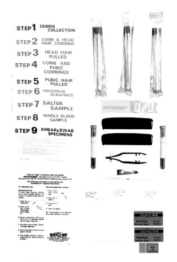

STEP **1** DEBRIS COLLECTION
STEP **2** COMB & HEAD HAIR COMBING
STEP **3** HEAD HAIR PULLED
STEP **4** COMB AND PUBIC COMBINGS
STEP **5** PUBIC HAIR PULLED
STEP **6** FINGERNAIL SCRAPINGS
STEP **7** SALIVA SAMPLE
STEP **8** WHOLE BLOOD SAMPLE
STEP **9** SMEAR & SWAB SPECIMENS

ABOVE Sex crimes investigation kit used by England's Metropolitan Police.

LEFT Array of blood samples being analyzed for DNA fingerprinting.

OPPOSITE PAGE Forensic scientist removes bloodstained material from clothing for DNA fingerprinting.

suspect sample for seminal fluid. The suspect trace is placed in one well of an electrophoretic plate, and the anti-p30 rabbit serum in the other. When an electric charge is applied across the plate, if the antibodies and antigens start to move toward one another and eventually form a visible straight line between the two wells, then the sample is seminal fluid.

More recently, these complex tests for different blood groups and the presence of different proteins and enzymes have been overtaken by the much more powerful technique of retrieving DNA from victims and suspects (see Chapter Fourteen). The DNA test produces an accurate and entirely individual result that can convict a criminal on the basis of the smallest trace of bodily fluid, quite independently of other corroborative evidence. As this technique becomes better known, of course, criminals are responding by adapting their methods of operation and leaving as few personal traces as possible.

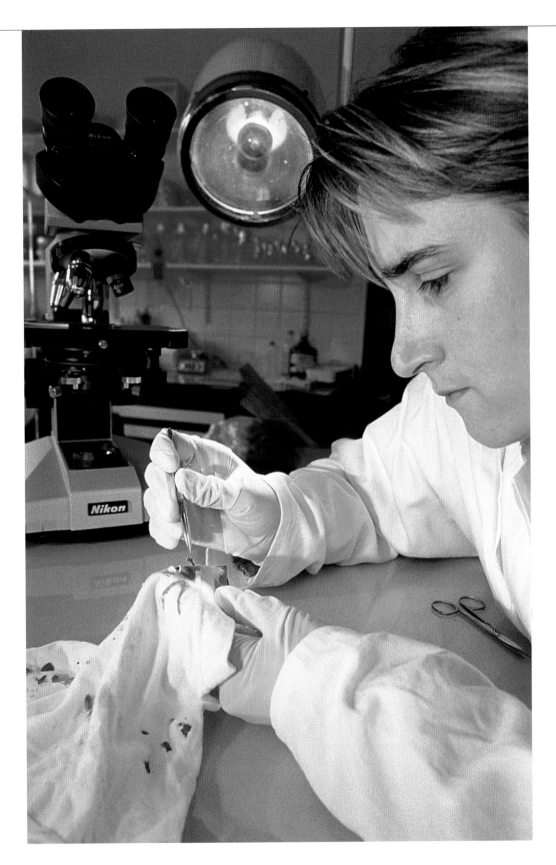

Lindy Chamberlain

ichael and Lindy Chamberlain took their two sons, aged six and four, and their nine-week-old daughter Azaria on a camping holiday to the interior of Australia in August 1980. The family pitched their tent at a site close to the huge and mysterious landmark of Uluru (Ayers Rock). The following day Michael climbed to the top of the rock twice, taking his young sons with him on the second climb.

On the evening of August 17, the baby was snugly cocooned in blankets in a baby carrier at the back of the tent where the younger boy was also asleep. Lindy Chamberlain was cooking supper for the older boy at the barbecue site some sixty feet away: the tent flap was left unzipped since the boy would be going to bed after his meal. Michael Chamberlain claimed he heard a short, sharp cry at around eight o'clock, and Lindy started back to the tent to check the baby.

Lindy Chamberlain later told of her astonishment at this point when she saw an Australian wild dog, or dingo, backing out of the tent and shaking something violently in its jaws. The dingo disappeared into the darkness, whereupon the horrified Chamberlains found their baby was missing. The alarm was raised and trackers mounted a search of the surrounding countryside, but no sign of the baby or the dingo was found.

To the surprise of many onlookers, the deeply religious couple seemed to accept their daughter's disappearance quite calmly, and to assume that she would not be found alive. Suspicions mounted when, eight days after the baby's disappearance, most of her clothes were found by a tourist walking through scrub to the west of Ayers Rock. The clothes were neatly folded, but the jacket was missing. The undershirt was inside out; the bootees were still laced up and were found inside the legs of the baby's jumpsuit. There were bloodstains around the neck of the jumpsuit and on the undershirt, but there were no signs of any human remains in the clothes or at the scene.

When the clothes were examined in detail, other curious facts emerged. There were no traces of dingo hair or dingo saliva on the garments, even in the area of the bloodstains. Controversial experiments were carried out in which dead animals of a size similar to that of the baby and clad in similar clothes were thrown into the dingo pen at Adelaide Zoo. The dogs' responses were observed and recorded. Investigators concluded that, since there were no pulled threads on Azaria's clothing or any other indications of a dingo being involved, the child must have been attacked by humans who had subsequently removed her clothes and left them several miles from the camp site.

BACKGROUND Lindy Chamberlain and her husband Michael, a pastor with the Seventh Day Adventist Church, entering the court at Alice Springs in 1982.

Tests on the garment bloodstains showed that the blood could have come from a child of parents with the Chamberlains' blood groups. The bloodstains also showed that the undershirt had been worn the right way round when the staining occurred and had then been turned inside out. It was also apparent that the top two studs of the jumpsuit had been unfastened, though they had been fastened when the bleeding took place. The pattern of the bloodstains suggested that the child's injuries had been inflicted by a cut to the throat with a knife rather than by any kind of animal bite. It was also reported that two bloodstained prints of small adult hands were found on the jumpsuit.

ABOVE Michael and Lindy Chamberlain with their attorney.

Suspicion began to center on the Chamberlains themselves. Stains of blood from a child less than six months old were found in their car: on the carpet, around the supports for the front seats and on the blade, handle and hinges of a pair of scissors in the vehicle. The couple were tried in September 1982 for the murder of their baby daughter, and though both partners pleaded not guilty, in October Lindy was convicted of the murder and Michael Chamberlain was convicted as an accessory.

The trial attracted continuing controversy, and much of the prosecution evidence came under attack. The "handprints," for example, were said to be random bloodstains; it was also difficult to see when and where the Chamberlains would have had the opportunity to kill the baby and dispose of the body on a packed campsite. Two appeals were mounted, but they were unsuccessful and Lindy Chamberlain remained in prison.

In 1986, controversy resurfaced with the discovery of the baby's missing jacket, now torn and bloodstained, in a dingo cave near the campsite. In the light of this new evidence, Lindy Chamberlain was released. There was apparently a wealth of evidence in this case, but too much of it was open to more than one interpretation, and ultimately too much remained unexplained to settle the important questions beyond reasonable doubt. In June 1987 the couple were officially pardoned, and in September 1988 their convictions were quashed.

RIGHT Lindy Chamberlain pictured in 1986 arriving at court in Darwin to attend the enquiry into her conviction.

DNA: the Ultimate Identifier?

ABOVE Laboratory culture dishes and glassware lying on top of a DNA profile.

From the earliest days of forensic science, those engaged in tracking down criminals of all kinds have longed for some universal identifier, some attribute entirely unique to each individual that would be difficult or impossible to disguise. At one time fingerprints seemed to offer the answer, until careful criminals learned to wear gloves, or to wipe prints off every surface they might have touched at the scene. At last, the answer has been found—and it lies in something more fundamental to the individual than superficial patterns on the fingertips: it lies in the cells.

Every human being is made up of vast numbers of living cells of different types. Inside the nucleus of every cell there is a string

of coded information in the form of a ribbonlike molecule of deoxyribonucleic acid (DNA) that contains the genetic blueprint of that particular person's makeup. Because everyone's genetic make-up is unique, this coded information is as individual as a perfect set of fingerprints with the added advantage to forensic investigators that the information is almost impossible to eliminate.

Each DNA molecule is actually a polymer, or a long-chain molecule made up of repeated units called nucleotides. Each one of these nucleotides consists of a molecule of sugar bound to another containing phosphorus and another containing nitrogen. The complete DNA molecule contains millions of these nucleotides, arranged in pairs on two long chains or strands, curved into a spiral or helix within the cell nucleus.

The amount of information contained in these codes is prodigious. Each human cell contains a string of twenty-three pairs of chromosomes, each of which contains almost one hundred thousand genes and DNA chains made up of one hundred million base pairs. So the complete human genetic code involves some three billion base pairs, controlling everything from height and build to color of hair and eyes.

BELOW James Watson (left) and Francis Crick, discoverers of the structure of DNA, with their model of part of the DNA helix in 1953. They shared the Nobel Prize for physiology or medicine with Maurice Wilkins, who specialized in X-ray crystallography.

ABOVE Computer-generated image of the DNA double helix.

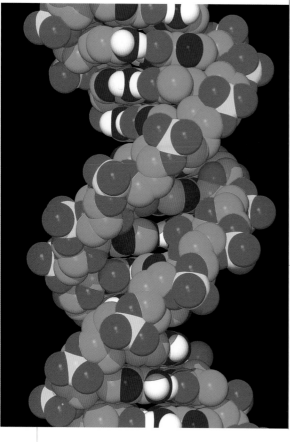

LEFT Computer graphic image of part of a DNA molecule with the atoms represented as colored spheres: yellow for phosphorus, red for oxygen, green for carbon, blue for nitrogen and white for hydrogen.

BELOW Nucleotides linking together to form the DNA strand, with S representing a sugar molecule, joined to a phosphate group to form the spine of the chain, and four bases (A for adenine, G for guanine, T for thymine and C for cytosine) that provide the links to the other half of the double helix.

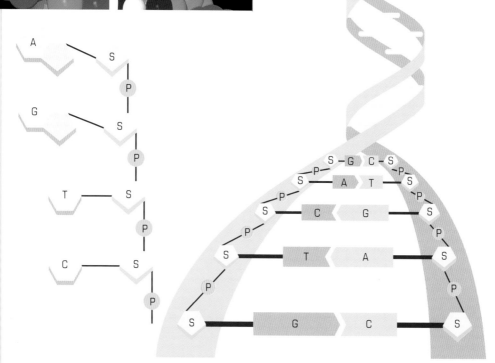

The DNA code

The DNA nucleotides are linked together to form the DNA chain with their sugar and phosphate molecules alternating. Each sugar molecule has one of four types of nitrogen compound molecules (or "bases") attached to it. These are adenine (A), cytosine (C), guanine (G) or thymine (T). The complete chain contains millions of these bases and uses these four basic building blocks in different combinations to draw up the blueprint for a complete living organism.

ABOVE Intertwined strands of DNA representing segments of two chromosomes—the one on the left has three repeating sequences of T, A and G bases, and the right-hand one has only two.

Inside each living cell, the double helix is formed by the bases of one DNA strand joining those of the other in specific combinations, rather like the rungs of an almost endless ladder. When the cell divides to form two new cells, the double helix splits into two single strands, each of which forms the nucleus of a new cell, combining with other nucleotides within the cell to form a new double helix identical to the original.

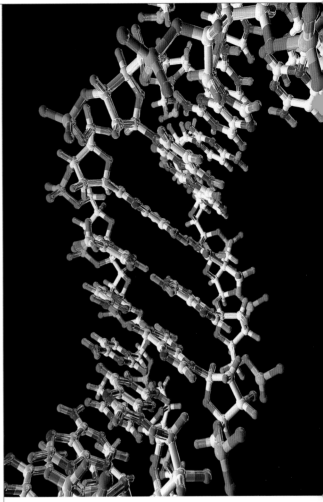

ABOVE Computer image of part of a DNA strand in all its complexity—in this case carbon is white, hydrogen pale blue, nitrogen is dark blue, oxygen red and phosphorus orange.

The DNA-coded sequence that specifies a single individual initially seemed to scientists to be an impossibly long and complex set of instructions. Yet it became clear that, since human beings share many basic characteristics, large stretches of the genetic code must be common to all individuals. The DNA elements that could actually single out an individual were those particular extracts responsible for specific details such as physical appearance, family traits and color of eyes or hair.

Genetic markers

Scientists realized that some form of marker was needed to allow these polymorphic pieces of an individual's DNA code to be isolated so that they could be recorded and eventually compared with corresponding information from other individuals or samples. By the 1980s, a team of genetics researchers at the Lister Institute of the University of Leicester in England, led by Dr. Alec Jeffreys, had isolated particular parts of the DNA code by taking cell nuclei from a sample and using a substance called a restriction enzyme to cut the DNA chain at particular points. The enzyme did this by recognizing a sequence in the code and cutting the chain at specific points to produce a series of fragments of different lengths. These were then sorted by a technique called gel electrophoresis, in which a high-voltage electric current was applied to the DNA fragments in a gel.

RIGHT A laboratory technician carrying out gel electrophoresis to sort and identify DNA fragments.

BELOW Dr. (now Sir) Alec Jeffreys working in his laboratory.

Gel electrophoresis causes the different DNA fragments to move through the gel at different rates. The shorter pieces move more quickly than the longer ones, effectively sorting the different fragments according to their length. The fragments are then transferred to a special nylon membrane in much the same way as an ink line might be transferred to a sheet of blotting paper.

Individual sequences are then identified according to the code they contain using a radioactive marker. This is a genetic probe carrying a code that automatically binds to the genetic material being looked for. For example, to identify DNA fragments that contain the code sequence A-G-T (for adenine, guanine and thymine bases), a radioactive marker with the sequence T-C-A (for thymine, cytosine and adenine) is used, since these two combinations automatically bind together.

Building the "genetic fingerprint"

The nylon sheet containing the DNA fragments is then placed on X-ray-sensitive film. A radioactive genetic marker will have bound to those fragments containing the code sequence being studied, and this affects the film at the points where they appear. The resulting plate, when developed, reveals the positions of the DNA fragments carrying the radioactive markers. They appear in a series of bars not unlike the bar codes used to identify different products at a supermarket check-out. Just as the arrangement of thick and thin bars and white spaces in a barcode identifies each different product, so samples of DNA show the coded sequences in arrangements unique to each individual, providing a genetic

BELOW Computer display from an automated method for decoding sequences of base-pairs in fragments of DNA extracted from the chromosomes in human cells—"DNA fingerprinting."

"fingerprint." The pattern on the "fingerprint" is different in every case, except where identical twins or other identical multiple births are involved.

In the future, this powerful technique will become faster and easier to use and the information it yields will be even more accurate. Existing methods of comparing the so-called "barcode" traces on an X-ray film are being replaced by a new technique developed by Dr. Jeffreys in 1991. This searches for short sequences of elements that are repeated within the DNA molecule. These sequences occur repeatedly throughout the DNA chain, and so can be retrieved from bodies or samples where the DNA has been degraded by decomposition or the passage of time, or from very small DNA samples that contain only incomplete material.

These sequences are isolated from the sample and amplified by a method called

BELOW DNA fingerprints used in paternity testing (top left) with prints of the mother's DNA shown in green, the child's in red and the potential father's in blue. Direct comparisons at the top right and bottom left show correspondence between all the bands in the child's DNA with either those of the mother or the true father, but the comparison with the DNA fingerprint of the alleged father at bottom right shows several mismatches, proving he could not be the father of the child.

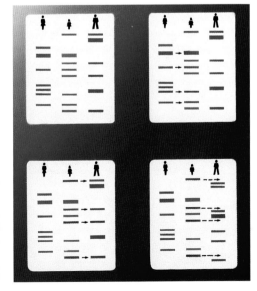

polymerase chain reaction (PCR) which can work with as little as a billionth of a gram of DNA material. The technique uses new knowledge about the way DNA replicates naturally in cell division and growth. PCR can magnify the amount of DNA originally extracted from the sample a million times in approximately an hour. The resulting DNA is then processed through gel electrophoresis to reveal the number of repeats of the basic sequence in each part of the sample.

Because there are hundreds of different types of these short sequences in human genes, a series of different searches extends into millions the odds against two individuals having the same DNA information. The information is now processed to yield a digital code of between fifty and seventy numbers. This precise record can be used to distinguish between DNAs from two or more sources found in the same sample, as they are sometimes in cases of rape or in the aftermath of a struggle. These digital records can also be stored in computer databases and transmitted virtually instantly across the world to be compared with others.

Rules of inheritance

Because each newborn child inherits half its chromosomes, together with their DNA, from each of its parents, any genetic fingerprint from the child's DNA must correspond in every detail with the equivalent genetic fingerprint of one parent or the other. The DNA of different offspring of the same couple have the

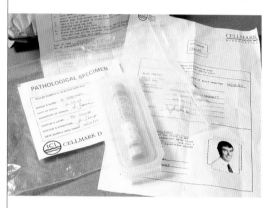

ABOVE A pathological specimen, bagged and waiting for analysis.

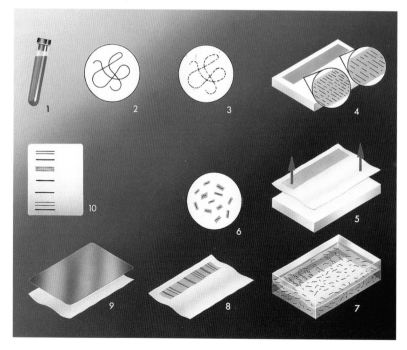

LEFT The DNA fingerprinting process—a blood sample (1) contains DNA (2) cut into fragments by a special enzyme (3) that are separated into bands of gel electrophoresis (4). A DNA band pattern is transferred to a nylon membrane (5) with a radioactive probe (6) which can recognize specific DNA sequences. The probe DNA binds to target DNA sequences on the nylon membrane (7) and excess DNA is washed off (8). An X-ray film is exposed to the radioactive DNA (9) and developed to reveal the characteristic bands that make up the DNA fingerprint (10).

same relationships with the parents' DNA. This creates the possibility of identifying individual DNA samples by reference to those of known relatives or descendants. It is even possible to reconstruct the DNA fingerprint of a missing parent from those of the remaining parent and their child.

This kind of investigation across the generations, or even the centuries, is made possible because of the extraordinary lasting qualities of DNA. Researchers have been able to extract DNA material from the bones of corpses burned long ago in an attempt to destroy their identity—and even from the mummified bodies of Egyptian pharaohs thousands of years old.

RIGHT Analysis and comparison of DNA fingerprints.

BELOW DNA testing used in anthropology research, to study family relationships and the transmission of hereditary diseases.

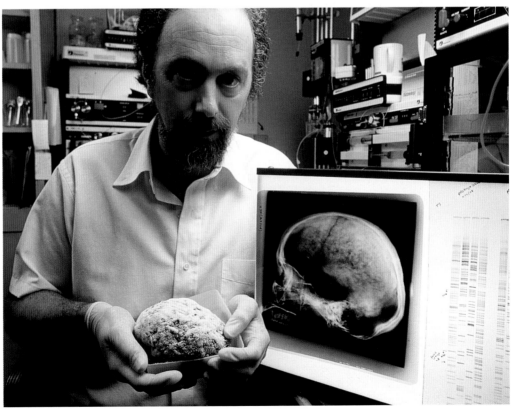

Colin Pitchfork

The rape and murder of fifteen-year-old schoolgirl Lynda Mann in the village of Narborough in Leicestershire in November 1983 horrified the local community. The only clue left by the killer was his semen which, even without DNA fingerprinting, proved to be of a type found in just ten percent of the adult male population. This at least allowed for the elimination of suspects, even if it could not be used for positive identification of the killer.

Because Lynda had been attacked and killed on a secluded footpath, police were confident that her murderer was a local man. Newspaper appeals for witnesses produced no helpful leads, however; nor did the police's door-to-door inquiries.

On July 31, 1986 another fifteen-year-old, Dawn Ashworth from Enderby, was raped and murdered on another quiet footpath, after having visited friends in Narborough. Soon afterward the police computer, searching for local people with records of sexual offences, identified a young kitchen porter at the Carlton Hayes mental hospital on the outskirts of the village. He was questioned by police and made a full confession, though this was later retracted. Nevertheless the police took a blood sample and asked Dr. Alec Jeffreys of Leicester University, the inventor of genetic fingerprinting, to compare the sample with that found on Lynda Mann's body.

The DNA evidence showed clearly that the kitchen porter was not responsible for either murder, but it also proved beyond all doubt that the same unknown man had killed both girls, and the police search was redoubled. With this precise DNA evidence on record, the police turned their attention back to the adult male population of Narborough and neighboring villages Littlethorpe and Enderby, only this time they were not just asking questions, they were asking for blood samples.

ABOVE Police collecting evidence at the scene of the murder of Lynda Mann.

BELOW Removing Lynda's body from the scene.

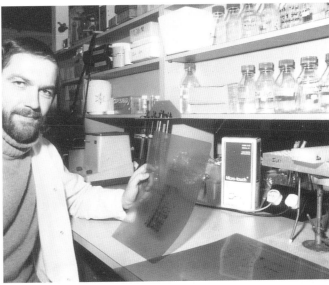

ABOVE Dawn Ashworth, the second murder victim.

RIGHT Dr. Alec Jeffreys analyzed the mass DNA samples in this case.

TOP RIGHT The pub where locals discussed Colin Pitchfork's payment to a fellow worker for giving a blood sample on his behalf.

In all, more than 4,500 men provided blood samples. According to the paperwork, one of these was Colin Pitchfork, a twenty-seven-year-old bakery worker who had been questioned earlier in the investigation. But on September 18, 1987, a policeman whose father was the owner of a local pub made an interesting report. Bakery workers had been heard discussing the fact that Colin Pitchfork had paid a workmate, Ian Kelly, to give a blood sample on his behalf. Police checked the signature at the blood test against Pitchfork's genuine signature, that appeared on the forms he signed during the original inquiry, and found the two did not match. Pitchfork was arrested and obliged to provide a blood sample: the sample confirmed that he was the double murderer. He confessed to the crime and in January 1988 was imprisoned for life.

ABOVE Colin Pitchfork.

Ian Simms

n the late afternoon of February 9, 1988, a twenty-two-year-old insurance clerk named Helen McCourt alighted from a bus and began the half-mile walk to her home in the village of Billinge in northwest England. Persistent local gossip linked her to Ian Simms, the landlord of the George and Dragon, the village pub, and it was likely she planned to pay him a call on her way home.

Whatever her intentions, the facts showed that after she got off the bus, Helen McCourt apparently vanished from the face of the earth. She did not return home and was never seen again, dead or alive.

Significantly, witnesses reported having heard a scream from the pub not long after McCourt left the bus, and police went to interview Ian Simms. There were scratches on Simms' face, which he told officers had been made during a fight with his wife. There was also soil trapped in the rings and a bracelet he was wearing, but he offered no explanation for that, nor could he account for the scream said to have been heard coming from his pub.

ABOVE Ian Simms.

RIGHT Local people join in the search for evidence after Helen McCourt's disappearance.

BELOW The jury outside the George and Dragon pub, where the murder took place.

Police took Simms' car for examination and found a bloodstained earring that had belonged to McCourt, together with long strands of hair. On searching Simms' rooms at the pub, they found a clip that matched the earring and patterns of bloodstains that suggested a fight had started inside the door, continued up the stairs and into a bedroom, and ended with the victim on the floor.

There were no signs of the woman's body, though one by one items that had belonged to her were retrieved from the countryside around the village. These included her purse, which was found with her coat and some other heavily bloodstained items of clothing. Hairs from Simms' two dogs were found on the coat, as were carpet fibers from his apartment, and the plastic bags in which the clothing was found were similar to those used at the pub. Also recovered was a knotted length of electrical cable that bore strands of hair matching those found in Simms' car. Both the hair samples were checked against samples of McCourt's hair taken from her bedroom at the family home, and both matched.

The remarkable feature of this case was the way in which DNA was used—in the absence of the victim's body—to prove that the blood in the apartment belonged to Helen McCourt. Blood samples were taken from both parents, and the DNA extracted from those samples was found to have very close similarities with the DNA extracted from the blood found at the George and Dragon. Using the parents' blood was one step away from using the blood of the victim herself, but Dr. Alec Jeffreys of the Lister Institute at the University of Leicester testified that the odds against any other sample providing as close a match were 14,500 to one. As a result, and in spite of the fact that Helen McCourt's body was never found, Simms was convicted of her murder and sentenced to life imprisonment.

BACKGROUND Helen McCourt, whose body was never found, but whose murderer was brought to justice through her parents' DNA.

Dr. Josef Mengele

ABOVE Dr Josef Mengele, taken in South America In 1960.

BELOW Wanted poster showing Mengele's photograph and an artist's impression of how he might have aged since the picture was taken.

At the end of World War Two, one of the most notorious fugitives from justice was the chief medical officer at the Auschwitz death camp, Dr. Josef Mengele. He was responsible for the deaths of hundreds of thousands of the camp's inmates. Many of them, including young children, had died as a direct result of his barbarous experiments.

Rumors abounded as to his eventual fate, but the facts appeared to be that he had evaded capture in Germany for four years before fleeing to Argentina, where the trail had disappeared. In the mid-1980s, when international efforts were being made to track him down in his South American hideout, reports were received that Mengele was buried in a Brazilian village in a grave bearing the name Wolfgang Gerhard. The occupant of the grave, whatever his real identity, was listed as having drowned in 1979 at the age of sixty-seven.

The grave was opened and the body removed in June 1985, and all the techniques available were used to try to provide a positive identification. The problem was that the only known personal information about Mengele was contained in his S.S. personnel file. This was short on detail, giving only basic information such as Mengele's overall height and the circumference of his head. When forensic anthropologists examined the bones from the grave they found the occupant was Caucasian, from the shape of the eye socket and nose. The pelvic bones suggested the body had been male, and characteristics of the arm bones indicated he had been right-handed. Judging by the wear of the teeth, the man had been between sixty and seventy years old when he died.

At that time, the only further checks that could be made to try to establish the body's identity involved comparing X-rays of the teeth with Mengele's dental chart from 1938, and using video superimposition to match the skull with an old photograph of Mengele. The results indicated the corpse was almost certainly that of the missing and much-sought criminal, but in the absence of any positive proof, some doubt remained.

Only in 1992, when DNA samples from the corpse were compared with samples provided by Mengele's living relatives in Germany, was a positive correlation confirmed. The corpse was indeed Mengele's, and though he had managed to evade justice for the remainder of his life, the hunt was over at last.

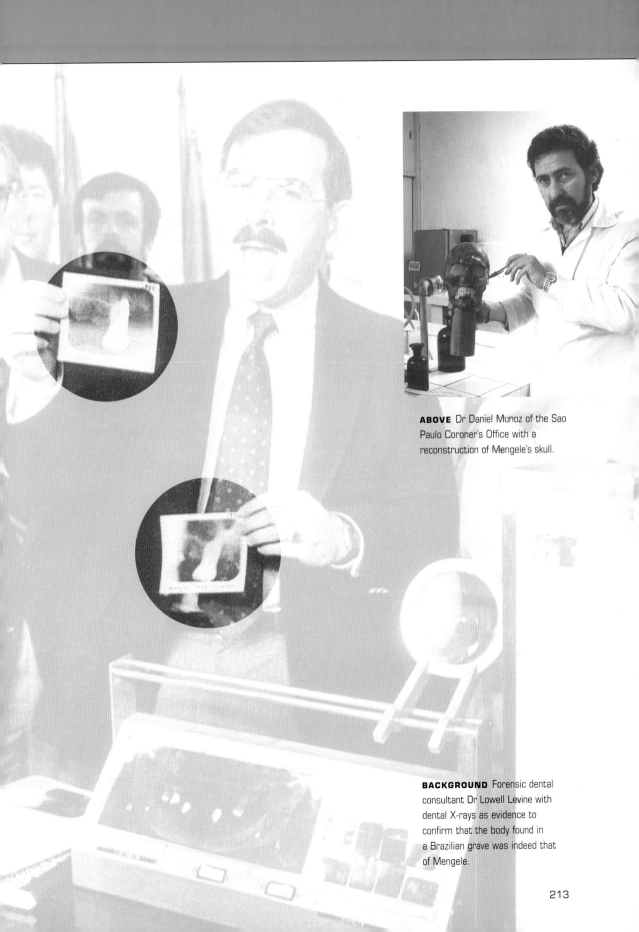

ABOVE Dr Daniel Munoz of the Sao Paulo Coroner's Office with a reconstruction of Mengele's skull.

BACKGROUND Forensic dental consultant Dr Lowell Levine with dental X-rays as evidence to confirm that the body found in a Brazilian grave was indeed that of Mengele.

The Tsar Nicholas II

BELOW Digging up the supposed remains of the Tsar and his family from marshy ground outside Ekaterinburg in 1993.

BELOW Tsar Nicholas II and the Tsarina Alexandra, with their children.

In the violent civil war that followed Russia's October Revolution in 1917, the position of the Tsar and his immediate family became very precarious indeed. To the Communists, the family represented valuable bargaining chips—but they could also be seen as a potentially dangerous focus rallying for the Communists' White Russian enemies. By July 1918 the Imperial family was being held prisoner in the Ipatiev House in Ekaterinburg in Western Siberia. Their captors heard that White Russian forces were closing in and orders were received to execute the Tsar, his wife, his children, and the other members of their party. The bodies were to be disposed of where they would never be found.

During the late 1970s, when the official Soviet blackout on any discussion on the fate of Nicholas II and his family was still firmly in place, the house where they had been executed was demolished in an effort to stem the increasing flood of sightseers. But some factions were still searching for the remains of the murdered family. An Interior Ministry official, Gely Ryabov, managed to track down the son of one of the guards, Yakov Yurovsky, who had witnessed the shootings in the cellar of the Ipatiev house. Yurovsky's son told Ryabov that his father had described the burial as having taken place in marshy ground on the outskirts of the town.

Ryabov eventually located a mass grave which was covered by a layer of logs with earth piled on top. Working at night with a team of helpers, Ryabov dug below the logs and retrieved a pile of old and fragile bones, together with scraps of clothing, all of which he placed in hiding.

Not until 1991 was the political climate sufficiently relaxed for the team to make their discoveries public. In an effort to establish the identity of the remains, photographs of Tsar Nicholas and Tsarina Alexandra were superimposed on photographs of the two largest skulls: the results showed a promising likeness. But by then there was the possibility that DNA evidence could provide final confirmation.

In order to identify any DNA samples taken from the remains as belonging to the Tsar's family, DNA samples from someone known to be a direct descendant of a family member were needed. Because the bones had decayed, only a small amount of DNA was available, so examiners had to rely on a special type of DNA called mitochondrial DNA, which is passed on through the female parent in each generation. This narrowed the field of potential donors, but DNA samples were finally provided by Prince Philip, Duke of Edinburgh and husband of Queen Elizabeth II, who was descended from the Tsarina's sister.

Among the skeletons were those of a man, a woman, and their three children. When the DNA samples were compared with those of Prince Philip it became clear that the woman was

ABOVE Forensic scientist examining the bones thought to be those of the Tsar and the Imperial family.

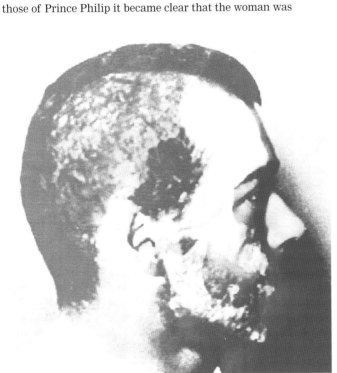

ABOVE Superimposing a photograph of the Tsarina on the second largest skull produced a close correlation.

LEFT Computer-generated image of a photo of Nicholas II superimposed on the largest skull found at the burial site, showing an equally close match.

RIGHT Chief researcher Dr. Peter Gill who verified the identity of the remains of the Imperial Family, was also asked to examine DNA from Anna Anderson Manahan, who claimed to be the Grand Duchess Anastasia whose remains had not been found (inset).

BELOW A medical expert locking the cases containing the remains of the Tsar and Tsarina and their children.

related to him, and therefore to the Tsarina's sister. This positively identified the bones as those of the Imperial family, though the skeletons of the young heir to the throne, the Tsarevich Alexei, and the Grand Duchess Anastasia were never found.

In a footnote to the main story, the fact that the bones of the Grand Duchess Anastasia were missing from the grave added new impetus to the story that the little girl had not been murdered with the rest of her family, but had escaped. It also focused attention on Anna Anderson, a refugee who had appeared in 1920 claiming to be Anastasia. Anderson's detailed knowledge of court life and of the Imperial family itself had convinced some of those who had known the family that her story was genuine.

Anna Anderson died in 1964, but by a remarkable coincidence some of her body tissue remained preserved in a hospital where she had undergone an operation shortly before her death. In 1994, DNA from her stored tissue was compared with that of the Tsar's children, and it was finally proved beyond doubt that she was not related to the family, and had certainly not been the Grand Duchess Anastasia. The mystery of Anastasia's eventual fate, like that of the Tsarevich Alexei, remains unresolved.

Anna Anderson's true identity was proved at last when members of the Schankowska family read of the DNA tests and claimed that the woman was a relative of theirs. She had been a penniless neurotic named Franzisca Schankowska who had reinvented herself as a member of the Imperial family and had earned a living from those she managed to dupe. Tests of DNA samples provided by the family showed that Anna Anderson had indeed been a close relative of theirs, and her true identity was exposed at last.

ABOVE Prince Philip, Duke of Edinburgh, a direct descendant of the Tsarina's sister, who provided DNA samples to help identify the remains.

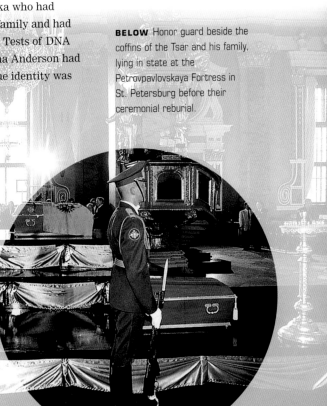

BELOW Honor guard beside the coffins of the Tsar and his family, lying in state at the Petrovpavlovskaya Fortress in St. Petersburg before their ceremonial reburial.

The Future
of Forensic Science

ABOVE A magnifying glass over two DNA sequences.
The sequences, also known as an autoradiagram, is
four rows of irregularly spaced black bands.

Forensic science is now more powerful than it has ever been, and the evidence it produces promises to be increasingly reliable in the future, provided legitimate concerns about accuracy and civil liberties are properly addressed.

An individual can now be positively identified by a number of techniques other than DNA or fingerprint analysis. These include the use of bar and contour voiceprints, retinal scanning and the analysis of chemicals present in perspiration. In theory, all these different identifiers could be used to build up a database of criminal records that could be crossmatched to check evidence or help identify suspects.

The recording, sorting and management of such complex databases—as well as the systematic searching involved in locating matches—has been greatly facilitated by the introduction of computers. When data was stored on paper only, the task of matching fingerprints taken from a crime scene with those held in police files was long and laborious, and had to be undertaken by officers with specialist skills. In addition, if criminals

LEFT Forensic scientists examining fingerprint files in the National Fingerprint Gallery at the Metropolitan Police Support Headquarters in London, England, which contains more than 4.4 million fingerprint records.

BELOW A specialist fingerprint examiner working in 1948 with a magnifying glass to examine the type of print and determine the number of ridges. The result is recorded on the card and placed in the fingerprint files.

moved from their original area of operations, their prints did not necessarily appear on police records in their new neighborhood. Where the files from different police authorities were merged in a central system, the resulting databases were so unwieldy that a systematic search of the entire collection was beyond the resources of most police inquiries.

Indeed, as forensic science became more wide-ranging in the information it collects on those who commit a crime, sorting and processing that information became more and more time-consuming. Much of that development might well have been wasted, without the huge increase in the power and speed of computers.

The role of computers in crime fighting

The first force to use computers for storing fingerprint records was the Royal Canadian Mounted Police, which completed the process of computerizing its fingerprint files in 1973. Sweden followed in 1975, and a year later Germany's seventeen million criminal police records were transferred to a computer database. As more countries added their records, the possibilities of identifying and tracking down criminals on the basis of their prints became truly global.

Computer programs quickly became more efficient at searching out the fingerprints' points of classification and comparison, and capable of faster processing. By the 1990s,

fingerprint records could be scanned at rates of tens of thousands per second and the area and time frame of the search could easily be modified or enlarged.

Police were able for the first time to undertake "cold searches," looking for matches with prints found at the scene of a crime without having a particular suspect in mind. Because the system would quickly reveal any matches with the prints on file, investigators could let the computer do the searching. In addition, because fingerprint records were increasingly being shared between police forces, matches were being made that identified suspects in previously unsolved cases.

But this was just one aspect of the development of forensic computing. By the late 1980s both the British and American police were making use of powerful mainframe computers. Because these were highly efficient at searching out and identifying patterns, they could be fed with enormous amounts of data collected during the course of an investigation and used to reveal any statistical quirks that indicated a particular suspect or group of suspects that may be worth investigating.

ABOVE A forensic optical comparator for matching fingerprints.

RIGHT Using a hand-held scanner to feed paper fingerprint records into the computer database, where they can be compared side-by-side with suspect prints.

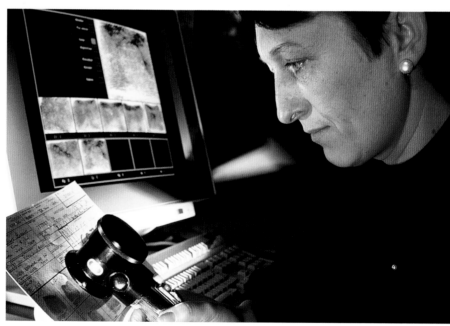

HOLMES and Floyd

In the United Kingdom, the first police national computer was developed during the 1970s to allow different forces all over the country to have access to a common bank of criminal records. In 1987 the British government introduced an additional computer system called the Home Office Large/Major Enquiry System (or HOLMES, after the great fictional detective). This allowed investigation teams to use the computer's pattern-sensing capabilities to suggest potential suspects, or to deliver a list of suspects who matched a series of characteristics revealed by forensic evidence at the scene of the crime.

In the United States, the FBI developed an "artificial-intelligence" computer system with the help of the Institute for Defense Analysis, part of the U.S. Department of Defense. This was called "Big Floyd," after the far-from-fictional Floyd Clark, head of the bureau's Criminal Identification Division, and it stored more than three million records belonging to the FBI Organized Crime Information System.

Big Floyd allows investigators to interrogate the computer to search for potential suspects or, if operators have a suspect in mind, the computer can reveal all the known information on that person. It can even suggest the next steps in investigating the subject, such as identifying known associates, approaching other sources of information or applying for permission for a wiretap for additional information in a particular area.

Some of the most difficult criminals to identify and track down are serial killers, who often find and strike their victims apparently at random. Two separate programs are being developed to help investigators generate psychological profiles of serial killers from the available evidence. One is run by the FBI's Behavioral Sciences Unit, which between 1979 and 1983 interviewed more than twenty convicted serial killers and their families. Detailed profiles were compiled and these are used to help identify other individuals showing similar patterns of behavior. The other program is the Violent Criminal Apprehension Program (VICAP) which was initiated by the FBI Academy in 1985. This records details of violent crimes, categorizing distinguishing features of each attack. Supplied with details of a new case, the program searches its records, comparing up to one hundred different features of each crime, to find the ten closest matches from its database. The resulting list is then analyzed by experts to assess whether the most recent crime may be one of a series committed by the same person.

TOP A technician using a barcode reader to enter fingerprint details into a computer file.

LEFT World War II poster highlighting a mass fingerprinting campaign for ordinary citizens.

ABOVE AND RIGHT An infrared viewer is used to examine a check. The numeral "1" has been altered to a "4."

Security screening

The one limitation common to all these computer records is that they can help to catch only those criminals who have had previous dealings with the police, so have had their details recorded. In several earlier cases (see pages 168 and 228), criminals were tracked down through mass fingerprinting and DNA testing that brought local people with no existing criminal records into the net. Suggestions that mass records such as these be retained and added to permanent police files invariably cause concerns regarding civil liberties. In today's increasingly security-conscious society, however, recorded evidence of individual identity is increasingly used to allow the ordinary citizen convenient access to sensitive parts of the workplace, to bank cash machines or other high-security areas.

For example, fingertip patterns can be scanned by computers to control access to secure areas of a plant or research establishment. A visitor simply presses a keypad, his or her print is automatically compared with the recorded prints of all authorized personnel, and if a match is found access is granted. Trials are already under way of futuristic cash-dispensing machines that use laser scans of customers' retinas in the same way to screen any user attempting to withdraw cash.

Equipment has also been developed that can detect forged signatures much more precisely than examination with the naked eye. The genuine signatory is required to sign on an electronic keypad that senses the pattern of the pressure and pen movements used. Although the pressure and pen movements may vary between consecutive signatures, the overall pattern remains the same. Though a skilled forger may be able to produce a convincing imitation of the genuine signature, he or she inevitably uses a different pattern of pressure and movement in doing so, and the equipment is able to detect this.

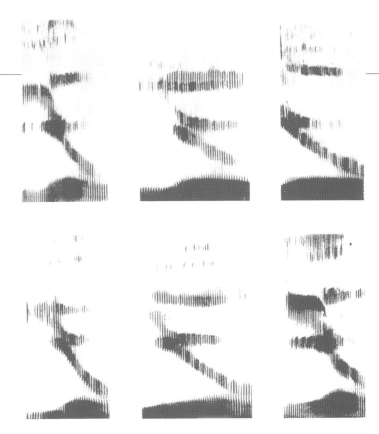

RIGHT Bar voiceprints showing a suspect saying the word "you" at top left. Five individuals repeated the word, and the positive match is shown at bottom right.

Bar and contour voiceprints

The characteristics of a person's voice, despite the prevalence of convincing mimics, are also highly individual. Voiceprints are made by recording two and a half seconds of a subject's speech on magnetic tape, then scanning the tape electronically to determine the different frequencies generated in the voice. The results are either displayed on a computer screen or drawn on a rotating drum by a moving stylus.

Two types of voiceprint display are used for security and identification purposes. Both show the time elapsed during the recording on the horizontal axis, and the different frequencies present in the voice on the vertical axis. The display most commonly used in giving evidence is the bar voiceprint, in which the intensity of the sound at different frequencies is shown by the density of the print at these different levels. The same information is presented in a different way in the contour voiceprint. Here the trace is presented as a pattern of lines joining together points of equal intensity, rather as contour lines on a map join together points of equal height to indicate three dimensions on a two-dimensional display.

In both cases, the patterns created by people with similar voices speaking the same words are still clearly distinguishable from one another. Moreover, when an individual attempts to disguise the voice by speaking at an unusually high or low pitch, the pattern may move vertically up or down the display, but it still shows the characteristic pattern and reveals the identity of the speaker when compared with the normal voice recording.

Voiceprints have been used in several cases in the U.S. to confirm the identity of telephone callers. They can also help identify, for example, a suspect who has made a ransom demand, left a threatening message or made a hoax call. The reliability of voiceprint identification was shown by tests carried out by the U.S. Air Force Systems Command in the early 1990s. A voice-recognition computer system was used to control access to secure areas. The system was found to be ninety-nine percent reliable, even when challenged by professional impersonators.

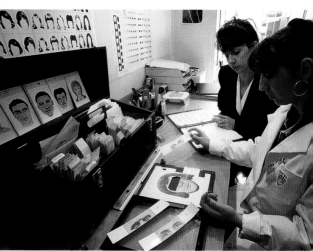

Individual identifiers

The need to identify individuals is not confined to criminal cases: a movement in the United States, sponsored by the American Dental Association in 1986, tried to persuade ordinary citizens to be "tagged" as part of a national register. Volunteers were invited to have a tiny disc bonded to a molar in the upper jaw. This almost indestructible identity marker would carry a unique twelve-digit code that could be read through a magnifier ... but so far only a minority of patients has taken up the offer.

In many cases, police have only witness descriptions on which to base their search for a suspect. Even now, some police forces use the services of skilled portrait artists who develop sketched likenesses of suspects from dialogue with the witness. However a more standardized system was developed as a result of suggestions by Hugh C. McDonald, chief of the civilian division of the Los Angeles Police Department, in 1940.

McDonald judged the traditional procedure to be both frustrating and time-consuming, and to speed things up he sketched a series of different kinds of eyes, noses, mouths, hairlines, face shapes and other individual features on transparent sheets so that they could be selected by the witness to assemble a picture of the suspect. This was the basis of

ABOVE LEFT A portrait artist developing the likeness of a suspect in discussion with a witness.

ABOVE RIGHT An Identikit researcher working with a crime victim to compose an image of the criminal's face.

the first Identikit system, which was commercially produced by the Townsend Company of Santa Ana in California. The original kit contained thirty-two different noses, thirty-three lips, one hundred and two pairs of eyes, fifty-two chins and twenty-five beards and mustaches. Using these elements together with different facial shapes it was possible to assemble sixty-two billion different faces. In addition, since each different feature was coded, information could be sent to other forces so that they could use the code to assemble their own equivalent Identikit portrait without seeing the original.

By the early 1960s, Identikit was being used by an increasing number of the world's police forces, but a successor was already being developed by forensic expert Jacques Penry from an idea he had conceived thirty years previously. In 1968, Penry was contracted by the Police Research and Development Branch of the British Home Office to produce a photographically-based facial identification system. Within a year, Penry produced a kit that had the potential to assemble five billion different male Caucasian faces. A year later he produced a supplement that could generate half a million Afro-Asian faces. Two years later, with the help of the Royal Canadian Mounted Police, he developed a kit that produced Native American faces, but the first Photofit kit for producing and identifying female faces took another two years to produce.

Since then, computers have played increasingly sophisticated roles in producing and identifying images. Specially designed software enables Photofit images to be produced in color and in three dimensions to give a more lifelike representation, and faces can be reconstructed from the blurred images retrieved from CCTV (close circuit television) security tapes by using image-enhancement facilities. Computer imagery has also been used—with some extraordinary success—in cases where the only physical likeness available is out of date and the image needs to be "aged" to resemble the subject's current appearance.

One program was developed by Scott Barrows and Lewis Sadler, two medical illustrators at the University of Illinois in Chicago. They used their anatomical

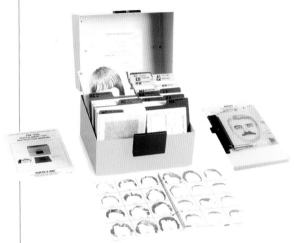

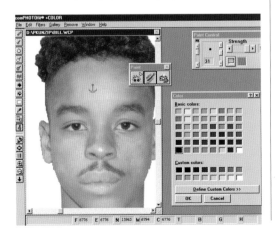

BELOW An E-fit composite picture created on computer using a blend of components of individual features from photographs of real people.

TOP A portable Photokit identification kit where the individual features are selected from photographs rather than Identikit drawings.

ABOVE A printer produces clear color images of a composite computer-generated likeness.

knowledge of how fourteen bones and more than one hundred muscles in the face develop as a person matures to project the probable appearance of a subject some years after the last known photograph was taken. The program is designed to suggest the physical changes that would naturally occur over time.

Researchers at the Louisiana State University have taken this technique a stage further in their Forensic Anthropology

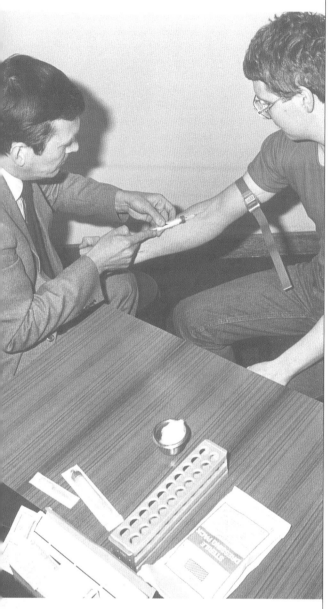

ABOVE A volunteer having a blood sample taken for police records.

Future possibilities— and pitfalls

Chromatography techniques are now so sensitive that they can produce a chemical spectrum of an individual's perspiration that is as unique as a fingerprint, and the possibility exists that the minuscule traces present in an individual's body odor may one day be enough to trigger a positive identification.

At present however, such information is useful only in proving that a known suspect was actually present at the scene where trace evidence was obtained. For these powerful techniques to assist detectives in finding their suspect in the first place, criminal records need to be redesigned and expanded to include all relevant information. Ideally, computers working from the evidence collected at the scene would be able to produce a short list of likely suspects in any given crime.

ABOVE A technician monitoring an analysis by high-performance liquid chromatography (HPLC).

Computer Enhanced System (FACES). This works by combining pictures of the subject with pictures of the parents, based on the concept that people from the same family tend to age in similar ways. The system has produced some remarkable identifications, especially in cases of child abductions where the child had been missing for some years.

There are already suggestions that criminals convicted of telephone offences—those involving threats, ransom demands or even just nuisance calls—should be required to have their voiceprints recorded at the same time as their fingerprints. In some states in the U.S., criminals give blood or saliva samples for DNA profiling as a standard part of their post-trial processing. However, extending this kind of record keeping to the wider public remains for the moment unlikely, given concerns over civil liberties and the potentially disastrous consequences of any errors made in the taking of samples or maintenance of records.

The increased sensitivity of the methods used in most fields of modern forensic science is not without its price. Those responsible for producing and assessing the evidence must be aware that their isolation of, or failure to identify, the merest trace of a particular chemical in a particular place can have direct and devastating consequences. The highest scientific standards must be brought to bear at all times to guard against the possibility of accidental contamination of laboratory equipment, materials, or samples.

Some samples must be kept under strictly controlled conditions, for example, since any fluctuations in temperature can result in misleading test results. Future advances in this most demanding of scientific specializations are likely to concern the improved reliability, as well as the extended capability, of the techniques involved.

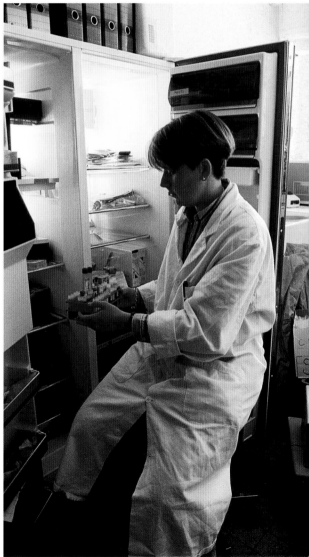

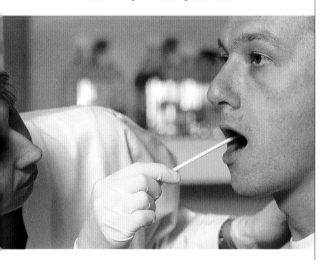

ABOVE Taking a saliva sample for DNA analysis.

RIGHT To prevent degradation and contamination of forensic samples, they are kept in secure refrigerators.

Richard Ramirez

Beginning in June 1984, a series of twelve violent murders were committed in Los Angeles. Each involved people being attacked in their homes in the middle of the night: male victims were shot, female victims raped. Several of the women were able to describe their attacker, named "The Nightstalker" by newspapers, as a tall, lean Hispanic man with bad teeth and body odor, but this information was not enough to provide promising leads when cross-matched with records of known sexual offenders.

There was a breakthrough in August 1985 when a victim managed to note down the number of the attacker's car as he drove away. A police hunt located the vehicle in a parking lot two days later; it had been stolen from outside a restaurant on the night of the previous attack. The car was put under surveillance, but the criminal did not return. Eventually it was searched by forensic examiners who found a single suspect fingerprint.

Because the Los Angeles Police Department's fingerprint records had been partly computerized earlier in the year, police were able to conduct a computer search, which retrieved a positive match. The subject was a Richard Ramirez, who had been fingerprinted following a minor traffic violation some years before. His photograph was circulated to the media, though Ramirez himself, who was out of town on a visit to Arizona to buy cocaine, was unaware of it.

On his return, he called at a liquor store on the East side of the city, to buy a can of cola and some doughnuts. Bystanders recognized him as the man whose face was printed on the newspapers in the racks at the store, and they chased him down the streets. Ramirez himself tried to evade his pursuers by stealing a car, but those chasing him were too close for his

BACKGROUND Richard Ramirez shows a pentagram on his left palm, a symbol of satanic worship, which had also been found at the scene of two of his crimes.

ABOVE Elyas Abowath was one of "The Nightstalker's" victims.

BELOW Ramirez after his arrest on August 31, 1985—police believe he committed 24 brutal assaults and 16 murders.

efforts to be successful. Finally he ran headlong into a waiting patrolman, also called Ramirez, and he was arrested.

Though Ramirez himself denied taking part in the crimes, during the three years it took for his trial to come to court he did all he could to change his appearance from the descriptions given by witnesses. It made little difference, as police searching the home of one of his friends had found the gun used in the murders, and jewelry belonging to his victims was found in the possession of Ramirez's sister.

On November 7, 1989, Ramirez was sentenced to death. He might never have been identified but for the computerized fingerprints records and his own date of birth. The records only covered criminals born since the 1st January 1960, and Ramirez had been born in February of that year.

Clifford Irving

By the 1970s the billionaire industrialist Howard Hughes had become a total recluse, living on a private island in the Bahamas. When in 1971 a writer named Clifford Irving claimed Hughes had agreed to his writing an authorized biography, publishers were skeptical. Only when letters signed by Hughes were pronounced genuine by Osborn, Osborn and Osborn, a company specializing in authenticating documents, did McGraw-Hill commission Irving to write the book and pay an enormous $765,000 advance to Hughes via a Swiss bank account.

The serialization rights to Irving's finished manuscript were sold to *Life* magazine. The magazine was then called by the Hughes Tool Company to arrange a telephone interview between Hughes and a group of radio, newspaper and television reporters. A conference call was set up in a Los Angeles hotel so that Hughes could answer detailed questions. For twenty minutes he was bombarded with queries, and his answers were recorded. Hughes insisted he had never met Irving, never given him permission to write his biography, and never received any payment.

Irving claimed the caller was an impostor, but since he had demonstrated detailed personal knowledge of Hughes in his answers to the reporters' questions, not everyone was convinced. The available evidence was re-examined. Letters purportedly from Hughes and amendments he had allegedly made to drafts of the book were shown to R.A. Cabbane, a document examiner for

BELOW Howard Hughes, pictured before his retreat into seclusion.

BELOW RIGHT Forged signatures of Howard Hughes shown on the top two lines showed several points of resemblance to Irving's own handwriting, shown in the remaining lines.

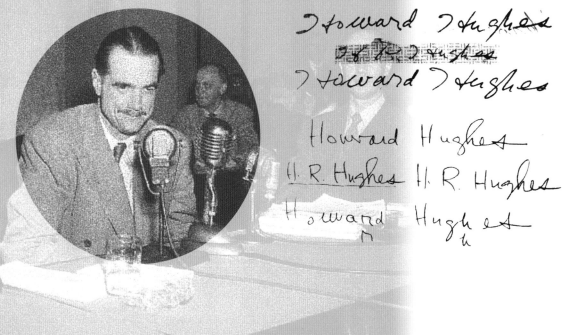

the U.S. Postal Service, along with samples of Irving's own handwriting. Though the signatures on the letters were very similar to the genuine article, they were now exposed as high-quality fakes. Experts also detected a resemblance between the formation of some of the letters in the forged signatures and that in Irving's own writing.

Investigators then set about establishing whether or not the conference caller had been genuine. Voiceprints made from the recorded interview were compared with voiceprints made from a recording of a speech Hughes had made in 1947 to a Senate sub-committee. The prints were compared by Lawrence G. Kersta, who had produced the first voiceprints while working at the Bell Telephone Laboratories in New Jersey in 1963. He found the two prints were almost certainly produced by the same person, and his findings were confirmed by Dr. Peter Ladefoged, Professor of Phonetics at U.C.L.A., whose assessment took into account the difference in the subject's age at the times the two recordings were made.

BELOW Clifford Irving and his wife Edith.

Finally, a report was received from Swiss bank officials who were alarmed that their establishment had unwittingly played a role in the fraud. An account had been opened at the bank in the name of Helga R. Hughes shortly before a check had been deposited by McGraw-Hill, made payable to H. R. Hughes. The account had been opened by Irving's wife.

The couple were tried for fraud and on June 16, 1972, and Irving was sentenced to two and a half years in prison. His wife, found guilty of being an accessory, was sentenced to serve eighteen months.

O.J. Simpson

On June 12, 1994, Nicole Simpson-Brown, former wife of football star O.J. Simpson, and her friend Ronald Goldman were found dead just inside the front gate of Mrs. Simpson's home. Both bodies were covered in blood and showed deep knife wounds. Simpson himself was ordered to report to the police, but he fled in a friend's car before eventually returning to give himself up.

When Simpson was eventually charged with both murders, it appeared that the forensic evidence against him was overwhelming and the outcome of the trial a foregone conclusion. Drops of blood were found at the scene that did not match the blood groups of either of the victims but had at least three factors in common with Simpson's blood—a trait shared by

RIGHT O.J. Simpson with his ex-wife Nichole Simpson-Brown and their children Sidney and Justin.

ABOVE The cut on Simpson's left hand that police noticed the day after the killings.

only one in two hundred of the population. When DNA profiling was carried out on blood drops found on the rear gate of Mrs. Simpson's property, the match with O.J. Simpson's blood was so close that only one person in fifty-seven billion could be expected to produce an equivalent match.

These incriminating drops were found near a set of bloody size twelve footprints that reproduced the sole pattern of a rare design of Bruno Magli shoes. Not only were these prints from shoes of Simpson's size, but photographs were produced at the later civil trial showing him wearing shoes of that particular design. When interviewed by police on the day after the killings, Simpson was also seen to have a cut on his left hand. A bloodstained left-hand glove was discovered next to the bodies and it bore traces of fibers from Goldman's jeans and shirt; the matching right-hand glove, with traces of Simpson's blood, was found outside his own home. Traces of the victims' blood were also found inside Simpson's car and home.

Unfortunately for the prosecution, the forensic evidence was largely wasted. Simpson's defense attorneys argued that the attitudes of the police officers involved implied a racist bias against their client, and hinted at police corruption. They also cast doubts on the methods used by the forensic laboratories involved and the professionalism of those responsible for collecting, preserving and testing the forensic evidence. Much was made of the absence of a murder weapon and the dearth of eyewitness testimony. Independent witnesses were also found

ABOVE Expert officer Gregory Matheson of the LAPD gave jurors a detailed explanation of the DNA testing methods, earlier believed flawless and foolproof in determining the guilt or innocence of O.J. Simpson.

BELOW Gregory Matheson shows a diagram of six EAP phenotypes to the jury, as part of his explanation of DNA methods.

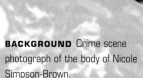

who testified to having seen Simpson on the day of the murders. The timing of their sightings indicated that he could not have been at the scene long enough to have carried out the killings.

Dr. Henry Lee, director of the Connecticut Forensic Science Laboratory, also appeared to admit under cross-examination that ambiguous blood traces found at the scene could have been partial shoe-prints made by a different sole pattern. If true, this suggested another killer may have been present, which clearly damaged the case against Simpson. Though FBI experts testified that the marks Dr. Lee referred to were not shoe prints at all, the prosecution case had lost credibility, and Simpson was eventually acquitted.

Nevertheless, a civil prosecution was later brought by the victims' families and the case was effectively retried: this time Simpson was found responsible for both deaths and ordered to pay huge sums in damages. This second trial appeared to confirm the value of the evidence, but the original case remains a powerful reminder that forensic science can be successfully brought to bear only when the evidence is collected, analyzed and presented according to the highest professional standards.

BACKGROUND Crime scene photograph of the body of Nicole Simpson-Brown.

BELOW Defendant O.J. Simpson wearing the gloves found by Los Angeles police. The prosecutors sought to prove that the gloves fitted Simpson's hands.

The New Bedford Highway Murders

O n July 3, 1988, outside Freetown near New Bedford,
Massachusetts, the partially mummified body of a young
woman was found close to Highway 140.

This victim seems to have been the first in a series of killings
now known as the New Bedford Highway Murders. On July 30,
1988, the skeleton of another young woman was found near
Interstate 195.

The first body was eventually identified from dental
records as that of Debra Medeiros. In the meantime a
third body had been found and, concerned that there
may be more undiscovered bodies in the area, police
from both Massachusetts and Connecticut mounted a
search using tracker dogs. A fourth body was found on
November 29, a fifth just two days later, and a sixth was
discovered on December 10.

Dental records identified the second body, and a partial
fingerprint identified the fourth victim. Several of the victims
had backgrounds of prostitution and drug addiction, as well as
links with the New Bedford Portuguese community.

Another body was found on March 28, 1989, body number
eight was found on March 31, and number nine was unearthed
on April 24.

ABOVE Fingerprint records.

New Bedford prostitutes were interviewed and a number of
women claimed to have been attacked by a man working in law
enforcement. The man had tried to strangle them. One woman
claimed that a man driving a white pick-up truck had raped her
near a highway exit close to where three of the bodies had been
found. A thirty-five-year-old man had been identified, arrested,
and charged with the rape, and police began to suspect that he
might also be responsible for the killings.

In spite of these leads, the forensic evidence from a total of
nine bodies has so far not provided a positive link to any one of
the suspects, and to date no one has been arrested and charged
with the New Bedford Highway Murders. The file remains open
after more than ten years. And this of course is not the only case
still waiting for a conclusion: the so-called Green River killer in
King County, Washington, is thought to be responsible for the
murder of more than forty prostitutes, but so far no one has been
found and charged. For all the power of modern forensic science,
some serial killers still manage to elude identification and
capture—just as Jack the Ripper did more than a century ago.

Acid phosphatase test: Test that uses two substances to reveal the presence of seminal fluid by the appearance of a purple color.

AFIS: Automated Fingerprint Identification Systems, which enable computers to make rapid and accurate comparisons between fingerprints and the vast numbers of fingerprints in police records.

Agglutination: The tendency of red blood cells to mass together in clumps in reaction to the presence of an antibody.

Antigens: Chemicals that are attached to the surface of the red blood cells to create the different blood groups.

Arches: One of the characteristic patterns of ridges in a fingerprint, possessed by around 5 percent of the population.

Ballistics: The examination of firearms and the projectiles they discharge, in relation to crime.

Benzidine color test: A test formerly used to reveal the presence of blood at the scene of a crime.

Bertillonage: A method of classifying human beings by a set of detailed body measurements, invented by Alphonse Bertillon, a clerk in the French Sûreté in 1883, but rendered obsolete by fingerprinting.

Big Floyd: The FBI supercomputer that contains software allowing it to search criminal records and draw conclusions from the available information in the hunt for those responsible for an individual crime.

Blasting cap: A small explosive charge triggered by lighting a safety fuse or applying an electric current, used to detonate high explosives.

Blood group: A classification system that divides human blood into groups A, B, AB and O, according to the antibodies and antigens carried by the red blood cells.

Bullet wipe: A dark ring-shaped mark made up of lead, carbon oil and dirt brushed from a bullet as it enters the skin, and found around the entry wound.

Caliber: The internal diameter of the barrel of a firearm, and the bullets it fires.

Choke: The constriction of the barrel of a shotgun to reduce the spread of shot as it leaves the gun, to increase its effective range.

Chromosomes: 23 pairs of threadlike bodies found in the nucleus of most human cells that carry the genes.

Comparison microscope: Two compound microscopes (see below) formed into a single unit, so that objects placed under each objective can be compared side by side in a single eyepiece.

Compound microscope: The basic microscope that uses two lenses (or combinations of lenses), an objective lens and an eyepiece lens, to focus a greatly magnified image of the subject on the retina of the observer's eye.

Concentric fractures: Patterns of cracks in glass pierced by a missile like a bullet, which run between the radial fractures (see below) and which originate on the side of the glass from which the impact came.

Cortex: The middle layer of human hair containing the particles of pigment that give the hair its individual color.

Cuticle: The protective outer sheath of the hair, formed by a series of overlapping scales.

Delta: A characteristic junction in the looped ridge patterns seen in the fingerprints of approximately 65 percent of people.

Density Gradient Tube: Equipment for measuring the distribution of particles of different density in a soil sample by determining the point at which they are suspended in a glass tube filled with successive layers of liquid of different densities.

Dental records: A standard system for classifying person's teeth according to distribution, displacement, and their appearance, together with any gaps or evidence of remedial work, useful for identifying bodies because of the virtual indestructibility of the teeth.

Depressants: Drugs that depress the action of the central nervous system such as phenobarbital, pentobarbital and alcohol.

Diatoms: Microscopic organisms found in lake and river water, which reveal by their presence whether a victim found in these surroundings died by drowning, or was already dead on entering the water.

DNA: Deoxyribonucleic acid, the molecules of which carry the body's genetic blueprint, and which provide a unique identifier for each individual.

Double action: A gun action where the pulling of the trigger to fire a round re-cocks the gun so that the next round is ready to be fired. (compare this with Single action, see below).

Dry drowning: Death caused by a body reflex from a spasm of the larynx due to the shock of the victim falling into the water, resulting in the heart stopping.

Electron microscope: A microscope that forms its image by the electrons emitted from the specimen when scanned by a focused beam of electrons.

Femur: The thighbone, which can be measured and used as a guide to the height of the person to whom it belonged.

Fingertip search: The careful, inch by inch combing of the crime scene by a team of searchers to turn up the smallest items of forensic evidence.

Forensic anthropologist: Specialist who can determine whether or not bones or other remains are human in origin and, if so, reveal details about how the victim died and how they appeared in life.

Forensic chemist: Specialist in the analyses of drugs, dyes, paint samples and other chemicals involved in crimes.

Forensic dentist: Specialist in examining the teeth of murder or accident victims for identification purposes, and for comparison with bite-mark evidence at crime scenes.

Forensic document investigator: Specialist in examining forged documents and forged signatures.

Forensic entomologist: Specialist in the different types of insect life which may be found on corpses or at murder scenes, as an indication of the time, season and weather when a crime may have been committed.

Forensic geologist: Specialist in the characteristics of soil samples, and what these can reveal in terms of the movements of a victim or a suspect.

Forensic pathologist: Specialist pathologist responsible for carrying out autopsies of murder victims and recording of evidence found on or in the body as to the manner and time of death.

Forensic photographer: Specialist who records forensic evidence on film at the crime scene or in the forensic laboratory.

Forensic psychiatrist/psychologist: Experts who evaluate a murder scene and victim to produce a possible psychological profile of the murderer.

Forensic serologist: Specialist in the study of blood and other bodily fluids in addition to DNA for identifying possible suspects.

Gas chromatography: A technique for separating complex mixtures of substances according to their movement when carried by gas through a thin film of liquid.

Gel electrophoresis: A method of testing for human blood by the movement of antibodies and antigens on a gel-coated plate subjected to an electrical field.

Hallucinogens: Drugs like marijuana, LSD, PSP and Ecstasy, which produce changes in mood, thought and perception.

High explosives: Explosives that produce an extremely intense explosive effect and a supersonic pressure wave when they detonate.

HOLMES: Acronym for the Home Office Large/Major Enquiry System, the UK mainframe police computer system.

Identikit: The first packaged system for reconstructing the appearance of suspects' faces, based on a wide choice of drawings of facial features.

Iodine fumes: The oldest method for visualizing latent fingerprints at a crime scene.

Latent fingerprints: Fingerprints at a crime scene that are present but not visible until visualized through one of several different techniques, including iodine fuming.

Liquid chromatography: Technique for separating complex mixtures into their constituents by dissolving the mixture in solution and passing it through a finely divided absorbent material.

Livor mortis: A coloration of the skin of the lower parts of a corpse, caused by the settling of the red blood cells as the blood ceases to circulate.

Low explosives: Explosives having a detonation less violent than high explosives (above) and that produce a subsonic pressure wave.

Luminol: A substance that can be sprayed onto furnishings at a crime scene to reveal traces of blood as spots of bright light.

Mass spectrometry: A technique for identifying the constituent parts of a mixture by passing their molecules through a high-vacuum chamber where they acquire a positive charge through colliding with a beam of electrons, which separates them according to their different masses.

Mitochondrial DNA: A type of DNA found in particular structures of the body and passed on intact through the female line of descent.

Narcotics: Drugs that have a painkilling or analgesic effect and can create a physical dependence among regular users.

Neutron activation analysis: Technique for identifying substances by bombarding a sample with neutrons in a nuclear reactor, and measuring the energies and intensities of the resulting gamma rays.

Nucleotides: The basic building blocks of the DNA helix, each consisting of one of four types of base (adenine, cytosine, guanine or thymine) attached to a sugar-phosphate group.

Phenolphthalein: A substance used with hydrogen peroxide to test for the presence of blood at a crime scene, which is revealed as a deep pink color.

Phrenology: A later discredited theory first proposed in 1796 that the shape of the head revealed different facets of the individual's personality through the presence of bumps and irregularities.

Plasma: The basic fluid constituent of blood, which carries the different blood cells.

Polymer: A complex long-chain molecule containing many repeated units or monomers.

Polymerase Chain Reaction (PCR): A technique that replicates part of a DNA strand outside a living cell, eventually producing millions of copies from the smallest original sample.

Portrait parlé: A system for regularizing verbal descriptions of a suspect's facial features introduced in the 1890s to aid positive identification.

Preciptin test: A test to confirm that a blood sample is of human origin by treating it with human anti-serum.

Prostate Specific Antigen (PSA): A substance contained in human seminal fluid that allows a test to confirm the presence of human semen.

Protein: Polymers made up of amino acids that are the basic building blocks of living organisms.

Pump-action: A shotgun carrying several cartridges in an internal magazine, and which can be reloaded by simply pushing a slider backwards and forwards.

Radial: A loop formed as part of a fingerprint pattern which opens towards the thumb.

Radial fractures: Fractures that form a star shape when a sheet of glass is pierced by a bullet, and which originate on the side opposite to the initial impact.

Rhesus factor: An additional way of differentiating between the blood of different individuals, who may be Rhesus positive or Rhesus negative, according to the presence or absence of a particular antibody.

Rigor mortis: The stiffness of the body after death, which helps in reconstructing the time at which death occurred.

Sciatic notch: Characteristic shape of part of the hipbone which can indicate whether a skeleton is that of a male or female.

Secretor: An individual who carries his or her blood group information in all their body fluids, including for example saliva and sweat.

Single-action: A type of revolver which needs to be cocked before each shot by pulling back the hammer (see Double action).

Stimulants: Drugs which increase the activity of the central nervous system, creating feelings of confidence and energy.

Striations: Fine lines in the internal rifling of a firearm caused by the cutting tool, which impart an individual identity to the gun, and to any bullets fired from it.

Superglue fuming: A technique for visualizing latent fingerprints on non-porous surfaces by using cyanoacrylate ester fumes.

Tattooing: A characteristic pattern in the skin caused by particles of unburned and partly burned powder from a shotgun blast at very close range.

TESTED: A mnemonic used by air accident investigators searching for the main parts of a crashed aircraft (Tips of the wings and tail surfaces, Engines, control Surfaces, Tail assembly, External devices like landing gear and Doors).

Thin-layer chromatography: Technique for separating a mixture into its constituent parts by the speed at which they move by capillary action up a plate coated with a thin layer of silica gel.

Tibia: The shin-bone, which can be used as a guide for calculating the height of a person.

Toxicology: The study of poisons, their effects and symptoms and tests to reveal their use.

Ulnar: A loop pattern on a fingerprint which has its open end towards the little finger (see radial).

Vitreous humor: The fluid that fills the eyeball and shows changes after death, which can be used as an accurate way of identifying the time of death.

Whorls: Fingerprint patterns where the ridges turn through at least one complete circuit.

X-rays: Electromagnetic radiation of high energy and very high frequency which can penetrate most materials to different extents and reveal their underlying structure.

Acknowledgments

It's always difficult to remember in the course of a book covering a subject as broad (and in many areas, as detailed) as *Hidden Evidence* all the many people who helped along the way with advice, encouragement and information. Starting with those who played a crucial role in bringing the book from an initial concept to a finished volume, in broadly chronological order, I should like to thank Roddie Craig for the original inspiration, Diana Steedman who turned the idea into a structured plan, Veneta Bullen who undertook the mammoth task of sourcing and identifying pictures, Diane Pengelly who subjected the text to detailed scrutiny and last, but most definitely not least, Toria Leitch for bringing the whole thing together in its finished form. To all of them, I send my sincere and grateful thanks, as I do to the anonymous but ever-helpful staff of the Reference Library of the City of Liverpool for tracking down the most detailed and elusive information for what has been a demanding but rewarding book to write.

David Owen - *January 2000.*

Bibliography

Air Accident Investigation: How Science is making Flying Safer, David Owen, *Newbury Park, California, Haynes Publishing, 1998.*
Beyond the Crime Lab: the New Science of Investigation, Jon Zonderman, *New York, John Wiley & Sons, 1999 (revised edition).*
The Blooding, Joseph Wambaugh, *New York, Bantam Books, 1989.*
The Casebook of Forensic Detection, Colin Evans, *New York, John Wiley & Sons, 1996.*
Criminalistics, Richard Saferstein, *New York, Prentice Hall (various editions).*
Detecting Forgery: the Forensic Investigation of Documents, Joe Nickell, *University of Kentucky Press, 1996.*
The Encyclopedia of Forensic Science, Brian Lane, *London, England, Hodder Headline, 1992.*
How to Solve a Murder: the Forensic Handbook, Michael Kurland, *New York, Macmillan, 1995.*
Lockerbie, David Johnston, *London England, Bloomsbury, 1989.*
Simpson's Forensic Medicine, Bernard Knight, *London, England, Arnold, 1996.*

Picture credits

The publisher would like to thank the following for permission to reproduce their images. While every effort has been made to ensure this listing is correct the publisher apologises for any omissions or errors.

Fotomas Index: p9(b), p10(l), p88, p97(b)
Black Museum: p 3(l and r), p10(t,tr), p16, p25, p29 and 5(l), p32, p49(t), p 58(t), p66(t), p83(b) and 7(t), p 97(t), p110(b), p116(r), p119(r), p126, p127(b), p133, 161(t), p166(b), p173(b), p175(t), p231
Science Photo Library: p11(t) Phillipe Plailly, p11(b) Peter Menzel, p20 Jean-Loup Charmet, p47, p62(t) Tony Craddock, p62(b) Gary Watson, p70(t) John Greim, p72, p73(t and b) Dr. Jurgen, p74 James King-Holmes, p85, p96, p103 Manfred Kage, p111(b) Professor Harold Edgerton, p114(c) and p115 Stephen Dalton, p119(l) and 7(c) Michel Viard, p146(b) Klaus Guldlbrandsen, p147(b) Robert Holgmren, p148(t) Volker Sleger, p151(r) and 1(r) Tony Craddock, p152(b) Geoff Tompkinson, p160 Alfred Pasieka, p163 Philipe Plailly, p177(t) and 1(l) Dr. Jurgen, p177(b) Andrew Syred, p178(c) Andrew Syred, p178(b) Dr. Jeremy Burgess, p179(bl) and p180(bl) Astrid & Hans Friedler, p180(br) Andrew Syred, p181(b) Manfred Kage, p187 Andrew Syred, p190(b) Dr. Jurgen, p191 P. Leca, p192(t), p192(b) Michel Viard, Peter Arnold, p193(t) Robert Longehaye, p193(b) CC Studio, p194(t) David Parker, p194(b) Peter Menzel, p196(cl) Carlos Goldin, p197 Dr. Jurgen, p200 Robert Longehaye, p201(b) A Barrington Brown, p202(t) and 3(c) Professor Ke Seddon & Dr. T Evans, p203 Alfred Pasieka, p204 and 1(c) Philippe Plailly, p205(l) and p207(b) Peter Menzel, p205(r) and p206(b) Michael Gilbert, p207(t) David Parker, p218, p219(t) Peter Menzel, p221, p224(r) and p227(r) Michael Viard & Peter Arnold, p226(r) Geoff Tompkinson
Science and Society Picture Library: p13(l and r),
Hulton Getty: p14(b and c), p15(bl), p17, p21(tr), p22, p24(t), p65, p69(t), p76, p77(t), p147(t), p149, p152(t), p158(t)
Roger Viollet: p15(r), p19, p21(bl and br), p23(l), p98-9
Frank Spooner: p2, p23(r), p44, p46, p48, p49(b), p51, p53, p60(t), p61(t), p63, p64(r), p67(cl and b), p68(b),

p69(b), p70(b), p71, p92(b), p106, p107(t), p108(t and b), p109(b), p113(tr), p114(t), p117, p120(t), p122(l and r), p123(c), p129(b), p135, p136(tl), p138, p139, p140, p141(t and c), p142, p143(c), p144, p145(t), p146(t), p153, p158(b), p167(b), p181(t), p188(b), p189(b), p204(b), p213(r), p214(t), p215(t), p216(t), p224 and 6(b), p227(l), p233, p235
Corbis: p24(b), p36, p37, p39(t), p42(tl), p43(r), p59(t), p60(b), p81(t), p86-7, p105(t), p112(t and bl), p120(b), p121(l), p123(b), p125(b), p128, p129(t), p171(tr), p172, p173(t), p198, p201(t), p212(t), p219(c) and 6(t), 220(b), p222(tl), p228-9, p230
Rex Features: p26, p27(t), p28, p33 and 7(b), p45, p53 and 6(l), p63, p64(r), p66(b), p68(t), p82 and 5(c), p84, p89, p95(b), p104, p111(t), p112(br), p113, p116(l), p118 and 5(r), p123(t), p127(t and c), p134, p136 (tr and b), p137, p141(b), p155, p174, p179(t), p189(t), p206(t)
Popperfoto: p27(bl), p38, p39(b), p40-41, p42, p43(l), p55(t), p56, p58(b), p59(b), p61(b), p77(c and b), p109(t), p143(cl), p145(b), p156, p157, p159, p170, p171(tl and b), p188(t), p212(b), p213(l), p214(b), p215(bl and br), p 216(b and tl), p217, p 232(r), p234
Sirchi Fingerprint Laboratory: p27(br), p31(b), p161(c and b), p162, p164-5, p166(t), p167(t), p190(t), p196(cr), p220(t), p222(tr), p225 **Oxford Scientific Films:** p30
International Civil Aviation Organisation, Quebec: p35
Jerry Young: p52 **Wilf Gregg:** p54, p55(m and b), p57, p75
The Art Archive: p67(t), p110(t), p121(r)
Topham: p78, p79, p124(t and b), p125(t), p169, p182-3, p184-6, p199, p210(t), p211 **Jonathan Goodman:** p90, 150
Solo Syndication: p81(b), p80
James Lawrence: p89(b), p102, p105(b), p176(t), p196(t), p202(b), p203(l) **Royal Society:** p 12
Robert Harding: p100, p107(bl and br), p130
Dr Nic Daeid: p131, p132, p175(r), p176(bl and br)
Foster & Freeman: p154(t) **British Textile:** p178(t)
Neville Chadwick: p208-9, p226(l) **Mercury Press:** p210(c)